UNCOMMON OPPORTUNITIES

The Report of the International Commission on Peace and Food brings together many of the issues central to the reflection on development which the United Nations is trying to encourage.... Once again, we see the inescapable relationships governing the goals of peace, development and democratization.

Boutros Boutros-Ghali, *United Nations Secretary General*

The end of the Cold War has created unprecedented opportunities for rapid progress on issues of concern to all humankind – peace, food security, economic development and the environment. Fresh thinking and fresh initiatives are needed to convert those opportunities into realities. I view the work of the International Commission on Peace and Food as an important step in promoting global peace and prosperity.

Mikhail Gorbachev

The Commissioners

A. T. Ariyaratne (Sri Lanka)

Dragoslav Avramovic (Yugoslavia)

Rosalynn S. Carter (USA)

Umberto Colombo (Italy)

Erling Dessau (Denmark)

Robert van Harten (Netherlands)

James Ingram (Australia)

Garry Jacobs (USA) – Secretary

Lal Jayawardena (Sri Lanka)

Mary E. King (USA)

Manfred Kulessa (Germany)

R. Martin Lees (UK)

Uma Lele (India)

Robert J. Macfarlane (USA)

John W. Mellor (USA)

Victor I. Nazarenko (Russia)

Alexander Niconov (Russia)

Her Majesty Queen Noor al-Hussein (Jordan)

General Olusegun Obasanjo (Nigeria)

Muhammad Abdus Salam (Pakistan)

Jasjit Singh (India)

M. S. Swaminathan (India) – Chairman

Brian W. Walker (UK)

Eugene F. Whelan (Canada)

Edward L. Williams (USA)

The International Commission on Peace and Food is an independent non-governmental agency established in 1989 by scientists and professionals from developing and industrial nations to evolve fresh perspectives, operational strategies and practical programmes to redirect resources from military uses to accelerate global progress on peace, food security, employment, social transition and human development.

For more information, please contact
International Commission on Peace and Food
2352 Stonehouse Drive
Napa, California 94558 USA
Tel: 1-707-252-4697
Fax: 1-707-252-8169
On CompuServe: 74721,2260
From Internet: 74721.2260@Compuserve.com

UNCOMMON OPPORTUNITIES
An Agenda for Peace and Equitable Development

REPORT OF THE INTERNATIONAL COMMISSION ON PEACE AND FOOD

Chaired by M. S. Swaminathan

ZED BOOKS
LONDON AND NEW JERSEY

Uncommon Opportunities was first published by
Zed Books Ltd, 7 Cynthia Street, London N1 9JF, UK, and
165 First Avenue, Atlantic Highlands, New Jersey 07716, USA,
in association with the International Commission on Peace and Food,
2352 Stonehouse Drive, Napa, California 94558, USA, in 1994.

Cover design by Andrew Corbett.
Laserset by Opus 43, Cumbria, UK.
Printed and bound in the United Kingdom
by Biddles Ltd, Guildford and King's Lynn

Contents

MESSAGE FROM THE UN SECRETARY GENERAL

The broad range of topics examined by the International Commission on Peace and Food demonstrates the interrelated nature of the challenges of peace and development. Your collective endeavour illustrates the fact that no longer can global peace and security remain the preserve of political and military specialists. Without an adequate development effort, there can be no lasting peace and security. Conflicts over resources, ultra-nationalism exacerbated by the tensions of unemployment, poverty and despair at home will inevitably lead to resentment, and resentment turns only too easily into armed conflict. The establishment of secure foundations for peace will be aided by development and post-conflict peace building.

Yet if there is a growing international consensus on the peace operations undertaken by the United Nations, there is no such consensus on its developmental work. Indeed, this lack of a consensus reflects a worldwide crisis in the field of development economics. As development becomes imperative, as we approach the turn of this century, we are faced with the necessity of giving new meaning to the word. Reflecting on development is thus, in my opinion, the most important intellectual challenge of the coming years.

Already, it seems clear that macro-economic growth can no longer be deemed sufficient for development purposes. Countries pursuing macro-economic growth paths have the necessary foundations for development, but that is only the first part. There can be no lasting development with the exclusion of social groups from the fruits of growth. Nor can there be long-term prospects for development when the environment is pillaged and the rights of future generations ignored. Finally, growth which is not accompanied by the improvement of the social fabric of society will be only a hollow shell. For economic and social development to take place, it is important to promote the expansion of employment opportunities, the improvement

vii

of educational and health networks, support for the role of women in development and the pursuit of equality between the sexes.

A hitherto ignored dimension of the development challenge is democratization: what I have chosen to call political development. There have been cases where development was accompanied by an authoritarian political system. But we have invariably seen that if the participation in the market place is not accompanied by political participation, development efforts are brought to naught by social and political instability. Political, economic and social development must be closely related, mutually supportive, deriving sustenance from one another. Once again, therefore, we see the inescapable relations governing the goals of peace, development and democratization – these are the goals of the United Nations.

The United Nations has, over the years, devoted great time and attention to the issues before the Commission on Peace and Food. In the research, analysis, debate, consensus-building and actual operational activities of the United Nations System, the issues of peace, development and democratization have been at the forefront. The Members of the International Commission on Peace and Food have interacted closely with the United Nations Funds, Programmes and Specialized Agencies. This report brings together many of the issues which are central to the reflection on development which the United Nations is trying to encourage, leading to the World Summit on Social Development to be held in 1995.

Boutros Boutros-Ghali
Secretary General
United Nations

FOREWORD BY THE DIRECTOR GENERAL OF UNESCO

The report of the International Commission on Peace and Food focuses on the 'uncommon opportunities' that have arisen as the world shifts into new alignments. These include the chance to tackle the problems of hunger and injustice at the root of so many of the global challenges confronting us – not the least, the overriding challenge of nurturing a worldwide culture of peace.

The Commission has put people first, recognizing that the greatest potential for change is within us, that with education and information we can mobilize the vast amounts of energy and skill which are currently wasted in the scramble for survival. It, nevertheless, also accepts that there are no easy solutions and that concerted action is necessary on many fronts in order to untangle the tortuous connections between, for instance, defence spending and food security, for no country can truly be said to be at peace while the violence of hunger blights the life of its citizens.

ICPF has no hesitation in putting forward ideas that are bound to unsettle, and it should be encouraged since imagination and daring are precisely what we need at the present time. Its calls for a standing world army, for the recognition of full employment as a fundamental right and for the elimination of protectionist trade policies – to mention but a few examples – will cause some sharp intakes of breath among world leaders. Indeed, the report contains many ideas that merit and should stimulate further reflection.

The situation of the countries in transition in Eastern Europe, highlighted in this report, illustrates perfectly the need for an integrated approach to development considered as a total human process. The Commission's report contains specific proposals in this regard as well as an overview pointing to existing domestic assets of various kinds which could help the countries concerned. It addresses the topic of job creation with innovative ideas on the roles of technology and trade, and emphasizes the significance of the developing countries and agriculture in the world economy. Its global education programme proposal – placing appropriate emphasis on the key issue of girls' and women's education – is one that particularly commends itself to UNESCO, which is already actively engaged in efforts along similar lines in conjunction with its UN partners.

This timely report should help to promote the idea of human-centred development within a culture of peace as a way forward to a better world. We are gratified that ICPF should have assigned UNESCO, as the intellectual arm of the United Nations, a prominent role in its recommended agenda for action, and we reaffirm our commitment to working with all possible partners in pursuit of the goal of global peace and sustainable human development.

Federico Mayor
Director General
UNESCO

PREFACE

The International Commission on Peace and Food began its work at a time of uncommon opportunities for rapid transition on a global scale to democratic ways of life, freedom of the media, and an independent judiciary; food, literacy, health and jobs for all; and sustainable life styles based on harmony between humankind and nature. The end of the Cold War and the consequent shift of expenditure from defence to development, the onset of the Information Age and the organization of information superhighways, the growth of mechanisms for regional cooperation, a renewed faith in the United Nations, and commitment to multilateral negotiations and action – all provided new opportunities for achieving global peace and prosperity. Rapid progress in the application of science and technology in agriculture, industry, and human health strengthened the hope that the concept of 'food, education, health and employment for all' can be converted from rhetoric into reality, provided the peace dividend can be deployed to achieve these goals.

ICPF had the advantage of building on the work of earlier independent commissions, particularly those chaired by Willy Brandt, Gro Harlem Brundtland and Julius Nyerere. We began our work with the conviction that, as Willy Brandt said, 'the problems created by men can be solved by men'. The ancient Indian scripture, *Bhagavad Gita*, expressed the same sentiment by stressing, 'Whatever man aspires to, that he can accomplish.' The achievement of food self-sufficiency by India – in a period when famine threatened millions of lives – through the power of political will and scientific action in a democratic society illustrates this truth.

In spite of such uncommon opportunities for a better common present, during the last six years the world has been witness to an escalation of ethnic and mini-conflicts, growing intolerance of diversity, the spread of small arms, an increase in violence – starting with violence to oneself through drug addiction – and damage to the life support systems of land, water, flora, fauna and the atmosphere. In addition, the current pattern of economic and technological growth is leading to gross social inequity and rising joblessness. The rich–poor divide is widening both within and among nations. At the same time, the spread of knowledge and information, particularly through the electronic media, has led to an era of rising expectations. The economically and socially underprivileged sections of human society are now aware that their future is not a question of fate, but of political and technological choice. If they are not given access to the information superhighways and other technological highways to progress, a new form of social and economic apartheid will spread, which will be even more serious in its consequences to the future of human civilization than the skin-colour-based apartheid which has just ended.

True education is leadership in thought. There are periods in human history when the progress of decades can be accomplished in a few years. It is the view of the Commission that we have arrived at one of these great, creative moments. Can the political leadership of all countries seize this moment and convert it into an opportunity for promoting job-led economic growth, rooted in the principles of ecology and equity? Can we make the gender inequity and the coexistence of extreme poverty on the part of a billion children, women, and men, and extreme affluence and unsustainable lifestyles on the part of another billion, an anachronism of the past? Can we foster love of diversity and pluralism in terms of religion, race, language, colour or political belief?

In our view, there are uncommon opportunities now to find the solutions to these basic challenges facing contemporary human society. We have tried to deal with them in a concise manner in this report, which concludes that commitment to the principles of democracy and human diversity, equity in terms of gender, economic condition and sustainable lifestyles, is fundamental to achieving both a better common present and a better future.

Personally, it has been a privilege working with a highly distinguished group of women and men, whose sole concern has been a better life for all. I wish to thank every member of the Commission, as well as the many others who have helped us, for their time and vision. The Member Secretary, Mr Garry Jacobs, however, merits a special mention for his total dedication to the principles which inspired the setting up of ICPF. Throughout the last five years, he has devoted his time and extraordinary talent to the work of the Commission. He has been the principal catalyst of the Commission's work. In his heavy responsibilities, he has been ably supported by Robert J. Macfarlane and Robert van Harten. I wish to record our sincere gratitude to this unique trio.

Our work has been largely supported by grants from UNDP and UNESCO. UNESCO also provided the services of Dr Maurice Goldsmith, Director, International Science Policy Foundation, to edit this report. It has been a privilege working with Dr Goldsmith, an editor of extraordinary wit and wisdom. I am indebted to Mr Boutros Boutros-Ghali, Secretary General of the United Nations; Dr Federico Mayor, Director General of UNESCO; and Mr James Gustave Speth, Administrator of UNDP, for their support and encouragement. A special word of thanks is also due to Mrs Robin La Brie-Jackson, who has helped throughout in managing the work of the Commission with great competence and courtesy. Finally, I must acknowledge the inspiration and encouragement provided by Mr T. Natarajan, Secretary, The Mother's Service Society, Pondicherry, India, from the very inception of the idea of the Commission. His emphasis on leadership in thought that leads to action has served as a guiding principle for the work of the Commission. A more complete list of the many individuals and institutions who have contributed generously of their time and resources to our work is contained in the Acknowledgements appended to this volume.

During 1994 and 1995, several major international events will take place. The International Conference on Population and Development at Cairo in September 1994, the World Summit for Social Development at Copenhagen and the Fourth World Conference on Women at Beijing in 1995, and the designation of 1995 as the International Year for Tolerance – all provide unique opportunities for promoting sustainable and equitable development. The past 50 years since the birth of the UN have marked striking progress in every field of human endeavour, except in the areas of ecological and human security. We should now concentrate on these aspects of security, so vital for sustained human happiness and fulfilment. It is our hope that this report will be of some help in accelerating the pace of progress in the evolution of a new human ethic conducive to human beings living in harmony with nature and with each other.

M. S. Swaminathan, Chairman
International Commission on Peace and Food
Madras, India, 6 July 1994

THE ORIGIN AND CONTEXT OF ICPF's WORK

Looking back, it is astonishing how much the world has changed since the idea of establishing the International Commission on Peace and Food was first conceived in 1987. Who had the foresight to imagine the monumental changes which have so radically altered the political, economic and social complexion of the world community – the end of the nuclear arms race and the opposing military alliances of East and West, the rising tide of democracy that dramatically and irreversibly transformed the USSR and the countries of Eastern Europe, the growing importance of the UN in peace keeping and peace making, the peaceful end of apartheid in South Africa, the first tangible steps toward lasting peace between Arabs and Israelis in the Middle East, the completion of global trade negotiations and the founding of the World Trade Organization, and concerted actions to stem the degradation of the environment?

The mid-1980s was a time when global military spending reached an all-time high of $1.2 trillion. Economic growth had slowed or stalled in much of the developing world, prompting some to term the 1980s the 'lost decade' for development. While there was little agreement on what steps were needed to reverse the arms race and provide a stable basis for world peace, a consensus was emerging that something must be done to address the urgent problems of hunger, famine and endemic poverty that continued to plague much of the developing world and constituted a gnawing source of instability that refused to be contained by national boundaries. The unconscionable loss of lives due to hunger in an age of plenty generated growing concern over the issues of food and famine. Starvation forced millions of people, particularly in sub-Saharan Africa, to flee their homes in despair. It undermined social stability, fuelled violence and in some cases led to war between neighbours and fellow-countrymen. The effort to glean more food from desiccated earth further ravaged the environment and aggravated shortages. To this was added the galling sight of hunger amidst plenty, when adequate food production was not matched by sufficient job opportunities to provide incomes to all who needed to buy food because they could not grow their own. These concerns motivated and were symbolized by the institution of the World Food Prize in 1987.

It was in this context that, on World Food Day in October 1988, a small group met in Washington DC and proposed the launching of a new initiative to utilize the growing consensus over food to press for more rapid and substantial progress on peace, disarmament and development. Without peace there could be no stable basis or fertile soil for development, without development there could be no lasting and assured peace. The inextricable linkage between war and famine, economic dislocation and unemployment, violence and social instability, fleeing refugees and migrating populations, high military spending and growing indebtedness argued compellingly against any uni-dimensional approach to resolving the problems of peace and development. In the rapprochement between the superpowers we saw an opportunity that demanded new perspectives, new attitudes and new approaches.

In constituting its membership, the Commission has brought together a highly diverse group of political leaders, scientists, economists, government administrators and businessmen, drawn from industrial and developing nations, with a wide range of experience in presiding over government ministries, administrative departments and agencies, international development and research institutions, prominent nongovernmental agencies and private companies.

The first official plenary meeting of ICPF was held in Trieste, Italy, in October 1989, within a few days of the fall of the Berlin Wall. Overtaken by the staggering pace of developments arising from the end of the Cold War, the world was being altered almost beyond recognition. Our ambition to slow the arms race appeared suddenly insignificant in the light of unfolding events. While we contemplated strategy, COMECON and the Warsaw Pact were breaking up, the USSR began to dissolve, democratic institutions began to spread, and command economies started transforming themselves into free market systems.

These monumental achievements were not purchased without cost. Peace was accompanied by partial economic collapse in Eastern Europe. It was evident from the outset that the transition in these countries would not be smooth or easy and that the destiny of the world in the twenty-first century would be influenced decisively by the outcome. Severe food shortages in the Soviet Union, which angered the long-suppressed population and compelled the government to take radical action, once again highlighted the linkages between peace and food. Production dropped precipitously as frantic efforts were made to reverse economic decline by radical measures. Although these events were closely observed and strongly assisted by top international experts, the world lacked both the conceptual knowledge and the practical experience needed to guide these nations through their crisis. At the invitation of the Soviet Academy of Agricultural Sciences, the Commission's next meeting, in November 1990, was held in Moscow: it would examine the challenges facing the USSR during the shift to democracy and a civilian market economy, and identify steps to improve the food supply, speed military conversion and ease the economic transition.

The immediate euphoria over the rapid reduction in tensions between East and West freed public attention to focus on other pressing problems and generated great expectations that a 'peace dividend' would usher in a period of rapid economic progress for developing countries. Yet, despite a remarkable one-third reduction in worldwide defence spending from peak levels in the 1980s, foreign aid budgets continued to shrink. This prompted us to examine the potential benefits that could be derived from transferring or redirecting scientific, technological, educational and productive resources from military applications to support development and the environment. At the same time, increasing pressure was mounted by donors on aid-dependent developing countries to reduce their own defence spending, often without consideration for the genuine security concerns of these countries. The need to improve mechanisms to protect all nations from external aggression has stimulated a rethinking of the competitive security paradigm which has governed relations between nations throughout the century, and the formulation of an alternative approach.

The slow expansion of world trade and economic growth in developing countries during this period, attributable to prolonged recession in industrialized nations and a drastic decline in demand from Eastern Europe, underlined the need for more effective and better-coordinated development strategies to address the problems of the world's one billion people who live in hunger and absolute poverty. Increasing the production and availability of food to meet the nutritional needs of a still rapidly expanding global population led us to propose steps to double food production in deficit regions.

In many countries, the problem of hunger has less to do with insufficient food production than with distribution or entitlement. The poor lack remunerative employment opportunities to generate the purchasing power needed to obtain the minimum essential requirements of food. In 1990, the Commission undertook a study of alternative strategies to eradicate poverty among the 300 million extremely poor in India, representing about 25 per cent of the poor worldwide, by more extensive development of commercial agriculture and agro-based industries. Following ICPF's third plenary meeting in Madras in October 1991, ICPF's Prosperity 2000 plan for creating 100 million jobs in India was presented to the Indian government, which incorporated the strategy in its Eighth Five Year Plan. The findings of that study and the strategic recommendations that emerged from it convinced us that eradicating the spectres of hunger, unemployment and poverty was possible even though these problems are present on such a massive scale in many developing countries.

Events continued to accelerate with the break-up of the USSR later that year, followed by the collapse of the Eastern European economies in 1992. Simultaneously, the slowdown in trade within this region and the high cost of Germany's reunification were having an unexpected and unwelcome impact on economic recovery in the industrial countries. Reduced military spending, large budget deficits and declining imports from Eastern Europe slowed growth and aggravated the already acute problem of unemployment in Europe and North America. Rising anxiety over prospects for employment in the 1990s posed a serious threat to global trade negotiations and to the prospects for growth in the developing world. Examination of the rising problem of unemployment in industrial nations led us to the formulation of a comprehensive strategy for full employment in the West. The Commission's fourth plenary meeting in Oslo during September 1992 focused on the issues of employment and transition.

Our effort to examine each of these problems, both in depth and in relation to each other, was aided by the constitution of six working groups to study a wide gamut of issues related to peace, disarmament, food, employment and human development in the emerging global context. This report is based upon the findings and recommendations of these groups, which were presented and discussed during the fifth and final plenary meeting at the Carter Presidential Center in Atlanta in October 1993.[1]

This narrative of ICPF's brief history illustrates the complex array of interrelationships that link the issues of peace, social stability, disarmament, democracy and environment with economic transition in the East, employment in the West and poverty elimination and

1 Most of the data cited in this book have been drawn from the seven papers prepared by working groups on the main issues covered in the report, and from several special reports prepared by ICPF for UN agencies – to be published as a separate volume.

population stabilization in developing countries. The necessity for understanding and addressing these issues as a complex whole rather than as disparate and independent parts has been an underlying principle of our work.

From the outset, it has been our intention to build upon the work of previous international commissions that have done so much to generate greater public awareness and support for coordinated global action. This report contains specific operational strategies for implementing many of their recommendations. Much of their work can come to fruition in the changed international climate, if only we shift the emphasis from preoccupation with cataloguing the problems to focusing on the opportunities available to eliminate them.

The work of an independent, self-constituted commission has the advantage of being unfettered by the necessity of conforming to any official policy lines. It is also faced with the challenge of making a real further contribution on issues which engage so many excellent minds and institutions worldwide. In formulating the ideas and recommendations incorporated in this report, it has been our objective to avoid utopian and idealistic prescriptions that are incapable of being translated into practice in the foreseeable future. At the same time, we have refused to be confined by what is presently considered realistic and practicable, because both intuition and recent experience confirm that our conception of what is real and achievable are themselves often the expression of limited and short-sighted perceptions.

Disclaimer

Due to the diversity and complexity of the views examined by the Commission, and the heterogeneous mix of Commission members drawn from a wide range of countries, backgrounds and professions, it has not been possible to arrive at consensus on all the views discussed in this report. Five years of research and discussion have created a much greater commonality of perspective, but there are still significant differences among members regarding specific views and recommendations presented in this report. However, all the Commissioners agree with the basic emphasis on social and gender equity, job-led growth and human security. Members share the conviction that a candid and challenging discussion of these issues is more valuable than representation of a consensus view.

2

UNCOMMON OPPORTUNITIES

The Next Millennium

We are on the threshold of a new millennium. All civilizations have recognized the special significance of new beginnings – the dawn of a new day, a new year, a new century. These are moments of new birth when fresh vision and greater energy are available for setting out in a new direction or accelerating progress along our chosen course. The dawn of a new millennium brings with it a tremendous power for renewal and advancement. It can mark a decisive transition or staging ground for speeding humanity's evolutionary progression.

The remarkable events of the past few years – the fall of the Berlin Wall, the turn to democracy in the former USSR and other countries of Eastern Europe, the peaceful end of apartheid in South Africa, and concrete steps toward lasting peace between Israelis and Palestinians – confirm this truth. In an age of incredibly rapid and revolutionary change, who can confidently claim the wisdom to predict what can or cannot be accomplished in the coming decade? Looking back on this moment ten years from now, we may well be able to chronicle what now appear as equally extraordinary achievements.

The glimpse of possible changes in the world over the next decade afforded in the box on pages 7–8 may appear outlandish and unrealistic to some. It is an indication of what is possible, not a prophecy or projection of what is inevitable. It presents a set of real opportunities that can be tapped, provided that we take best advantage of the present situation. The progress it heralds is no more inconceivable and remarkable than the chain of recent achievements seemed seven years ago – yet those we have already come to take for granted and, under insistent prodding by the media, to replace in our consciousness with ever new concerns.

Prospects for the Year 2005

- According to the provisions of international treaty, the final batch of nuclear weapons has been destroyed, ushering in a world free of nuclear, chemical and biological weapons.

- Global military spending has fallen by nearly 50 per cent since 1994 to $400 billion per annum (in 1990 US dollars), half of which is now contributed to a global military force responsible for enforcing a total ban on war between nations.

- Not a single inter-state or civil war is raging due to the extension of the UN's mandate to prevent all forms of war and its vastly strengthened military capabilities.

- International drug trafficking has declined by more than 80 per cent since the signing of the UN declaration granting the UN special powers to eradicate the drugs trade.

- An accelerated schedule for dismantling trade barriers and the formation of regional economic unions, such as the Middle East Economic Area that incorporates Israel and the Arab states, and other initiatives to promote larger bilateral trade between countries and regions, have helped to more than double the growth rate in world trade.

- With the assistance of the UN's World Development Force, proposed in this report, food shortages have been eliminated from the last famine danger zones in Africa, and total food production on that continent has doubled within a decade.

- Poverty in its direst forms has been eradicated in China and India by strategies that have led to the creation of hundreds of millions of new jobs.

- Rapid economic growth in developing countries has acted as a powerful engine for vigorous expansion among the industrialized nations.

- In partial fulfilment of their common commitment to generate Full Employment Economies, the member states of the OECD have announced that unemployment in industrialized countries has dropped to the lowest level in half a century.

- Most of the nations of Eastern Europe and Central Asia have achieved a significant measure of political and economic stability combined with unexpectedly high growth rates ranging from 5 to 10 per cent. This

➡

region has emerged as an important source of trade and economic growth for the industrial nations.

- Global expenditure on education and training as a percentage of GDP has doubled during the decade. One remarkable result has been the complete eradication of illiteracy and universal enrolment in primary education.

- Scientists report that the ozone layer is being restored to pre-1970 levels far more rapidly than had been anticipated. This has been aided by a worldwide rush to renewable energy power generation led by such regions as California, which now produces 10,000 megawatts of electricity from wind power and has mandated an increase in pollution-free motor vehicles from the present level of 5 per cent to 25 per cent by 2010.

Common sense tells us it is not possible simply to wish away the serious problems barring these achievements. We need the technology vastly to improve productivity in poor countries. We need the organizational know-how to create effective administrative and political systems in transition states and to restructure international institutions. We require enormous investments in constructive economic activities – as opposed to lavish arms spending – to generate jobs and higher incomes for hundreds of millions of people in the developing world, and by extension to stimulate further economic growth and job creation in the West.

All these essential ingredients are available in abundant measure, if only we choose to employ them for our common benefit. Yet even this is not enough. Otherwise, we would already have accomplished many of our goals. Above and beyond these material, social and financial resources, we need a new vision, a new perspective and new attitudes about what can and must be done. If the events of the past seven years prove anything, it is that a massive change of attitude and perspective, such as the one brought about between East and West, is imminently possible and incredibly powerful. The one we have all been party to has immensely altered the world's political and economic landscape – sweeping away at a single stroke the very real danger of another world war and widespread nuclear destruction.

The recommendations formulated in this report call for profound changes in the way we think, feel and act to meet the challenges and tap the opportunities of the coming decade. We should not underestimate the magnitude of the changes required or the collective effort needed to bring them about. Nor, as recent events confirm, should we underestimate the capacity of humankind to make these changes and realize the benefits.

During the twentieth century, humankind has achieved an unprecedented mastery of its physical and social environment – soaring into space and landing on the moon, exploring the ocean floors, harnessing the power of the atom, delving into the secrets of the human brain and creating machines that imitate many of its functions, unravelling our own genetic code, generating unimagined wealth for many, proliferating national and global institutions, evolving the rudimentary foundations of world governance. Yet the very magnitude of these accomplishments has generated a sense of dependence and even helplessness. Our own creations have cast a spell over us. Impressed by the power of our works, we feel obliged to submit to our own incomplete and sometimes faulty constructions, rather than to complete or modify them to better meet our needs.

Instead of marvelling at the wondrous achievements of the modern era, we should marvel at the unlimited human capacity for invention and progress. The beginning of the third millennium is an opportunity for us to rediscover the ancient truth that human beings, individually and collectively – not material resources, nor the technology we invent, nor the institutions we fashion – are the primary resource, driving force, centre-piece and ultimate determinant of our development. The key lies within us.

Some Common Challenges

Listing future achievements does not mitigate the very real and pressing problems that confront us now. A brief catalogue suffices to indicate the magnitude of these challenges.

- *Population*: In spite of the continued decline in birth rates, world population is expected to rise by nearly three billion people or 50 per cent over the next three decades, making the task of achieving food security, employment and education for all even more daunting than it is today.

- *Poverty*: The incidence of poverty continues to increase both in relative and absolute terms. Presently, 1.4 billion people, constituting 26 per cent of the total population of developing and developed nations, live in poverty. The poorest 20 per cent of the world's population share a minuscule 1.4 per cent of the world's income. According to current projections, 300 million people, representing nearly 50 per cent of the population of sub-Saharan Africa, will live below the poverty line at the turn of the century.

- *Environment*: Unsustainable lifestyles and consumption (in industrial countries) and population growth, along with rising levels of production and consumption (in developing countries), will place strenuous demands on the environment of the planet. Growing damage to the basic life support systems of soil, water, flora, fauna and the atmosphere is taking place in all parts of the world.

- *Unemployment*: In the West, rising levels of unemployment have increased resistance to free trade and immigration. Rising levels of long-term unemployment and youth unemployment in inner cities are associated with the increasing incidence of crime. In developing countries, rapid population growth continues to outpace job creation in most regions, resulting in high levels of unemployment, increasing social unrest and large scale migration from rural to urban areas and internationally.

- *Gender discrimination*: Gender remains a major determinant of privilege and discrimination worldwide. Women still suffer from unfavourable sex ratios, lower wages and restraints on property ownership, as well as higher levels of illiteracy and lower educational attainments.

- *Rising violence*: Violence is on the increase, especially violence within society in the form of civil wars, crime and drugs. During the first half of 1994, 36 armed conflicts were in progress. During the past year, more than half a million people perished in Somalia and Rwanda alone. Nearly 100 less-known conflicts rage at the present moment.

- *Refugees*: Violence, poverty and environmental degradation are displacing people on a massive scale. Today there are more than 18 million refugees, far more than the number immediately following the Second World War. A rising tide of immigration is increasing ethnic tensions and intolerance in both industrial and developing countries.

- *Debt*: Outside the industrial countries, global growth in the last two decades has come from a limited number of countries in East and

South East Asia. Income inequalities are increasing rapidly, even between developing countries. More than 60 countries are unable to meet their debt obligations. Many are facing depressed prices for primary commodities, upon which they rely for their export earnings and debt servicing.

- *Economic collapse in Eastern Europe*: The enormous spread and depth of economic decline among the former communist countries of Eastern Europe during the period 1990–3 exceeds in magnitude the catastrophe that engulfed the capitalist economies during the Great Depression of the 1930s. Falling production and incomes coupled with soaring prices are combining to cause political instability, social unrest and extreme hardship to the populations of these nations. If not remedied, this could result in a reversal of the remarkable progress towards world peace achieved during the past seven years.

- *Arms exports*: The cutting of defence budgets has generated increasing pressure on arms manufacturers to seek export markets. Although the value (in 1992 US dollars) of arms exports fell by more than 50 per cent from 1988 to 1992, it still represents nearly $20 billion annually. These weapons, over 80 per cent of which are supplied by the five permanent members of the Security Council, directly contribute to the growing instability and violence. During the last decade, 40 per cent of these weapons were sold to trouble spots such as Afghanistan, Iraq, Somalia and Sudan.

These are, indeed, severe challenges that call for urgent and determined action by the global community on a scale unprecedented during times of peace. But the lessons of the past decade should caution us against accepting as a *fait accompli* statistical projections that predict the outcome of our effort over the next ten years before it has even begun. *No such determinism exists, except in our minds.* Given the right leadership, we can change the course, amend the rules, alter the structures and accelerate action to achieve an entirely different and more favourable set of outcomes. *Our future is not a question of fate. It is a question of choice.*

Evolutionary Opportunities

What then is the justification for predicting a bright future? There are political, economic, social and technological forces active in the world today that can override the causality of past trends and combine together to make this a time of unprecedented opportunity.

- *Intellectual synthesis:* War is the result of a conflict that leads to a forceful resolution followed by a fresh period of progress. The end of the Second World War marked the defeat of fascism. It gave birth to the United Nations, followed by the dissolution of colonial empires and freedom for more than forty subject nations. The end of the Cold War marks the end of a seventy-year confrontation between two opposing ideologies – capitalist and socialist – that reflected a more profound conflict between two fundamental aspects of human existence – individual freedom and social responsibility. The posing of these two as opposite and mutually exclusive forces has for long limited our freedom of thought and action and prevented us from boldly experimenting with new ways to reconcile them. The peaceful termination of this confrontation has lowered the mental barriers. It provides us with an opportunity to synthesize these forces in a manner which balances individual freedom with collective action to eradicate the blatant manifestations of poverty, social injustice and inequity.

- *Economic liberalism and rising investment in developing countries:* One immediate result of this reconciliation has been the recent movement of economic liberalization spreading throughout the developing world, accompanied by the relaxation of bureaucratic constraints that impede growth. This trend has stimulated a dramatic increase in foreign investment in these countries, which has risen nearly six-fold during the past seven years. Private loans and foreign direct investment together are now approximately twice the level of total overseas development assistance. This investment provides additional benefit in the form of increased transfer of technology and management skills, increased access to export markets and a reduction in the cost of capital.

- *Defence cuts:* The monumental and extravagant waste of human, material, scientific and financial resources resulting from the preparation, execution and consequences of armed conflict are too staggering to quantify. In financial terms alone, direct expenditure on defence over the past decade was roughly equivalent to the value of the entire world's gross annual product. The $400 billion reduction in global military expenditure achieved during the past seven years can be matched by a further saving of equal or greater magnitude, representing four times the current combined annual levels of foreign aid and international capital flows to developing countries. The freeing of an additional $400 billion a year for development would be sufficient to finance the eradication of poverty worldwide.

Less than 3 per cent of this saving is sufficient to eradicate the diseases that now claim the lives of 25,000 children every day.

- *End of war:* Cessation of war and of the threat of large-scale warfare are essential preconditions for more rapid social progress. The end of East–West confrontation and withdrawal of support for proxy wars fuelled by superpower rivalry provide us with the opportunity to build upon and extend peace in the Middle East and South Africa to all regions, to eliminate the use of war as an instrument of policy, and to impose peace within and between nations as a condition for membership and participation in the world community.

- *Expansion of world trade:* The end of international political confrontation has given a strong impetus to global economic cooperation. The successful conclusion of the international trade negotiations, culminating in the establishment of the World Trade Organization, opens up vast potential for nations to increase mutually beneficial economic activity, predicated on the understanding that more trade is good for everyone. Studies cited by the World Bank estimate that the removal of trade barriers by the industrial nations would increase the exports of many developing countries by as much as 50 to 100 per cent, representing a gain in real income of $40 billion to $80 billion annually. For the least developed countries, these gains could be double the amount of official development assistance. The International Monetary Fund (IMF) has cited reasons for concluding that actual gains may be significantly higher than these estimates.

- *New engines for global economy:* Economic growth in the developing world is projected to remain strong throughout the decade, averaging 4 to 5 per cent per year in low- and middle-income countries. At a time of slackened demand and low levels of growth in most industrial nations, developing countries have become the principal engine driving expansion of the global economy and employment generation, whereas until recently the Third World was perceived primarily as a drag on the world economy or a threat to jobs in the West. The potential for much higher rates of growth in these countries, as recently achieved by China, can result in much larger flows of capital, technology and organizational know-how. Recognition of this opportunity should be central to the strategy of industrial nations for stimulating their own job growth.

- *Advancing technology:* The pace of technological development continues to accelerate. The application of biotechnology in agriculture offers significant opportunities to raise productivity and generate higher incomes for farmers. Medical biotechnology is opening up the prospect of longer, healthier lives of better quality for the elderly. Over the next 40 years, child mortality is expected to fall to half its present level and life expectancy is projected to rise by 10 per cent. The shift to renewable energy sources and reduced material consumption in manufacturing can lighten the environmental burden of economic growth. Concerted action now could bring these benefits much sooner.

- *Information superhighways:* Information is a catalyst and stimulant to social development. The speed of information, like the speed of transportation, is a critical determinant of economic activity. Innovations brought about by the marriage of computers and telecommunications will make possible more, faster and better communication in developing countries at substantially lower cost through global computer networks and satellite-linked telephone systems. In some areas, such as finance, news and sports, the barriers to the flow of information are already crumbling. The increasing quality, quantity and speed of information flows about markets, technologies and significant events are quickening growth of the global economy. One consequence has been the globalization of financial markets, resulting in increased financial transfers to developing countries. The technology exists for similar achievements in many other fields related to development.

- *Global consciousness:* The impact of the 1992 Earth Summit goes far beyond the decisions taken to protect the global environment. By focusing on critical threats that can only be met through common action, it has changed the way people and nations think about the world and each other. A consciousness of One World is emerging above the din of individualistic and nationalistic self-interest. This new perspective will enable us to generate effective strategies for addressing many problems that have thus far defied solution.

In addition to these nine factors, two powerful revolutions are redrawing the landscape of the global society and generating an unparalleled dynamism for rapid progress on the issues of critical concern to humanity.

Democracy, Peace and Development

The first is a revolutionary movement from authoritarianism to democracy that has travelled around the world during the past decade.

The initial wave swept through Latin America in the early 1980s, replacing military regimes in Peru, Argentina, Brazil, Uruguay, Chile, Paraguay and Bolivia. In 1979, 12 out of 19 Latin American countries had authoritarian governments. By 1993, every country except Cuba and Haiti had a democratically elected government. *Glasnost* and *perestroika* in the USSR initiated a second and more powerful tide of freedom that expanded rapidly through Eastern Europe and then to other continents, in the same way that India's attainment of freedom from colonial rule gave birth to a host of freedom movements and new nations after the Second World War. The number of single-party or military states and people under autocratic rule has fallen dramatically since 1980, and the trend continues.

This shift to multi-party democracy, when coupled with a free press and an independent judiciary, vastly reduces the threat of large-scale wars similar to those that have twice shaken the world in this century. Three factors are at play in most conflict situations: the absence of developed democratic institutions, the absence or abuse of fundamental human rights, and the inability to make those choices in the management of public policy on which good governance depends. Authoritarian governments find justification for their existence in the presence of external threats to national security, in times of war and during periods of imperialist expansionism. They have a vested interest in maintaining a state of tension or initiating conflicts. In contrast, empirical evidence shows that liberal democracies do not go to war against one another. A study by Dean V. Babst of 116 major wars from 1789 to 1941 revealed that 'no wars have been fought between independent nations with elective governments'. The reasons for this are several. Democracies tend to be more prosperous and better educated. They share common political cultures based on individual rights and liberties. They establish orderly and peaceful processes for conflict resolution within society. In addition, elected governments find it extremely difficult to win public support for initiating and sustaining wars in which the country's own citizenry must fight, except in order to rebuff or forestall external aggression, as illustrated by domestic opposition to America's role in Vietnam.

War is the engine of dictatorial power. Peace is the social dividend of democracy. Peace is not merely the absence of war. It is a settled, stable, secure condition which thrives on a foundation of political maturity, social freedom and economic well-being. A world in which all major military powers – with the present exclusion of China – have democratic governments removes the ideological basis and political pressure for confrontation between states. If it is maintained, the adoption of democratic forms of government by the nations of Eastern Europe and the developing world will help ensure peaceful relations between states, which is the most fundamental precondition for accelerated economic development. The marriage of democracy and disarmament can transform the world – abolishing wars, eliminating nuclear arsenals, liberating hundreds of billions of dollars for building a better common future.

In economic terms, the shift to democratic government presents an opportunity for more rapid development in these countries. During the post-war period of technology-driven industrialization, there is a strong correlation between a representative form of government and rapid economic development. This relationship is reciprocal. In democratic countries freedom of expression and exposure to independent media awaken people to expectation of a better life and encourage them to take initiatives that lead to prosperity. At the same time, the democratic tendency is strengthened substantially by rising standards of living. As democracies distribute political power, they also tend to distribute the benefits of science, technology, information and education, which are the essential building blocks of economic development. Democracies provide greater access to resources, permit greater social mobility, and encourage institutional innovation. Not surprisingly, today all of the high-income industrial nations, as well as the top 25 ranked nations on UNDP's Human Development Index, are liberal democracies. In contrast, only eight of the 43 poorest nations have multi-party democratic political systems.

Even among the poorest countries, democracy has served to protect the population from the worst scourges of war and poverty that have ravaged many authoritarian countries. Economist Amartya Sen was one of the earliest to observe that no country with a democratic government and a free press has suffered from famine during the last four decades. India, the world's most populous democracy, suffered its last major famine prior to independence in 1943. Although a major famine threatened ten million lives in India during the mid-1960s, it was averted by the government's emergency measures and timely launching of the Green Revolution. In contrast, as many as 30 million persons may have died of famine in China during the late 1950s. The political necessity of maintaining popular support and the threat of exposure by the media force elected governments to take all necessary steps to ensure sufficient food supplies.

Modern democracy is the political counterpart of the market economic system. Historically, democracy broke the monopoly of the aristocracy over governance of the people, giving freedom and rights to the individual politically. The market system – basing itself on property rights and self-determined initiatives of the individual producer and consumer – is an economic expression of the same principle. Both democracy and market-oriented economies decentralize authority and decision making, providing the essential legal and regulatory framework and empowering the individual to choose and act with minimum direction or interference from above. Both depend for their success on the quality of those choices, which means on the quality of education and information possessed by the mass of people, and on the freedom and dynamism of the population.

In contrast, authoritarian systems and command economies centralize decision making, restrict the flow of information to the public, foster vast unresponsive bureaucracies, limit individual freedom and initiative within narrow bounds, and encourage obedience and conformity rather than innovation. The spread of education, which fosters independent thinking, and dissemination of information through the media were important factors in undermining public acceptance of communism in Eastern Europe. In a real sense, it was Gorbachev's policy of *glasnost* that brought down the Iron Curtain. It opened up an insular society and exposed it to an avalanche of new information, new ideas and new possibilities, which released a fervent aspiration in the people for a better life.

Over the last few years, democratization has been especially dynamic in Africa, where it has been dubbed Africa's Second Liberation. During the first three decades of post-colonial independence, almost all of the continent's 54 states had come under either single-party or military rule. The preference for authoritarian rule was often justified by the need for rapid economic development, which could be impeded by opposition to government policies and by the need to contain regional and tribal conflicts. Neither of these claims has proven true. Living standards have actually declined in most African countries during the last two decades. Regional and tribal politics have flourished. Dozens of civil and inter-state wars have been fought, accounting for millions of lost lives. Food production and employment have lagged far behind population growth. In the absence of legal channels of protest, opposition parties have frequently resorted to violence. By the end of the 1980s the lack of material progress and the emergence of young educated professionals in leadership positions had fostered, on the one hand, a revolt against single-party rule and, on the other, popular pressure for multi-party democracy that have together resulted in a democratic domino effect, similar to the spread of communist rule which Western democracies had feared would overwhelm South Asia twenty years ago. As recently as 1989, only four African countries could be considered stable democracies and three more were moving in that direction. Only three years later, 18 African nations could be classified as democratic and a number of others were in the midst of far-reaching political change. The peaceful end of apartheid in South Africa is one remarkable outcome of this process. There are even winds of change in the Middle East, where Jordan has recently shown the way by conducting free elections.

The role of democracy in development would be even more compelling were it not for the apparently contradictory evidence posed by the recent experience of Russia and China. Russia hastened to introduce democratic reforms in the hope that they would lead to rapid economic advancement. China preferred to postpone political reforms until the economic transition was much further advanced. As an immediate result, China has the highest economic and employment growth rates among the nations of the world, while Russia has experienced three successive years of steeply declining national income. These differences are of vital importance, but they centre around the issue of the best strategy for the transition in human terms, not on the ultimate importance of democracy to continuous economic development. The opening up to foreign trade and investment, the spread of higher education which is essential to achieve global competitiveness and the rising living standards which the market system will generate – all serve to undermine the legitimacy and staying power of the single-party system. China has released a social movement that is rapidly shifting power from the Party to market-responsive institutions and special interest groups, which include wealthy entrepreneurs, provincial officials, workers and peasants. Final assessment of China's strategy will be determined by the further response of the political system to rising social expectations and growing pressure for greater individual freedom.

Restructuring the UN

The movement towards democracy is not merely a question of idealism. In some countries, particularly in Africa, it is an essential step towards overcoming the desperate economic conditions that threaten the lives of millions of people. In many others, it can vastly accelerate the development process by releasing greater social initiative. In his message to the ICPF quoted earlier, the UN Secretary General emphasized the importance of democratization – what he chose to call political development – as an essential foundation and complement to peace, and to both economic and social development.

> There have been cases where development was accompanied by an authoritarian political system. But, we have invariably seen that if the participation in the market place is not accompanied by political participation, development efforts are brought to naught by social and political instability.... Once again, therefore, we see the inescapable relations governing the goals of peace, development and democratization – these are the goals of the United Nations.

In order for this revolution to have its full beneficial impact on the world's political and economic affairs, its principles need to be extended to cover all nations and international institutions. The end of the confrontation between democratic and autocratic superpowers within the UN system opens up the possibility of finally translating the idealistic aims of the UN into practical realities. First and foremost is the prospect of extending representative government to all nations. This effort will be given strong impetus by establishing democracy as a minimum condition for membership and participation of states in the affairs of the UN. It is true that the UN stands for diversity and pluralism, but not when it comes to freedom and human rights. True pluralism and diversity can only be exercised and enjoyed by people in freedom.

Recognizing the considerable effort that will be needed to prepare still subject people and to train national leaders in democratic institutions and processes, all possible support should be extended by the international community to make available the knowledge and skills needed to build viable political institutions. The UN should establish a graded, time-bound programme for the transformation of authoritarian states. Should the people of any country themselves prefer an alternative system, let them freely make that choice by electoral process. Suspension of voting rights or of the privileges of membership should be the ultimate penalty for the failure of governments to comply with this condition within a reasonable period of time.

The affirmation of democratic principles cannot and will not stop with the domestic governance of member countries. It is inevitable that the same principles be extended to the relationships between the nations that make up the international community. The present structure of the UN system is a product of the Second World War, just as the League of Nations was of the First. The Allied powers conceived it at the height of the war and evolved its structure to reflect the immediate post-war realities. Russia, the USA, France and the UK emerged from the war as the arbiters of the world order. The defeated

Axis powers, Germany and Japan, were relegated to the background. Mainland China had become communist and was therefore excluded from the power structure. India and the other colonies had not yet gained their freedom. In recognition of the mutual suspicions between Russia and the Western powers, the rule of unanimity usually adopted by political conferences was applied to decisions made by the five major powers that became the permanent members of the Security Council. The rest of the world was poorly represented. Only 51 nations – including only two African states, two East Asian nations and three Soviet republics – out of the current total of 184 UN members were present at its founding. This structure is based on political realities that no longer hold true. As the limitations of the League led to renewed conflagration two decades later, so the arrangements underlying the establishment of the UN contained within them the seeds of the confrontation between the superpowers and the Cold War.

The present international system of governance is as far from being truly representative and 'democratic' as many erstwhile authoritarian governments that incorporated the popular adjective in the names of their parties or states. The UN Charter assigns primary responsibility for the maintenance of international peace and security to the Security Council of 15 members, of whom five are permanent members with veto power over all matters. In no other constitution or organization founded on democratic principles is it accepted that a few members may thus invalidate the decisions of the majority. The General Assembly, in which all members are represented and which is headed by an elected Secretary, is only an advisory body, constituted to 'discuss any questions relating to the maintenance of international peace and security' and to 'make recommendations with regard to any such questions to the state or states concerned or to the Security Council or both'. This authorization is restricted by the provision that in regard to any dispute or situation in which the Security Council is exercising its functions under the Charter, the General Assembly will *not* make any recommendations with regard to the dispute or situation unless the Security Council so requests.

It may have been the wisdom of the great powers to fashion this non-democratic structure and maintain it, so long as the superpowers and the military blocs stood in firm opposition to each other, and so long as military power was a primary factor in world affairs. Equally, it will be wisdom now to recognize that this system is no longer justifiable or tenable. The end of the East–West confrontation, the rise of economic power and economic issues to a dominant position in international relations, the proliferation of new member countries from the developing world, and, most importantly, the emergence of development alongside peace as a primary mission of the UN system, are all arguments for radical change.

The same rationale that warrants an insistence on the adoption of democratic institutions and democratic rights within all member countries also justifies their adoption by the international community. A system that is not truly representative will not have the credibility and cannot generate the necessary participation and cooperation required for effective action on issues of crucial importance to the whole world. The rule of unanimity or veto power cannot be an effective principle of governance in a world of complex and diverse interests, as the recent conflict of interests within the European Union also illustrates. Those nations that regard themselves as the standard bearers of democracy and human rights within nations cannot justify denying these principles between nations. World peace and prosperity in the coming decades will depend on our willingness boldly to confront this issue. At the end of the Second World War the victorious nations joined together to found the UN. At the end of the Cold War, the organization needs to be re-founded, and restructured according to democratic principles, to give a more active role and more equitable representation to people of all nations.

To deem such considerations unrealistic given the present alignment of power in the world is a short-sighted view. It ignores the incredible speed and scope of changes that have radically transformed international relations over the past half decade. It assumes that the present system has the backing of the international community and that it can and will sustain itself regardless of whatever steps we may contemplate. A fundamental change in structure is essential and inevitable. The break-up of the Soviet Union and the end of the Cold War have resulted in the demise of the bipolar system which dominated international relations after 1945. The United States is now recognized as the sole superpower and the primary determinant of actions by the UN Security Council. But neither America's culture nor its historical economic and political development and present outlook will permit it to take on the extraordinary responsibilities and overseas commitments which fulfilment of this role necessitates, as its reluctance to get involved in Bosnia and Rwanda, and its quick withdrawal from Somalia illustrate. Indeed, no one nation can or should assume such responsibilities on behalf of the whole world. The rapid shift of Eastern European and former Soviet republics to radically different political and economic systems demonstrates that changes of even greater magnitude than this can be brought about rapidly.

There is likely to be far greater support for this change than may at first appear possible. Russia may actively support and China offer only nominal resistance, once a clear conception of the new structure has emerged. Ironically, the major opposition to this change is most likely to come from the past defenders of democratic principles in the Western world, rather than from the newly liberated nations of Eastern Europe. If so, this will follow the normal law of social development in which the vanguards of previous revolutions become the principal opponents of the next stage of progress. Even here it is likely to come primarily from entrenched vested interests, not the general public.

A mere tinkering with or modest amendment to the structure of the UN will only perpetuate the inherent inadequacies of the present system and postpone its maturation into a truly effective instrument for global political, economic and social integration and collective accomplishment. Many proposals are being floated to modify its workings, mostly by expanding representation on the Security Council. As an interim measure and first steps, the immediate addition of five more permanent members to the Security Council, based on the criteria of population and economic status, and the abolition of the veto power are fully justified. However, these changes do not go far enough in furthering the interests of global peace and development. They will not fundamentally alter the out-dated, non-representative structure which perpetuates the *status quo*. It is time to devise a new formula and a new structure for international governance that will reconcile and harmonize the political rights and economic interests of all the world's peoples. The institution that had come to symbolize the Cold War must be restructured in such a manner as to symbolize the abolition of all war and the establishment of peace and democracy as the foundations for global development.

Global Social Revolution

A second revolution also possesses tremendous transforming power to accelerate human progress – the revolution of rising expectations. This revolution is not new in conception or expression, but what is new is its rapid extension to encompass people and nations around the globe. Although the term was first applied to describe the growing aspirations of the middle class in North America forty years ago, it is now widely applicable to all social and economic groups in both developed and developing countries.

After countless centuries of slow, often imperceptible progress, humanity everywhere is on the move. A rising tide of technological advancement has brought with it wave after wave of social innovation. Democracy has liberated long suppressed populations from military or political oppression. With the passing of colonialism, a new generation of youth has come of age in developing countries that never lived under the fear, compulsion and humiliation of colonial rule. The knowledge imparted by the spread of universal education has removed much of the ignorance and superstition, the submissiveness and sense of inferiority that limited people's mental and social horizons in the past. The elimination of deadly epidemic diseases has replaced an ever-looming shadow of fear with vibrant health and prolonged vigour for billions. Improved methods of cultivation have converted food shortages into abundance or surplus in many countries which until recently suffered from chronic hunger. Advanced production technologies have made accessible to greater numbers the comforts and conveniences that until recently were exclusively in the purview of the élite. Vast sections in developing countries now have access to wristwatches, bicycles, televisions, travel, houses and motor vehicles of all descriptions. Although China produced only 178,000 refrigerators between 1949 and 1979, production has now soared to the highest level in the world to meet the surging demand. More than 39 million households, representing 56 per cent of all urban households, have acquired them in the last fifteen years. Similarly, between 1981 and 1990 India's production of televisions rose more than ten-fold from 450,000 per year to 4.8 million. Exposure to lifestyles elsewhere through the media, cinema and travel has created greater awareness of possibilities and generated higher hopes. The enormous recent achievements of East Asian countries, which are quickly closing the economic gap that separates them from the wealthiest nations, act as a constant reminder and goad to those who have achieved less. In the new atmosphere of peace and greater freedom brought about by the end of the Cold War, all these factors combine to add urgency and intensity to the aspirations of the lower and middle classes everywhere.

Not long ago most people expected to end their lives in the same place and largely in the same position as they and their predecessors began. Growth was confined to the advancement of a small number of individuals, mostly within existing levels of the established social order. Development was a slow, haphazard and largely unconscious result of countless individual efforts. Today, people in most developing countries are motivated by an expectation, an urge, a feverish drive for rapid advancement that has acquired the characteristics of a social revolution. The search for greater comfort, convenience, security and enjoyment motivates entire societies to embrace progress as their primary goal and collectively dedicate themselves to achieve it. The race for development has become an intense preoccupation of every nation. The slow pace of trial and error growth is no longer adequate to meet the rising demands of the people.

The awakening of this compelling urge has unleashed a powerful social force for human progress. That force refuses to be bound by either rationality or morality. Revolution means to bring future results more quickly, sooner than they would come through normal evolutionary processes. In earlier ages, people revolted when their most basic needs were not met, when they were denied rights or oppressed. Today, vast sections in developing countries are stirred to action because their expectations are not fulfilled. Economic liberalization has unleashed people's expectations: witness the rush of Chinese peasants to invest in the stock market and the increasing demand of Indian villagers for a range of consumer goods. The same movement continues in the West as increased physical and social mobility, the growing demand for higher education and the widespread urge for greater recreation and travel.

These expectations are the seed and driving force for social progress. They provide the energy and create the openness and willingness for change. But they also increase the danger of frustration, disappointment and violence. The end of the Cold War was expected to usher in an age of peace, but actually violence is on the rise in both developing and developed countries because of the widening gap between human expectations and achievements. This growing gap between expectations and achievements is at the root of contemporary turbulence worldwide. The popular and sometimes violent demand for freedom and participatory democracy, the return of religion in politics, surging ethno-nationalism and intolerance, and rising urban crime are disparate expressions of this phenomenon.

In Eastern Europe, where a peaceful revolution from within has broken the shackles of statism that long confined the energies of people, these energies now surge forward in high and eager expectations of a better life. Already there are growing signs of impatience, disappointment and frustration arising from the greater hardships that have come in place of the greater benefits that all expected. It is essential that these energies be channelled into constructive pursuits that generate tangible improvements. Otherwise they may recoil from the effort and look backwards to a failed system or be guided by false prophets on a path that once again poses a threat to other nations.

The phenomenon of growing violence in an age of increasing affluence seems to contradict the thesis that poverty is one of the major causes of violence, until we realize that the increasingly visible signs of prosperity the world over raise the expectations and aggravate the sense of deprivation and revolt among those that have been by-passed by the general progress. Greater political and social freedom can only further magnify this tendency. This suggests that violence at the international, national and community levels cannot and will not be eradicated before poverty itself has been abolished, and that, if poverty is left unaddressed at its source, further economic progress is likely further to aggravate conflict in society, unless we are able to extend the benefits of progress to everyone. This realization would be quite disconcerting were it not for the fact that we are fast approaching the time when both these persistent ills of humankind can be banished forever – the way slavery and colonialism were banished in the past. The recognition that it is neither desirable nor possible to go backwards adds urgency to our efforts to move forward.

Revolutions of the past have been partial and localized negative reactions against an existing social order, and benefited only a small part of society that, in turn, blindly resisted change. They resulted in war and usually much destruction. The revolution of rising expectations is a positive, constructive movement spreading to encompass people at all levels of all societies around the globe, and pressing for the establishment of a higher social organization that can meet the expectations of all humanity. But the energies liberated by this revolution have to be properly converted into an evolutionary effort for development, otherwise they will fly off in unwanted directions. Society must provide the conditions and opportunities for these energies to express themselves positively and constructively in pursuit of their own fulfilment.

Education is the most essential ingredient for this transformation. It is a great leveller of social hierarchy. It has the power to transform the propensity for violent revolution into ordered evolution. It can temper and mature aspirations and enlighten expectations by an understanding of what can reasonably be sought after and achieved. It can impart knowledge of opportunities, attitudes that support constructive initiative and skills for productive application. Production technologies that make consumer goods available at lower and lower cost to more and more people also level social differences by extending the benefit of development more widely and evenly.

The soaring of human aspirations is a natural and irresistible result of goals that humankind has been striving for over the last century. It is a direct product of the great advances in freedom and democracy, human rights, social equality for women and minorities, health and education, science and technology, the rule of law, social institutions and social welfare. Society has no alternative but to meet these growing expectations by channelling the awakened energies into productive pursuits. For that we need to acquire a greater understanding of the social and psychological process that has already enabled so many to achieve so much. *The challenge and the opportunity now presented is to make conscious the previously unconscious process of development, to accelerate it, and to convert the revolution of rising social expectations into a positive energizing movement of the entire global society.*

This is the all-powerful driving force that has so radically transformed the social landscape during this 'century of the common man'. This is the ultimate 'rationale' behind the inevitable claim of the poor everywhere that will be made with ever-growing insistence and impatience until it is finally granted – as the birthright of every human being – *freedom, food, education, employment, prosperity and fulfilment for all.*

Perspectives for the New Millennium

The individual effect, complex linkages, mutually supportive inter-actions and consequent cumulative impact of these two revolutions and the nine other factors propelling global change are incalculable. They make this a rare moment in history for a quantum leap forward, which many have dreamed about but few believed achievable. Seizing this opportunity requires, most importantly of all, a change in aware-ness, attitude and perspective. Several ideas will be of abiding value in our endeavour to make the most of this rare moment.

- Our present problems and future potentials can only be understood when viewed from a wider historical perspective that avoids getting lost in the media-driven drama and intensity of momentary crisis and short-term trends. As recent global action to protect the environ-ment amply demonstrates, public awareness and understanding are growing too rapidly and becoming too important in global affairs for us to rely on the present positions of governments or current public sentiment as gauges of what may be achieved in the near future. More reliable indices of what is possible are the underlying currents that are rapidly raising the value of the human being, bringing nations together in ever-closer cooperation and mutual inter-dependence, and pressing the international community to raise its goals.

- The world is blind to the measure of its own accomplishments. We need fully to recognize the astonishing magnitude of the achievements of the present century and fully to understand the process that made them possible. This process expresses itself as scientific, technological, commercial, political, economic, social and cultural development. But its driving force is social and psychological. Its prime mover is human beings. Becoming conscious of the process of society's past achievements is a key to more rapid future progress.

• There needs to be a two-fold shift of our attention and emphasis from solving problems to tapping opportunities and from seeking to meet minimum needs to achieving our maximum potential. Preoccupation with studying problems often becomes an excuse for not dealing with them, while sapping our enthusiasm for action. Recognition of opportunities releases fresh energy and constructive initiative. Setting goals to achieve minimum needs ensures that the minimum is the most we will accomplish. Seeking to tap the maximum potentials challenges us to strive unceasingly for higher goals.

• The world possesses the technology, resources and organizational abilities needed to eradicate poverty from the globe. Positing material constraints becomes a justification for non-action. The true constraints are not material, but psychological and social. Recognizing the real barriers will help us overcome them.

• Human beings are our most creative, productive and precious resource. Human capacity increases the more it is drawn upon. It can never be exhausted. Developing the human resource should be the centrepiece of all development strategy.

• We can solve today's most pressing problems if we adopt a total approach which takes into account all the interrelated factors – political, economic, technological, social and environmental – rather than relying on partial strategies. Partial remedies, however welcome or desirable, can always generate side-effects – such as the increase in social tensions and violence observed when increasing political and social freedom are not matched by increasing economic opportunity, or the rise in unemployment and arms exports that accompany a reduction in defence expenditure. The success of the Green Revolution was due to its integration of technological, institutional, commercial and public policy measures, while its shortcomings arose from its failure to integrate environmental factors, which are now being incorporated in agricultural development strategies. Comprehensive measures can eliminate the side-effects of partial progress.

- The progress of the whole depends on the progress of all its parts. Humankind is infinitely enriched by the qualitative diversity of culture and individual expression, but it is immeasurably impoverished by the quantitative abyss which separates the more fortunate from the rest of humanity. The most prosperous levels of society cannot fully and finally rise to higher levels of accomplishment and enjoyment without first ensuring that the less fortunate and less productive are helped to obtain the full fruits of life at the present level of social achievement. Social equity, apart from its moral value, is an essential condition for continued progress.

- A proper balance has to be found between the principles of freedom and social responsibility, competition and cooperation, and between public good and private profit.

- All individual achievement is based on prior social accomplishment. The courageous pioneer and talented individual who achieve more for themselves always draw upon a rich social legacy and build on the ideas, knowledge, discoveries, inventions and innovations of countless people and societies who have come before. Policies should be formulated to reflect the contribution of the collective to all individual achievement.

3

THE PEACE IMPERATIVE

The main prerequisite and condition for the fulfilment of the world's many different potentials is peace. As democracy supports peaceful relations between states, economic prosperity and fuller development of people, peace makes possible the development of stable political institutions, more productive economic activity and a more civilized and enlightened social life. Without establishing a stable climate of peace, human rights cannot be safeguarded, democratic institutions cannot function effectively, prosperity cannot flourish, and human beings cannot discover their higher capacities for external achievement and inner fulfilment. Peace is imperative for a thriving democracy. A comprehensive perspective and integrated approach to these inter-related issues can lead to a major breakthrough on multiple fronts.

We are poised at what can become a turning point in the role of war in human affairs. The momentous consequences at stake call for decisive action. Historically, war has been a means of territorial expansion and economic conquest that strengthened and enriched the conqueror while draining the energy and diminishing the wealth of the conquered. War and economic development co-existed and sometimes complemented each other. Technological progress increased defensive and offensive capabilities. The demands of war and the associated destruction stimulated greater economic activity and spurred organiza-tional innovation, especially for the benefit of those not directly engaged in the conflict. Guns were one of the first products of mass production.

In the modern era, society has become the principle target and victim of war. With the advent of the Industrial Revolution, technology and economic activity in support of fighting forces became an increasingly significant factor. As a result, more and more effort was directed at eliminating or crippling the enemy's economic and industrial capacity and the 'national will' to wage war. Targeting of civilian populations became increasingly common. In the two world wars in this century, opposing sides waged all-out war against the military, political, economic and social resources and capacities of the enemy society. The strategic bombings of the Second World War, the fire-bombing of Tokyo, and the nuclear devastation of Hiroshima and Nagasaki took this concept to the extreme. As a result, the ratio of military to civilian casualties in military conflicts changed dramatically. In the First World War, there were 20 military casualties for each civilian death. In the Second World War, the ratio was one to one. In the Korean War, civilian deaths outnumbered military losses five to one. In the Vietnam War, this ratio rose to 20 to one. Advances in the sophistication and dissemination of modern military technology have fuelled this trend. The Iran–Iraq War, the war in Afghanistan and the Gulf War involved the use of ballistic missiles against civilian centres. In all, over 5,000 surface-to-surface missiles have targeted population centres during the last five decades.

The devastating effect of even conventional weapons on economic activity and society in general is so great that today no developed nation can afford the costs of military confrontation, either at home or overseas. No longer can non-combatants sit quietly on the sidelines or work productively undisturbed. War both between and within states has come to involve and affect all of society. Infrastructure and production facilities have become a principal target of military action. Food supplies are frequently the first major casualty and most lethal weapon. A single explosion can paralyze a major metropolis or contaminate an entire region with toxic material, dwarfing the devastation caused by the industrial accidents at Chernobyl and Bhopal. The disruption of trade resulting even from regional conflicts such as the Gulf War or the war in Bosnia, impacts not only on the economies of the belligerents, but also on neighbours, trading partners and global economic performance. Neither the victor nor the victim can any longer afford to resolve conflicts violently.

Political states may still be able to survive wars, but developmental achievements cannot. So long as the benefits of development are confined to one or a few sections of society, the costs of militarization and war may not prevent economic and social progress. But when the need is to fulfil the rising expectations of the masses by extending the benefits of development to the entire society – thus enabling the society as a whole to move to the next higher level of collective affluence and fulfilment – every social resource must be garnered and harnessed for this purpose. The colossal cost of armaments and the catastrophic destruction of war are incompatible with the achievement of prosperity for all. *Peace has become the fundamental imperative for development.*

War as an Instrument of Policy

Humanity has lived with war for so many millennia that it is difficult to imagine a world without it. Even in the four decades of 'peace' following the Second World War, approximately 160 inter-state and intra-state wars, including 100 major conflicts, have been fought in developing countries, leading directly to 20 million deaths – half of them caused by the armed forces of developed countries in Korea, Indochina, Algeria and other anti-colonial wars – and to another 20 million war-related casualties. These massive casualties during a time of 'peace' are roughly equal to the total casualties incurred by all the countries of the world during the last world war.

An equally disturbing phenomenon has been the expansion of violence within society for political purposes. Of the 82 armed conflicts between 1989 and 1992, only three were between states. During 1993, 42 countries were involved in 52 major conflicts, and another 37 experienced political violence. Terrorist warfare, whose principal aim is to threaten social peace, has become the model for conflicts in Northern Ireland, the Middle East and the drug war in Colombia. Modern means of communication, increased vulnerabilities of inter-dependent, integrated civil societies, and modern instruments of violence make these forms of war extremely destructive.

The expansion of war to encompass society poses one of the most serious challenges to national and international security and development and raises fundamental questions regarding war as an instrument of policy. For more than two centuries, war has been rationalized as an appropriate instrument in international affairs. The increasing destructiveness of violent conflict to society in general has resulted in a shift in military strategy from actual fighting to preventive diplomacy. The Helsinki Process, the Stockholm Document, the Conference on Security and Cooperation in Europe, the Warsaw Treaty's adoption of the doctrine of 'non-offensive defence', and most recently the UN Secretary General's *Agenda for Peace* – all give highest priority to war prevention.

While welcome, these incremental measures do not fully recognize either the extent of the danger of the continued application of violence to achieve political ends or the extent of the opportunity which the end of the Cold War has brought for radically altering the way in which humanity settles domestic and international disputes. There was a time when war could be justified as a necessary expedient. Now the potential human and economic costs of even limited terrorist war – especially if it involves the use of nuclear or biological weapons, but even otherwise – are so great that the risks are no longer tolerable. Because the potential risks far outweigh the possible advantages of continued reliance on this means of achieving national and international security, *war has become obsolete as an instrument of policy.*

At the same time, there is no longer an insurmountable political conflict within the UN system to prevent all member countries from agreeing to a total ban on the use of violence against each other. *It is time for the UN to declare war itself a crime against humanity and to ban from membership any nation that engages in aggression against another.* Even if this intention cannot immediately be made effective, the adoption of this Peace Imperative would mark a milestone in human affairs. There is no rational or practical obstacle to the immediate adoption of this measure. *As a starting point, it can be demonstrated that with the right perspective, courage and commitment, practical immediate solutions are possible for any and all of the conflicts presently raging.* Recent failures of international diplomacy do not contradict this assertion, they confirm it. War must, and can, be abolished.

Nuclear Weapons

The threats to future peace come in many forms and at many levels, but unquestionably the most pernicious and potentially devastating is the peril from nuclear weapons. The end of the nuclear arms race between the superpowers may have removed the looming fear of all-out nuclear war and annihilation that surfaced in the artistic drawings of young American school children in the mid-1980s, but the horrible genie of Hiroshima and Nagasaki will continue to haunt us until every nuclear weapon has been destroyed. The very existence of the nuclear stockpiles carries its own inherent dynamism for their utilization, which is likely to be expressed intentionally or accidentally sooner or later.

There have been repeated efforts by the non-aligned nations to move a resolution in the UN General Assembly that the use of nuclear weapons should be declared a crime against humanity and outlawed. One hundred and twenty-six nations have voted for the resolution. It is ironic that the opposition to this resolution and justification for the continued possession and possible use of nuclear weapons come solely from the most militarily, politically and economically powerful group of nations, which are militarily without adversary and at the same time in the best position to afford and institute alternative means for their national security. Here lies the real key: the insistence of the few most powerful nations on perceiving security in their own terms, and their insatiable urge to achieve ever more of it for themselves at the expense of greater insecurity for others and the world as a whole, even though their goal can never be achieved on this unilateral basis.

During the Cold War, nuclear weapons were legitimized by the five permanent members of the Security Council which are the nuclear weapon states. Now that it is over, the governments of these nations seek to justify continued possession and the option to use these weapons, even while exerting every possible pressure to stop proliferation to other countries. The very logic which the nuclear weapon states rely on to support this policy, however, makes the acquisition of these weapons extremely attractive to non-nuclear powers. So long as their possession and possible use is tolerated and justified, the relatively low cost of production and high threat potential of these weapons offer strong incentives for other states to acquire them. It is unrealistic to expect that any system of international controls or inspections can prevent their eventual acquisition by states that decide to develop them and have the advanced scientific capabilities to do so.

From the inception of nuclear weapons, two things have been clear. There can be no victors in a nuclear war and there is no credible defence against these weapons. Confidential studies by NATO in the 1960s concluded that the costs of a nuclear exchange to either party would be so great that the weapons were essentially unusable. No satisfactory answer has ever emerged for the question: where and under what circumstances can these weapons be deployed beneficially? The continued expansion of nuclear stockpiles over three decades may have added to the self-importance of the military and political leaderships, and perhaps of the general public, in states that possessed them, but there is little evidence that it ever added to national security. The unusability of these weapons helps to explain why predictions of rapid spread of these weapons to other states proved to be so wildly exaggerated. The irrelevance or unusability of nuclear weapons is evident in all the wars involving major powers during the past four decades. A greater understanding of the environmental impact of these weapons has further strengthened the perception of unusability. It is time that psychological posturing gave way to a mature recognition that these weapons have no place in the civilized world and must be banished from it.

The continued build-up of nuclear arsenals was an attempt by the superpowers to maintain parity or superiority over each other as a deterrent against being attacked. Although the nuclear powers may argue that their arsenals have protected them from any such danger, there is little rationality in a strategy that compelled adversaries continuously to take steps to offset each other's measures, without either party actually achieving greater real security. In addition, this strategy was pursued at the cost of increasing insecurity to other nations. The acquisition of nuclear weapons generates a ripple effect and acts as a powerful force for proliferation.

The arms build-up has been reversed, but at least 40,000 nuclear weapons are still in stockpiles with a combined explosive force at least 1,000 times greater than all the firepower used in all the wars since the introduction of gunpowder six hundred years ago. START-I and START-II will bring down the number of warheads of the United States and the former Soviet Union by 90 per cent from a combined 55,500 total to 6,500 over a ten-year period. But this reduction could, in fact, be achieved within months rather than years by deactivating delivery systems and separating their warheads, which could then be stored under multilateral control. Nor do these agreements, long overdue and greatly welcome, remove the fundamental dangers and questionable legitimacy of these weapons. Even without a decision to abandon completely their use under any circumstances, a further drastic reduction to somewhere between 20 and 200 warheads is more than sufficient to meet any security need. Immediate steps can, and should, be taken to negotiate reductions to this minimum level.

The relaxation of tensions has drawn public attention away from this issue and reduced the momentum for progress at the very time when there is the greatest opportunity finally to eliminate this threat completely. The Nuclear Non-Proliferation Treaty, which ensures the military superiority of the nuclear powers over other signatories, is an instance of rule by strength forcibly imposed by the major powers on the rest of the world community in the name of peace. It is neither equitable nor justifiable. Already, 156 countries have signed the treaty, owing either to coercion or indifference, and the number is expected to increase to 170 out of 179 states by 1995. The acceptance of non-proliferation by these countries further delegitimizes the continued possession of nuclear weapons by any country. All of the treaty non-signatories can be persuaded to sign in exchange for annihilation of these weapons by those that now possess them. Under these circumstances, refusal to sign the Non-Proliferation Treaty could be considered sufficient grounds for expulsion from UN membership. Without a universal ban, the efforts of the nuclear powers to stop proliferation lack moral authority.

Arguments are often advanced that nuclear weapons cannot be 'disinvented', and that the danger of a rogue state or terrorist group acquiring and threatening use of these weapons necessitates that the present nuclear powers retain them for such a contingency. With the massive conventional firepower already available, nuclear weapons are not needed for defence, even against a rogue state with nuclear capability, and they do not represent a credible defence against terrorism under any circumstances. How could nuclear weapons conceivably be used to retaliate against terrorism? Alternative solutions can be found to address these threats far more effectively.

Similar arguments were made in the past against complete eradication of chemical weapons. The new treaty for the abolition of chemical weapons provides a useful model. Chemical weapons technology is far easier to acquire and violations of the treaty are far more difficult to verify. The fact that a comprehensive universal treaty to abolish one category of weapons of mass destruction is now a reality proves that political will rather than technical factors is the crucial element. The Chemical Weapons Treaty also shows that negotiation of such a treaty need not take decades.

The demise of the Cold War offers a unique opportunity to eliminate nuclear weapons while the political atmosphere is favourable. If the world now intends to uphold democracy and human rights as inalienable values, then the human right to live without the threat of a nuclear holocaust must be proclaimed and made inviolable. A durable non-proliferation regime can only be constructed on the basis of the universal abolition of nuclear weapons. Manufacture and possession of nuclear weapons must be banned. Use of such weapons must be outlawed as a crime against humanity. First use of such weapons by any power should automatically invoke the strongest collective security measures under the UN Security Council.

The decision on whether to permit the continued existence of nuclear weapons is of too great importance to the future of humanity to be left to the discretion of one or a few member nations of the international community. Under the present structure of the UN, the only body with authority to act is the Security Council, but the veto power of the five permanent members deprives other nations of an effective voice. *The proposal to ban completely the possession and use of nuclear weapons should be put before the Council. The right of veto should be rescinded with respect to this most crucial issue. A time-bound plan should be drawn up by the UN for complete and total nuclear disarmament by all nations.*

Ban on ballistic missiles

Nuclear devices are the most lethal class of weapons, but much of their threat arises from the development of ballistic missile technology which can deliver them to distant targets unmanned and without risk to the aggressor. Even if nuclear weapons are eliminated, these vehicles can be utilized to carry large conventional payloads that strike terror in a distant population. The danger to all nations of unexpected and unprovoked attack from near or distant powers can be vastly reduced by declaring an immediate ban on the use of ballistic missiles of all types, including those carrying conventional warheads.

This proposal, first put forth by US President Reagan in 1986, would eliminate the discriminatory provisions that deny missile acquisition to some, while preserving the right of others to maintain and develop this purely offensive capability. It would also eliminate the need for missile defence systems, which no nation can afford and which are the only possible defence against ballistic missile weapons. The ban on use should be followed by urgent measures to dismantle and scrap this entire class of weapons worldwide. Technically, a prohibition on testing and deployment of ballistic missiles would be far more verifiable than any limits on nuclear proliferation. Monitoring stations at missile production facilities and existing surveillance systems can restrain manufacture and detect test flights. Evading a ban on testing would be practically impossible.

Small Arms, Drugs, Crime and Terrorism

Four decades of preoccupation with nuclear weapons have blinded policy makers to an extremely dangerous and destabilizing threat to nations and their citizenry from the other end of the weapons spectrum – the proliferation of small arms. The shift in the nature of conflicts from massive wars between states by regular armed forces over a wide region or encompassing the globe to small, inter-state or intra-state warfare by irregular forces, insurgents, criminal or terrorist groups infiltrating and often indistinguishable from the general population has led to a frighteningly swift and widespread proliferation of small arms. This category includes weapons up to 50 mm calibre, high-powered automatic personal weapons such as the AK-47 Kalashnikov, sophisticated explosives, and shoulder-fired rockets, grenades and surface-to-surface missiles.

The transfer of small arms takes place through diverse channels – formal and clandestine trade, legal and black or grey markets, and local manufacture. These weapons provide the means to support and sustain low-intensity (but highly lethal) conflict. The contemporary international scene is replete with examples – Peru, Central America, Northern Ireland, Bosnia, the Caucasus, Angola, South Africa, Somalia, the Middle East, Afghanistan, Tajikistan, Kashmir, Sri Lanka, Myanmar and so on. Recently, they have been used more widely to support ethnic conflicts around the world.

These weapons are often targeted against the society itself. The high rate of violence in Washington DC and other American cities, and the internecine conflicts of the Mafia and other criminal operations, all depend on the use of these deadly weapons, of which there are more than 200 million in the United States alone. Coping with this threat is made more difficult because, more often than not, such weapons in the hands of non-state actors, especially militants and terrorists, are superior to those available to security forces and law enforcement agencies of the state, and because detection and control of their distribution pose serious problems. No serious efforts are being made to stop this cancerous proliferation. In fact, many states have actively fostered proliferation as an instrument of their own policies.

One of the most serious consequences of this trend is the linkage between small arms proliferation and the drugs trade. The use of and trade in narcotics represents a menace not only to the health and well-being of individuals and societies, but also to international security. The scale of the problem can be judged by the reported fact that Americans, who represent five per cent of the world's population, consume fifty per cent of the world's cocaine. In Pakistan, where there were virtually no drug addicts a decade ago, it has been reported that as many as 3 per cent of the population are addicted and thrice that number use drugs frequently. The CIS has now been added to the traditional drugs routes emanating from the Peru–Colombia–Panama, Pakistan–Afghanistan, and Myanmar–Thailand–Laos regions.

The drugs menace is transnational in character with far-reaching implications for societal and international peace and security. The countries and regions which produce these drugs, and through which the trade flows, have been afflicted by endemic violence and social turbulence. A similar impact occurs at the point of concentrated consumption, especially in the inner cities of America, where crime and murder rates have soared due to drug-related violence. Inevitably, drug trafficking is linked with illicit arms, terrorist groups and the Mafia. Criminal elements are increasingly gaining control over the administrative and political structures of drug-producing states, where drug-related corruption permeates the military and government.

Neither the proliferation of small arms, nor the proliferation of drugs, nor the growth of terrorist and criminal activity can be solved as isolated problems, or by the independent initiatives of individual states. No country is exempt from the danger, which will continue to multiply unless checked and eradicated by concerted international action. Urgent steps are needed to classify and register small arms production and trade, to monitor and control their manufacture and limit their export. Agreements are needed to reduce production and severely restrict sales. Strong sanctions must be instituted to discourage states from actively or passively aiding or abetting small arms proliferation. The scope of the UN Conventional Arms Register should be expanded to cover small arms, but at the same time its provisions must be greatly strengthened in order to make this an effective mechanism. Reporting must be made mandatory rather than voluntary, and an independent surveillance system should be established to monitor compliance. The five permanent members of the Security Council, which together account for 80 per cent of the world's arms sales, should also set up a system for mutual consultation on all large weapons orders.

Mahatma Gandhi once explained that his efforts to suppress the natural aggressiveness of the people during India's freedom struggle resulted in an explosion of violence between Hindus and Muslims when the country was partitioned. Today, in the absence of opportunities for venting aggression in global wars, pent-up energies are finding other outlets for expressing violence. The only possible way to manage these innate aggressive forces is to meet them firmly. The international community has already shown, in the case of airline hijacking, that it is capable of effective action on a global scale when the necessary political will and commitment are forthcoming. By concerted measures, the rapid proliferation of hijackings has been virtually eliminated. Similar results can be achieved today drastically to curtail small arms proliferation and the drugs trade. The anti-social forces supporting these activities must be handled with the same firmness and determination applied to hijackers, regardless of whether they are governments, military, criminal or terrorist groups, corporations or banks. *The power of these measures lies not in the enactment of laws but in their enforcement. Enforcement should be made mandatory and automatic.*

At the same time, it must be recognized that force alone can never eliminate these problems at their roots. Aggressive energies must be given constructive channels through which to express themselves positively in economic development. Unless and until famine and poverty are eliminated, both in developing countries and in the inner cities of the North, these energies will continue to find negative expression through violence. Therefore, a comprehensive approach is called for. The measures proposed here must be viewed in conjunction with recommendations made elsewhere in this report to eradicate hunger and unemployment.

Linkages to commodity trade

Isolated and independently pursued policies, which appeared highly beneficial at the time enacted, often result in unexpected and unwanted consequences that negate the benefits of the original measures. The refusal of high-income nations to meet the demands of developing countries for protection of commodity prices is an example. During the 1980s, the debt crisis forced many developing countries to increase exports of basic commodities – often at great cost to the environment – in an effort to make loan repayments. This resulted in a self-defeating downward commodity price spiral. The increased exports of these commodities pushed world prices lower, thereby forcing debtor nations to export ever larger quantities to earn the same amount of foreign exchange to repay debts. Defaults on these loans have resulted in huge losses by the world's major banks and write-offs of billions of dollars by donor governments.

One consequence has been to increase the attractiveness of drugs cultivation as an alternative source of income for farmers in developing countries. At the height of the drug wars, the then President of Colombia, Virgilio Barco, argued that farmers in his country would readily give up cocaine production if the international price of coffee could be stabilized at its former price level. His call unheeded, the United States has been forced to spend billions of dollars fighting drugs crimes and expanding prisons due to the rapid increase of drugs consumption in America. By a strange circuitous mechanism, the savings to consumers in developed nations by the refusal of their governments to negotiate international commodity agreements favourable to developing countries has cost these governments and their economies tens of billions of dollars in the form of loan write-offs and crime fighting. If an international commission in the 1970s had tried to point out this linkage between low agricultural incomes in Colombia and drug-related crime in New York, London or Moscow, it would have been readily dismissed. But this is the type of understanding and perspective needed by governments and international agencies today to formulate effective policy measures in an interdependent world.

Cooperative Security

Eliminating nuclear weapons, ballistic missiles and small arms proliferation are practical measures whose time has come. But by themselves these steps will only mitigate the most pernicious threats to international security. They will not provide an effective system for ensuring the peace and security of all nations that is so vitally needed, and now so imminently possible, as a basis for accelerating the political, economic and social development of humankind. The end of the Cold War provides us with the opportunity, and pressing global issues provide the urgency, for more significant measures. These measures cannot be conceived within the perspective of international security that has dominated our thinking in the post-war period, or from a half-hearted desire to modestly improve what to some still appears an adequate and acceptable system. This is an occasion that demands visionary and courageous leadership to usher in a better world. The children of the next millennium will judge us by our response.

Historically, all landmark changes in the international political and security system have been the result of armed conflicts, wars and revolutions. In each case the victors who emerged from the ashes of war sought to build on a static formula for enforcing peace in a dynamic world. In each case, the arrangements for conflict termination contained a dynamism that would produce the tensions, disputes and conflicts of the future. These in-built limitations and imbalances resist adjustment until a new round of fighting sweeps away the old framework and replaces it with another, fashioned in much the same way.

This has been true of the arrangements for international security which have governed international affairs during the present century and which provided the underlying dynamism for the First World War and, when the failed attempt at forming a League of Nations left the world unprepared to deal with fascism, for the Second World War as well. The skewed division of powers allotted under the UN Charter contained the seeds for the bipolar, intensely adversarial relationship between the two military blocs that resulted in the Cold War and the arms race between the superpowers.

All these arrangements have been based on the concept of competitive security. The competitive security paradigm is a state-centred, egocentric approach in which the security of each nation is perceived in terms of its military superiority over potential adversaries. The push of each nation for unlimited security through military power is inherently destabilizing, since it inevitably increases the level of insecurity of other sovereign states. In practice, the effort of nations to arm themselves against perceived external threats generates a sense of insecurity among other nations and compels them in turn to increase military preparedness, thus initiating a vicious spiral, as it did during the Cold War. When NATO and the Warsaw Pact had armed themselves to the point where direct confrontation became too risky, mutual suspicion and insecurity led them to fight each other through proxy wars in the developing world. Every move by either side was perceived as a potential security threat, prompting a counter by the other. Compounded by the inherent instability of nuclear weapons, this doctrine led to the anomaly of increasing military power and steadily decreasing national and international security.

This highly militarized approach contains an in-built mechanism for escalation that was responsible for the growth of global military expenditure to an all-time peak of $1.2 trillion in 1988. Even when effective in controlling direct aggression between major powers, it encouraged proxy wars and it completely ignored the security needs of countries not aligned with one bloc or another. This is one of the reasons why all the wars in the last forty years have taken place in developing countries. Taken to its extreme in the nuclear competition of the superpowers, it 'logically' led to the astonishing doctrine of mutually assured destruction (MAD) as the cornerstone of national security policy.

While there have been efforts by the West to claim 'victory' in the Cold War and arrogate to itself the right to determine the post-war dispensation, in reality neither side won or lost, but a failed international security system was intelligently abandoned because it was extravagantly wasteful of resources, dangerously unstable and actively promoted violence in other regions.

Failure to anticipate the future and to structure policies and instrumentalities to meet future needs has been the dominant characteristic of all previous attempts at forging an international security framework. Now, once again, there is a manifest tendency to forge a framework based on the supremacy of might, rather than right, and determined by the present balance of powers. This framework is likely to be even more tenuous and short-lived than previous compromises, because it ignores revolutionary forces that are reshaping the world for the twenty-first century. *We now have the opportunity and responsibility to evolve a more flexible and far-sighted framework. This requires a fundamental shift in perspective, a new vision of global security.*

Clearly, the competitive security paradigm cannot provide a stable basis for global peace and security. A significant reduction in global military expenditure is a welcome development. Reducing the quantity and destructive power of weapons arsenals will certainly reduce the actual and perceived risks of conflict. But, at the same time, a tendency is emerging to perpetuate the 'we–they' syndrome of competitive security by shifting the axis from East–West to North–South. This has resulted in increasing pressure on developing countries by multilateral and bilateral aid agencies seeking to bring down military expenditure among aid-dependent countries even further. In doing so, *it ignores the right and responsibility of these nations to provide for their own legitimate security needs at a time when no alternative mechanism exists at the international level to ensure the inviolability of their borders.*

There is truth in the claim that military spending by developing countries has increased dramatically during the past 30 years. This increase is partially explained by the fact that more than 100 new sovereign nations have emerged, many of which were protected, prior to independence, by the colonial powers that have now withdrawn. The acquisition of even modest defensive capabilities may consume a significant portion of national income when the economic base is small, as it is for many of these nations. In addition, the increasing incidence of war, terrorism and drug-related violence in the developing world has heightened the sense of insecurity among these countries. However, a closer analysis reveals that half of the military expenditure of the developing world is incurred by a small number of oil-exporting countries in the Middle East and North Africa, and another quarter is incurred by other high-income developing nations, mostly in East and South East Asia – whereas the 84 developing nations with lower and lower-middle incomes, including such large nations as China, India, Indonesia, Pakistan and Bangladesh, comprising 72 per cent of the world's population, incur roughly 6 per cent of global military expenditure, on average less than 3 per cent of the total GDP of these countries.

International pressure for defining acceptable levels of military expenditure and reducing defence budgets is entirely warranted, provided that it is applied equitably to all countries, takes into account the varying conditions between regions and nations, and places corresponding limitations on arms exports by industrialized nations. Placed under the control of an impartial international agency specialized in security issues, rather than being left to development banks or made an instrument of bilateral policy by donor nations, these measures could effect a further 50 to 75 per cent cut in global defence spending and thereby generate $400 billion to $600 billion per year for non-military purposes, equal to roughly ten times current levels of overseas development assistance. The international community should commit itself to a minimum goal of reducing global military expenditure to $400 billion (in 1992 constant dollars) by 2000 AD.

Military expenditure mitigates but does not resolve the underlying problem of security. *Today, the most pressing security threats are social, not military. The appropriate response to them is greater investment in sustainable human development, not more arms.* However, preservation of physical security against external aggression is a primal instinct of nation states that cannot be rationalized away. Nations will continue to arm themselves as long as that is the only effective means to ensure their security. What is needed is a quantum shift from the competitive security paradigm to a cooperative security system in which countries mutually and collectively agree to refrain from acts of aggression and to protect each other from such acts by any nation. This principle served to protect the NATO and Warsaw Pact countries in the past, but on an exclusive basis which promoted a polarization of alliances into military blocs and, most importantly, left more than one hundred countries outside the security orbit and vulnerable to proxy wars. It should now be restructured on a global basis as a collective security system that offers protection to all nations from external aggression.

A whole range of new security challenges is rising to confront the global society. The increasing number, complexity and unpredictability of security threats cannot be managed effectively and in time without international cooperation based on a fundamental change of attitude. *We are now at an historic crossroads: one path leads us back to a static, unstable and exclusive competitive security paradigm; the other leads to a far more stable and dynamic cooperative security paradigm inclusive of all nations and responsive to future needs and challenges.* A global cooperative security system is needed that seeks to strengthen national security without increasing the insecurity of other states. It should be based on the fundamental principle that force will no longer be tolerated by the international community as a legitimate instrument of national policy.

World Army

The limitations of the competitive security system have given rise to numerous calls for the establishment of various types of standing international military force. The role of UN peace-keeping forces has been expanded dramatically in recent years to maintain peace in Eastern Europe, the Middle East, Africa and Asia. At the same time, the scope of its activities has been enlarged to include limited forms of peace making as well – disarming guerrillas, conducting elections and enforcing human rights. Article 42 of the UN Charter also empowers the Security Council to take direct military action where necessary to maintain or restore peace and guarantee international security. Article 43 pledges member states to make armed forces available to the Security Council, not only on an *ad hoc* basis but also as a permanent standing military force. This provision has never been activated due to the intervention of the Cold War. In the wake of the invasion of Kuwait, a proposal was placed before the UN General Assembly on behalf of a group of small and militarily weak nations seeking the protection of an international 'security umbrella' against the threat of invasion by mercenary forces, terrorists, drug traffickers and warlike neighbours. The proposal was supported unanimously by the UN's 166 member states.

In *Agenda for Peace*, the UN Secretary General has recommended broadening the peace-making, peace-keeping and peace-enforcing capabilities of the UN by establishing a standing UN military force. With the end of bipolar confrontation within the Security Council, this proposal is practicable and should be acted upon immediately by establishing a strong permanent force drawn from 20 to 30 member states, trained and equipped for rapid deployment. Such a force, if established, is likely to be relatively small, however, and unequal to the task of dealing with threats from a major army equipped with sophisticated weapons. In addition, its deployment would always be subject to veto by any of the five permanent members of the Council. For both these reasons, it cannot constitute a reliable mechanism for guaranteeing the security of UN member countries. Although a strengthening of the UN's peace-keeping capabilities is highly desirable, it cannot serve as an adequate foundation for a cooperative security system unless the UN's political structure is radically modified. Because it is essentially an addition to national forces rather than a substitute for them, funding will be a perennial difficulty and there will be strong resistance to its expansion on economic grounds. Furthermore, as recent events have demonstrated, nations contributing their forces will have a strong propensity to resist their active deployment in situations that involve significant risks. Even after the Security Council decided to send a peace-keeping force into Rwanda for strictly humanitarian purposes, none of the leading military powers, with the exception of France, were willing to contribute the modest amount of military equipment urgently needed to protect UN troops.

Similar efforts are in various stages of maturity for establishing standing international forces at the regional level in Western Europe, Latin America and other places as part of collective security arrangements. The limitation of these proposals, like that of NATO and the erstwhile Warsaw Pact, is that they are fundamentally exclusive in nature and could easily become competitive with other forces as the East and West blocs have in the past. The strong resentment voiced by Russia at the proposal that some Eastern European nations would join NATO illustrates the danger of expanding exclusive military clubs. For NATO to overcome these legitimate concerns, it would have to be thrown open to all nations that seek to join and abide by its charter. The great reluctance of the West to shoulder the burden of responsibility for security enforcement in Eastern Europe under a widened NATO umbrella highlights the basic inadequacy of exclusive blocs for meeting global security needs.

If the structural limitations of the UN cannot be immediately overcome, the alternative would be to build a cooperative security mechanism in parallel with the UN but structured along more democratic lines similar to NATO. *A World Army could consist of an international peace force that would unconditionally guarantee the security of its members against external aggression based on the following provisions:*

- Membership in the World Army would be voluntary and open to all countries, provided that they have and maintain democratic, multi-party political systems. Since membership is not exclusive, it could be merged at any time with other like-minded organizations such as NATO, or be integrated into a UN military force when the necessary changes in UN political structure have been made.

- As a condition for membership, each country would by legal enactment forego war as an instrument of policy and undertake not to commit any act of external aggression against any other member or non-member for any reason whatsoever. Any violation would be grounds for immediate expulsion.

- Members would agree to contribute an assessed sum of money, equipment and military personnel towards the maintenance of a standing military force under the command of a centralized military leadership. In addition, the peace force could be granted the right to recruit personnel directly from member countries.

- Members would also agree to limit their own overall military spending within norms fixed by the organization.

- Members would be banned from possession of nuclear weapons and ballistic missiles. Existing weapons would be destroyed or turned over to the peace force.

- As in NATO, members would agree by treaty to consider an attack on one member as an attack on all. The peace force would intervene automatically and unconditionally – defensively and, if necessary, offensively – to protect the sovereignty and international borders of any member country, provided that it conformed to the rules under the charter.

- The organization could also assist members in fighting drug trafficking and terrorist activities.

The benefits of this cooperative peace-keeping mechanism would be manifold:

- Since the charter would bind members and the alliance to eschew the use of force and aggression for any reason, it would represent a stabilizing, non-provocative, non-offensive defence. Its charter could also include specific provisions for close association with other international forces.

- Its combined strength and technological capabilities would exceed those of any of its members and constitute a substantial deterrent to aggression against any member country.

- It would significantly reduce the costs of security for members, possibly by up to 50 or 75 per cent, without compromising their legitimate security needs. The more members, the lower the defence expenditure required by each, both because the collective force would be larger and because the number of potential adversaries would be reduced proportionately.

The organization of a World Army, run on well-defined and transparent lines with appropriate mechanisms for control and responsiveness, would help eliminate the need for countries to maintain their own large standing armies. Ultimately this could enable other nations to follow the lead of Costa Rica, which abolished its military forces several decades ago.

National Sovereignty and International Responsibility

The recent calamities in Rwanda and Somalia following the outbreak of civil and ethnic war, and in Bosnia following the breakaway of several Yugoslav republics, demonstrate the need for substantially improving international mechanisms for war prevention, peace making and peace keeping, and for protection of basic human rights both between and within states. The effort of the international community to deal with these events has brought to the fore fundamental issues regarding national sovereignty and the responsibilities of the world community. The very definition and sanctity of the state have been blurred by the determination of ethnic groups in various nations to declare independence from their parent bodies, and the inability or unwillingness of national governments to maintain law and order and provide basic security for their citizens. The role of other states, regional organizations and international agencies in giving explicit or implicit support to these movements has further complicated the task of formulating just and practical solutions.

These events raise questions about the rights of both nations and their citizens that have to be addressed theoretically before the role of international organizations in these affairs can be determined properly. Does a minority group within a country have the right to proclaim itself independent on the basis of its desire for self-governance and in defiance of the claims of the majority on the property and resources they possess? Does a national government, whether elected or in power by force, that is unable to protect its citizens against famine and civil strife have the right to insist on its sovereignty and independent action in the face of the persecution or extermination of its own people? What is the responsibility of the international community for preventing or alleviating crises within societies? What should be the limits placed on international involvement in the internal affairs of countries that, at least momentarily, are unable to help themselves?

The sanctity of the sovereign state, like the sanctity of private property in a capitalist society, is a fundamental principle of the nation state system on which the present world community is based. Like the protectors of private property, the guardians of the sovereign state vigorously resist each attempt to limit its scope or qualify its power – although in both instances there are obvious and well-recognized limits and qualifications. The sensitivity over the issue of sovereignty – especially among former colonies and victims of imperialist aggression – is quite understandable in view of the fact that the emergence of modern nation states over the last two centuries occurred during a period when imperialist wars and colonial conquests were accepted as part of the normal conduct of international relations. It is a measure of the world's progress in this century that this standard of conduct is no longer tolerated by the international community. The formulation of current policy on racial memories of past exploitation or persecution is no more appropriate or conducive to human progress, however, than the false conception of policies based on an exaggerated sense of pride or egocentric self-importance derived from the glory of forceful conquest in the past. In both instances, attitudes of the past must give way to fresh attitudes oriented to the future.

Some member states are understandably wary of raising these issues, out of concern that their re-examination could become an excuse for outright political interference in the internal affairs of sovereign nations, a concern which is reinforced by the non-representative character and lack of impartiality of the Security Council. Other nations are reluctant to assume the greater responsibilities that a clearly enunciated doctrine might impose on them. All would agree, however, that neither an infinite fragmentation of nation states along ethnic, cultural, religious or linguistic lines, nor a blind indifference to persecution or unconscionable neglect of its own citizens by a state government, can be justified by either reason or lofty legal principles, or be permitted by the human heart and conscience to go unchecked.

The UN is precluded under article 2(7) of the Charter from intervening in 'matters which are essentially within the domestic jurisdiction of any state'. It must be possible to define objective criteria for identifying instances in which action in apparent disregard of this provision is fully justified. The deaths of hundreds of thousands of people in Rwanda and Somalia due to famine, ethnic strife and civil war surely qualify, even if errors in the method of intervention, and lack of public support among nations asked to contribute troops, complicate these precedent-setting initiatives.

The sovereignty of a nation derives ultimately from the fact that it represents the will of its own people and the right of those people to freedom of action over their own lives and territory. National sovereignty is limited on two sides: on the one, by the inalienable human rights of a country's citizens and, on the other, by the rights of other member nations of the world community and the citizens they represent. In past centuries the sovereignty of nations may have been based on the principle that might is right. In our more enlightened age, however, the only acceptable basis for a nation's sovereignty is that it expresses the will of its own people, and this condition can only be met under a freely chosen form of government that enables people to express their own free will and determine their own destiny. Therefore, *the decision of the UN to insist on the operation of democratic processes in member countries is an essential step toward resolving the dilemma of sovereignty*. When the representative nature of a national government is in question, its claim to sovereignty over its own people under all circumstances is also questionable. Hitherto, it has not been possible to address this issue forthrightly, because the evolution of the international community had not yet come to accept in practice, as opposed to merely in principle, the fundamental human rights so frequently espoused in constitutions and ignored in actions. This situation has changed, especially after humanity's bitter experiments with totalitarian regimes during this century. It is now recognized that the democratic principles of political freedom, social equality, self-determination and related human rights are inalienable and must be extended to all people everywhere.

The second factor that naturally imposes limits on national sovereignty – the rights of other nations and their citizens – has also gained substantially wider acceptance, has been enshrined by international law, and has become accepted doctrine governing many facets of international relations. Common security against transnational threats and common prosperity for all humankind cannot be based on a 250-year-old concept of nation sovereignty. Over the last half century, *national sovereignty has been maturing into international sovereignty*. As the evolution of the international community proceeds towards the establishment of an effective system of world governance in one form or another, the collective rights of the international community of nations must inevitably come to be regarded as another inalienable truth, alongside individual human rights and the rights of each nation. The right of the nation state to self-determination has to accommodate the rights of other nations and the common shared rights of every human being.

This approach establishes criteria for determining when claims of national sovereignty must be ignored. Every right is accompanied by a responsibility. A government that fosters external aggression or cannot contain domestic violence and civil strife, that cannot create conditions in which its people can feed themselves or even receive outside assistance, fails the test of sovereignty. *Under these circumstances, the international community, through the UN, should have the right and accept the responsibility to intervene appropriately.*

The need of the hour is not to undermine the legitimate right of nations to self-determination, but rather to protect that right by more clearly demarcating its legitimate boundaries against the highly visible challenges being posed by forces of disintegration and fragmentation from within. The current tendency for states to fragment along ethnic lines cannot be handled by any abstract principle of international law. It depends on the understanding and will of people. The evolution of larger, heterogeneous national units functioning under principles of equality is an outstanding product of civilization that should not and cannot be reversed without great damage to the general welfare of humanity. The only solution is to work constantly to educate the public in all countries to understand the benefits of national integration and international cooperation. The implications of this view will be endorsed by some and opposed by others. Acceptance must be fostered through education and discussion rather than unilateral forced initiative.

Preventive Diplomacy, Peace Making and Peace Building

The answers to the questions regarding national sovereignty and international responsibility will determine the scope of UN preventive diplomacy, peace making and peace building in years to come. They must be addressed with a view to evolving valid principles of international law, rather than remaining subject to frequent reversals of public policy by member states based on the short-term impact of the media on current public opinion.

Granted that a consensus is reached regarding these larger issues of principle, there still will remain immense problems relating to implementation, as illustrated by the recent failure of international intervention in Somalia. Whatever may be the limits placed on the UN's mandate for action, it is clear that it cannot carry out that mandate effectively under the current constraints imposed on it by member states through indecisiveness, narrowly defined interests and lack of political commitment. Once again the inherent weaknesses in the structure of the UN organization impact negatively on its capacity to perform the tasks rightfully allotted to it. The absence of a unified chain of command for national forces placed under UN command – culminating in the outright refusal of field forces to follow the commands of UN field staff, inadequate training and equipping of both military staff and fighting units, poor coordination between field units from different countries and between member states and UN headquarters – and a failure to vest sufficient authority in the UN Secretary General are among the most blatant weaknesses of the present system.

Substantive measures are needed to strengthen the UN's capabilities to handle crises. First and foremost, the position of the Secretary General, who now has the diplomatic status equal to that of a prime minister of a member state, should be upgraded to that of a head of state, with full authority over the forces placed under his command by member states to carry out the decisions of the Security Council. Problems of control over the armed forces of member states argue for the constitution of a standing international military force, as described in the previous section of this report.

Lesser measures can be implemented immediately, such as provision of appropriate training to UN Secretariat personnel responsible for conflict prevention, expanding the staff of the Department of Political Affairs, and establishment by the UN of its own independent international surveillance capability, including a satellite system to monitor its work worldwide. Meanwhile, advanced computer, satellite and communications technology should be made available to the

Secretariat by member states. A comprehensive system is needed to monitor military movements. Through its resident representatives, the UN should openly monitor political, ethnic, nationalist and religious developments that increasingly lie at the heart of conflicts in order to understand the complexities of local events and to anticipate potential turbulence. The right to sovereignty should not include the freedom to privacy in cases which involve support for terrorist groups, instigating border conflicts, arms build-ups, torture and genocide. In addition to the role of the UN in consensus fact-finding, it must also acquire the jurisdiction to order fact-finding missions relating to both domestic and regional conflicts in which this type of violation is suspected.

Cessation of violence and conflict settlement often leave unresolved the root causes of conflict, resulting in potential for renewed fighting or social turbulence. Peace-building activities should address underlying economic and social factors that prevent the establishment of a stable and secure peace. In instances such as Cambodia, Rwanda and Somalia, the vacuum created by the complete collapse of political and economic institutions necessitates a broader role for the UN in re-establishing the peace. Peace building has thus far been defined as post-conflict actions to support reconstruction and to strengthen and solidify peace. The concept needs to be broadened to include pre-conflict actions and expanded to encompass a wider array of potentially destabilizing factors that lead to conflicts. The Commission supports the establishment of an International Centre jointly operated by the UN Security Council and UNESCO to implement peace-building programmes.

Peace-building activities should be expanded to address security threats issuing from environmental degradation, poverty, migration of population and refugees. Many cases of ethnic conflict have an underlying basis of economic deprivation that must be addressed before tensions will permanently subside. Others can be mitigated by the introduction of positive economic incentives for cooperation. Economic cooperation is already dissipating ethnic tensions and conflict in the Middle East. It can be creatively fostered in the Balkans and elsewhere. In other cases, the modification of the electoral and constitutional systems in a culturally appropriate manner can reduce or eliminate tensions in ethnically divided countries. International assistance is also needed for coping with tensions arising from the sharing of natural resources – particularly water resources – and chemical or radioactive pollution of air, soil and waterways. Resolution of these issues requires the mediation of international experts for impartial assessment and formulation of equitable recommendations. Regional security organizations can play a leading role in this capacity.

An effective international judicial system is vitally important to the expanded role contemplated for the UN in dealing with arms and drugs trafficking, terrorism and crimes against humanity. This requires, as a minimum step, either that the International Court of Justice be granted mandatory jurisdiction over such cases by member states, or that an International Criminal Court be established with jurisdiction over these offences and other crimes under international law, thus strengthening both the preventive and enforcement capabilities of the international community against non-traditional threats to security.

Alternative Use of Military Resources

National and international security can no longer be conceived in narrow military terms. Ethnic conflict, drugs, environmental degradation and pollution, famine leading to civil unrest or massive migrations of refugees, high levels of unemployment, urban crime and violence constitute threats to both social stability and the preservation of a productive material base. Curbing drug traffic, preventing nuclear and chemical contamination, stopping soil degradation and deforestation, augmenting food production capabilities in deficit areas – all directly and substantially contribute to the security of society.

The attention given to the anticipated monetary savings from reduced military spending has directed attention away from the potential benefits of utilizing other resources controlled by the military for addressing these threats to security, particularly for the alleviation of poverty, protection and restoration of the environment, and management of natural disasters. The military possesses a vast array of resources – human, educational, scientific and technological, medical, organizational and logistical; in training, in engineering and production, in communication and transportation, in construction, land and housing – that can be employed to meet non-military security challenges. Many of these resources can be utilized for these purposes without necessarily removing them from military control. Especially in many developing countries, the organizational and managerial capabilities of the military far exceed those of other agencies and represent a precious resource for addressing these other security threats. Participation of the military in these activities necessitates a wider conception of both security and the role of the military in meeting security needs.

Coping with the serious challenges from environmental and developmental security threats requires the mobilization of a wide range of scientific, technological and physical resources presently utilized for military purposes. There are significant precedents for the utilization of the military to support the environment and development – for construction of roads in Ethiopia and Yemen, bridges in Guatemala, as well as harbours, canals, railways and airfields; for afforestation projects and monitoring wildlife in India; for training of mechanics, electricians, and other productive skills; for urban renewal projects and drug enforcement in the United States, harvesting of crops in the USSR, flood rescue operations in Bangladesh, nuclear clean-up at Chernobyl, damage limitation after the vast oil spills and oil fires in Kuwait, humanitarian relief for Kurdish refugees, distribution of food and medicine in Bosnia and a host of other activities.

In many developing countries the military can assist with efforts to improve social services in rural areas on a war footing – to spread literacy, primary education, basic vocational skills, health care and access to safe drinking water. The military have at their disposal scientific and technological resources which in many cases can be applied to environmental protection with the minimum of adaptation, such as information and monitoring systems that track changes in the atmosphere, in the oceans and on earth's surface. These resources can be applied to environmental monitoring and impact assessment, protection of endangered species, quick response to disasters and accidents, energy conservation, and the minimization and management of waste. The appropriate role for the military in these various activities will depend on the country, the urgency of the circumstances, and the cost-effectiveness of military involvement compared with available alternatives. In some instances, it may be feasible to establish international 'Earth corps units', specially trained and equipped to carry out certain types of environmental protection and restoration, such as India's eco-battalions, which seek to conserve the Himalayan habitat by restoring tree cover and constructing small dams and canals.

International development force

The goals of peace, prosperity and fulfilment for every human being represent formidable challenges – intellectual, attitudinal, organizational and technological. We cannot hope to reach such lofty achievements if we waste and squander the precious and abundant resources – mental, psychological, social and material – placed at our disposal. A massive reduction in emphasis on weapons production and military establishments, made possible by recent political events and demanded by the pressing unmet needs of people everywhere, represents both a great opportunity and a considerable challenge. The opportunity is not only further to reduce the threat of war by reducing the capacity for waging war, but also to redirect and utilize for other purposes the resources now dedicated to war making and prevention. The challenge is to do so at a time when rising unemployment and economic stagnation in many countries make further cuts in the size of the military unpopular domestically. Since 1990, the total number of military personnel worldwide has declined by two million or about six per cent. By 1998, a further decrease of at least two million is anticipated. A large proportion of these demobilized people have already joined, or will soon join, the forces of the unemployed. Some may be tempted to market their military skills elsewhere.

Just as the present efforts of the UN to make and keep the peace are severely constrained by the lack of a standing professional military force under its own direction, so also the prodigious efforts of the UN's development agencies to accelerate development among member countries is hampered by a lack of well-trained, disciplined and highly organized personnel for implementation, especially in those countries with the greatest need of assistance. The Commission recommends that, as a complement to the establishment of an International Force for Peace, an International Force for Development be constituted, comprised of former military personnel who, after appropriate training, will work to accelerate economic development to provide food, health, literacy and jobs for all. A UN Peace Force and UN Development Force, functioning under a democratically restructured UN, can make a lasting contribution to achieving the major goals of the UN system.

Conclusion

Seven years ago the threat of nuclear war between the superpowers loomed large in the minds of people everywhere. The euphoria generated by the end of the Cold War led to high expectations of peace and a 'peace dividend' the world over. Yet excitement soon turned to disappointment as the full anticipated results of these magnificent accomplishments did not immediately materialize. Then, as attention turned to more mundane problems closer to home, the sense of relief and celebration was replaced by growing concern over the increasing prominence of other threats to international security: some of these were aggravated by the new positive developments, while others had not previously seemed so serious by comparison with the threat of nuclear annihilation. The end of political confrontation between East and West, the sudden conversion of authoritarian communist states into democratic market economies, and substantial cuts in global defence spending were accompanied by increasing political instability and ethnic violence in the many parts of Eastern Europe and the former Soviet Union, by the horrendous loss of life due to civil and ethnic strife in several African countries, by growing concern over drugs and violent crime in the West, by the danger of nuclear terrorism resulting from potential theft of Soviet weapons, and by pressure on defence producers to compensate for reduced domestic defence budgets by increasing arms exports.

This surprising turn of events has led some to re-examine the incredible achievements of the period and conclude that they were either vastly overstated or, perhaps, even illusory. Others have come to take these achievements for granted. Still others have simply forgotten how much things have really changed. But the most important realization to be derived from these events is of the inherent defect in attempts to address the factors underlying international security in a piecemeal manner. Over the past five years the Commission encountered reminders of this truth in virtually every field that it took up for examination. It is this experience that has convinced us of the need for wider perspectives and total solutions. The marvellous achievements of the past few years are neither fortuitous nor illusory. The Berlin Wall has been brought down and demolished. The Iron Curtain has been lifted and obliterated. But we still proceed with our heads turned back, looking for shadows behind us at a time when the future demands our full attention in order to capitalize fully on what these events have prepared and made possible.

In this report, the Commission is calling for a comprehensive, multi-pronged approach to the problem of international security that defies and will continue to defy partial solutions. That approach recognizes the critical importance of the linkages between the establishment of democratic political systems at the national and the international level, the abolition of war as an instrument of policy, the elimination of highly destabilizing weapons of mass destruction, substantial additional cuts in defence spending by *all parties*, and the constitution of a cooperative international security system that is not state-centred and is supported by a standing international peace force. Taken separately, each of these elements can substantially contribute to improving the international political and security environment. Taken together as a cohesive whole, they can transform global political affairs and create a highly conducive atmosphere for the eradication of the pressing economic problems confronting us.

Recommendations on the UN, Peace Keeping, and Arms Control

1 Establishment and maintenance of a multi-party democratic government should be made the minimum condition for membership and participation in the UN. A graded, time-bound programme for the transformation of authoritarian states should be drawn up by the UN in cooperation with concerned governments. The UN should provide assistance to nations in making the transition.

2 A major UN Conference should be convened to examine UN institutional reform, including the composition and powers of both the Security Council and the General Assembly. The objective should be to restructure the UN according to the same democratic principles advocated by its members for national governments.

3 As an interim step in this necessary restructuring, the Commission recommends expanding the membership of the Security Council from 15 to 20 members by adding five new permanent members. The veto power of the five permanent members of the Security Council should be abolished and the diplomatic status of the UN Secretary General should be elevated to that of a head of state.

4 A detailed plan should be drawn up by the UN for a further 50 per cent reduction, to a maximum of $400 billion, in global defence spending before the end of the decade. Spending quotas for member states should be established according to the principle of non-offensive defence.

5 The peace-making, peace-keeping and peace-enforcing capabilities of the UN should be strengthened substantially. A permanent, well equipped UN force made up from 20–30 member states should be placed at the disposal of the Secretary General for rapid deployment in conflict zones under Article 43 of the UN Charter to enforce the decisions of the Security Council. Either the Military Staff Committee of the UN could be revitalized to give strategic direction to any enforcement action, or a new structure should be created of member states supplying troops to any UN operation, chaired by the Secretary General. Member States should earmark national troops for use in UN Chapter VII enforcement action, the scope of which should be expanded to include humanitarian intervention under circumstances when national governments are either unable or unwilling to protect their populations from imminent threats to their survival.

A cooperative collective security framework must be evolved that is inclusive of all nations and guarantees their security against acts of external aggression. A standing international military force or World Army should be established under a democratic framework to provide unconditional security guarantees to member countries against aggression by other nations. If such a force cannot be established at the present time under the UN, then there is need for a separate organization similar in constitution to NATO but open to all nations that practise democratic principles of national governance, contribute financial and defence resources to a common armed force, accept ceilings on national defence expenditure and eschew the possession of nuclear weapons. The army should consist of both a directly recruited standing force and forces placed on call by member nations.

The use of nuclear weapons should be declared by the UN a crime against humanity. First use by any nation must automatically invoke the strongest collective security measures by the UN Security Council. Based on the precedent of the Chemical Weapons Treaty, the proposal for a universal ban on the possession of nuclear weapons by any nation should be placed before the Security Council for a vote. The five permanent members should agree to the suspension of their veto power on this issue so crucial to the future of humanity.

The danger to all nations of unexpected and unprovoked attack from near or distant powers can be vastly reduced by declaring an immediate ban on the use of ballistic missiles of all types, including those carrying conventional warheads. This would eliminate the discriminatory provisions that deny missile acquisition to some while preserving the right of others to maintain and develop this purely offensive capability. It would also eliminate the need for missile defence systems, which no nation can afford and which are the only possible defence against ballistic missile weapons. The ban on use should be followed by urgent measures to dismantle and scrap this entire class of weapons worldwide.

9 Highest priority must be given to controlling and reversing the proliferation of small arms in line with the determined international measures employed to curb hijacking. As an immediate first step, these weapons should be classified and a UN register created to monitor their manufacture and sale. Agreements should be negotiated between major arms suppliers to severely restrict production and sales. Strong sanctions must be instituted to discourage states from actively or passively abetting small arms proliferation, especially to non-state actors.

10 UN action to curb the international trade in major armaments needs to go further than the existing Arms Register. Arms exports to areas identified by the UN as trouble spots should be banned by international law. An independent agency should be established to verify the submissions from arms-exporting states. Major arms exporters should agree to consult the Security Council in advance about large orders received for destabilizing weapons and, where appropriate, coordinate actions to limit the size of arms transfers.

11 Narcotic drug production and trafficking must be treated as threats to international peace and security. The strongest possible sanctions should be instituted under the UN against countries that permit or support these activities. UN forces must be made available to assist member countries with eradication of these activities within their borders. Economic measures must be supported internationally to provide attractive commercial alternatives to drug growers through special trade agreements for agricultural commodities. International criminal proceedings should be instituted against violators under a new International Criminal Code.

12 The UN should create its own international surveillance system, including its own satellites, to monitor and report on potential trouble spots and troop movements. It should also develop its own appropriate and effective logistics units. Criteria to allow UN fact-finding missions in respect of intra-state conflict should be negotiated and codified by the General Assembly. At the same time, the UN should integrate fact-finding into enforcement action taken under Chapter VII of the UN Charter. A UN Staff College should be established to develop and maintain administrative procedures for governing UN peace-keeping, peace-making and peace-enforcing operations and to train an effective corps of personnel for these purposes.

Utilization of Defence Resources for Development and the Environment

1 The concept of 'peace dividend' should be expanded to include manpower, educational and training capabilities, scientific and technological resources, production facilities, land and abandoned military bases that can be redeployed to combat rural and urban poverty as well as national and global environmental degradation. An inventory of these resources should be compiled and efforts made to identify alternative uses through the UN's specialized agencies and by national governments. All nations should advise the Secretary General of the human, technological and productive resources they are willing and able to place at the disposal of the UN.

2 Each government should draw up an inventory of its military manpower, science, technology and other facilities which could be used to sustain the natural resource base, prevent environmental degradation and cooperate with other countries in combating regional and global threats to environmental security. The information should be shared with the UN Environmental Programme and the Sustainable Development Council. In each case it will be necessary to show how action implemented by the military will be more cost-effective than using traditional resources.

3 A UN International Force for Development should be constituted under a democratized UN structure, consisting of demobilized military personnel and young professionals from different countries, which will be trained and equipped to promote people-centred, environmentally sound development initiatives that integrate political, social, economic and cultural factors.

4 Global security is threatened by mass population movements, potential changes in sea levels, drought and famine. Greater international cooperation is needed in the sharing of national military manpower, under the auspices of a new UN Earth corps. Article 43 of the UN Charter, which was originally drawn up for dealing with the threat of conventional war, can be interpreted to apply to threats to environmental security as well. In parallel to a UN Earth corps, national Earth corps units should be constituted to operate within each state and for service internationally under the UN. Vocational skills imparted through these agencies will be of subsequent use to the community at large.

5 A greater degree of cooperation in the sharing of environmental data is essential if global security is to be enhanced, particularly that gained from military remote-sensing devices. This is especially relevant to the majority of nations which do not have such equipment at their disposal. The need for secrecy, always stressed in the Cold War period, has been superseded by the need for openness.

6 An international system should be instituted by the UN to assist in the transfer of environmentally beneficial technology, as recommended by the Royal Society and the United States National Academy of Sciences, both from the developed to the less-developed nations, and from the military to the non-military sectors. This applies in particular to the field of information technology, where there is scope for dual use of existing military capabilities. Closer links should be established between research and development teams in the military and civilian sectors at the national level.

7 A greater degree of regional cooperation is desirable between states which share natural resources and common environmental interests. This is of particular importance where regional peace and stability is at stake, as in the Middle East, over the question of access to water supplies. Where national environmental resources may lead to dispute and conflict, agreements should be drawn up between potential belligerents and the good offices of the UN's specialized agencies used to anticipate and avert future conflict.

4

Full Employment

Peace and democracy can provide only the foundation for stable and productive social life, not its fulfilment. For that, political security has to be complemented by economic security and a blossoming of individual and cultural potentials. Yet here our optimism seems to flag. Our thoughts of the new millennium do evoke images of greater peace and stability internationally, more individual freedom and democratic rights, growing international cooperation, exciting new technologies, increasing cultural interaction. But they also evoke images of more people and less work – meaning fewer jobs! No sooner has the threat of nuclear annihilation receded, than the spectre of chronic unemployment and unrelenting poverty has risen to replace it, giving renewed justification to humanity's deepest anxieties by transferring them to a new source of apprehension.

In recent years, unemployment has emerged as a major cause of concern for governments around the world. In industrial countries, the subject evokes pessimistic prophecies of a fast-approaching future in which tens of millions of people will never find jobs, technology eliminates the need for human labour, cheap imports replace domestic jobs, welfare systems collapse under an unbearable burden, children have less economic opportunity than their parents, a widening abyss divides the rich and poor, and both markets and governments are powerless to do anything about it. In developing countries, it dashes hopes of ever conquering hunger, eradicating widespread rural and urban poverty, and bridging the gap that separates these nations from the prosperous West.

The very same deterministic mentality that until recently made us feel that a nuclear war was inevitable now leads many to conclude that rising unemployment, chronic poverty and social alienation are unavoidable. Yet the enormous gains of peace and democracy that we contemplate cannot be secured and brought to fruition if this other

62

apprehension is allowed to become a settled reality, as war between nations has been during past millennia. The peace and security we seek internationally depend directly on our ability to promote and maintain domestic peace and tranquillity within nations, which in turn are dependent on the ability of countries to provide food and economic security to their people. Poverty and unemployment are closely linked to most instances of social unrest – tribal wars, civil wars, urban crime, drugs and violence. There is clear evidence from the US and UK that crime is economically related to lack of job opportunities. Unemployment is also a major cause of massive migrations, both to urban areas within countries and across borders, which has become a highly destabilizing factor in many regions. Without sufficient purchasing power for food and other material essentials and non-essentials, there can be no assurances of lasting social peace and political stability.

The linkage between peace, political stability and economic development will be even stronger in the future than in the past, due to the democratic and social revolutions that are in the course of encompassing the globe. The greater access to information and freedom of expression which characterize democratic societies and the rising expectations of people at lower economic levels combine to generate a powerful pressure on society to provide economic opportunities as well as social freedoms to every citizen. If the greater freedom and higher expectations are unable to find means for their positive fulfilment, they can lead to rising frustration, tension and violence, which threaten the prosperity of those at higher levels and the stability of the society as a whole. Democracies can only thrive and the revolution of rising expectations can only fulfil itself peacefully, when economic opportunities are provided to every human being. The recent rise of the political right, ethnic unrest and opposition to immigration in Western Europe, and the surge of crime in the United States, are sufficient evidence of the corrosive impact that unemployment can have, even on mature democracies. Increasingly, those excluded from the benefits of modern society reject its standards of justice and ignore its laws.

The end of the ideological confrontation between capitalism and communism leaves the market system exposed at its weakest point – its impersonality and insensitivity to human needs and suffering – with no longer any lesser alternative to point at in self-justification. Having rejected the inadequacies and abuses of authoritarian socialism as a solution, we are compelled to find other methods to achieve social equity. In the present context, employment is the most effective way to distribute the fruits of development among people. The world is now capable of producing sufficient food and other basic necessities to feed, clothe and house everyone; but without opportunities for employment, people lack the purchasing power needed to buy them. Economic entitlement, rather than a shortage of food or food production capacity, is the key to global food security. Lack of employment opportunities is also directly linked to destruction of the environment, both rural and urban. The destruction of tropical rain forests has been one result. The greatest security challenges of the twenty-first century are economic, not military or political. Employment is a *sine qua non* for meeting these challenges.

A thorough examination of facts and a dispassionate analysis reveal grounds for hope and opportunities for action. The possibility of more rapid economic growth and rising incomes in both developed and developing countries – spurred by further substantial reduction in defence spending, the diffusion and application of new technologies, economic liberalization leading to growth of international trade, the globalization of financial markets, and the emergence of new engines for global expansion among developing countries – indicates that our apprehensions need not prove justified, provided society acts courageously and decisively to meet the challenge. A global overview of employment cannot do full justice to the special circumstances, problems and potentials of specific regions and countries, but it can dispel the growing concern that employment has become a problem beyond the means of governments or the global economy to eradicate or even contain.

In the final analysis, creation of jobs for all is not a question of possibility. It is a question of necessity. Neither logic nor self-interest justify a detached attitude or a half-hearted effort to address this issue. As in the case of the recent global response to the threat of global warming from depletion of the ozone layer, it simply is not acceptable for us to remain indifferent or claim that we are powerless to act where the entire world's vital self-interests are at stake. When war threatens a nation's borders, technology threatens its environment or unemployment threatens the livelihood of its people and the fabric of its social existence, there is only one acceptable response – that is, action.

The greatest achievement of this century has not been technological, economic or political, but rather the growing concern and intolerance for the slaughter, persecution or impoverishment of other human beings. This marks the awakening of our collective, human consciousness to the full value of human life and the consequent rejection of physical strength, political power and money as the governing values of society. This evolution of consciousness has led to monumental changes in the accepted rules of social existence. Slavery and colonialism were abolished because society evolved to the point where it would no longer tolerate them – not for economic reasons, but because they were a disgraceful blot on the conscience of humanity. Similarly, the acceptance of famine, poverty and unemployment as necessary or inevitable by-products of economic life should no longer and need no longer be tolerated. Social charity and welfare were necessary inventions to mitigate the worst effects of economic development over the past few centuries, but they are signs of a defective system that humiliate the recipients and deprive them of self-respect, rather than equipping them with the capacity and self-confidence to help themselves. *As freedom has finally been recognized as an inalienable right of every human being, we are fast approaching the time when society must recognize and ensure the right of every individual to gainful employment.* Given the right leadership and policies, 'Jobs for All' is an achievable goal for all industrial nations within a decade and for all of humankind early in the twenty-first century. A change of attitude is the prime necessity for this accomplishment.

Global Survey

A survey of unemployment in different regions of the world makes evident the reason for the mounting concern over this issue. Unemployment in the industrial countries is at its highest level since the Great Depression. The official figure is around 6.4 per cent in the United States, but the actual number, including those who have given up seeking jobs, is probably above 10 per cent. More than 35 million Americans, constituting 14 per cent of the population, are living on incomes below the poverty line, including 30 per cent of all blacks and Hispanics. Western European unemployment rates are at the highest level in 30 years. They are projected soon to reach 12 per cent or 18 million people and remain high throughout the decade, prompting the outgoing European Union President, Jacques Delors, to call employment Europe's 'Achilles heel'. Youth unemployment rates (aged 16–19) in the European Community average nearly 20 per cent and nearly 50 per cent of the unemployment is long-term (more than one year). The emerging situation poses a challenge to the European concept of the welfare state.

Employment in Eastern Europe and the republics of the former Soviet Union has been severely disrupted by the break-up of COMECON, the dissolution of the USSR and the movement of these countries from centrally planned to market economies. From the beginning of 1990 to March 1992, registered unemployment grew from 100,000 to over 4 million and it has continued to rise steeply since then. The unemployment rate for ten Eastern European countries now averages around 17 per cent. Recent projections indicate that joblessness in Russia could reach 15 million persons or 18 per cent of the workforce in the near future.

By far the most serious problem lies in the developing world, where unemployment rates average 40–50 per cent in many countries. In Latin America, 192 million people representing 46 per cent of the population live under the poverty line, and 22 per cent of them are considered 'extremely poor'. Urban unemployment is around 8 per cent, but average industrial wages in the region fell by 17.5 per cent during the 1980s and the number of workers in the lower-wage informal sector doubled. Although population growth has slowed, a 72 per cent increase in labour participation rates for women is causing the workforce to continue to expand rapidly. This region needs to double its employment growth rate to create 89 million new jobs during the 1990s in order to provide full employment opportunities for all its people.

In sub-Saharan Africa, home to 20 of the 25 poorest nations in the world, urban unemployment afflicts some 14 million people, representing 15–20 per cent of the workforce, and is projected to more than double in the next ten years. Typically, youth comprise 65 to 75 per cent of the total unemployed. With the region's population still growing at 3 per cent annually, these countries need to create 100 million new jobs in the coming decade just to maintain their present levels of unemployment.

High population growth and a severe economic slowdown have generated high rates of unemployment in the Arab countries, estimated to exceed 25 per cent during the early 1990s, in spite of the very low labour participation rates among women in this region. In the aftermath of the Gulf crisis, labour-supplying countries such as Jordan, Lebanon, the Sudan and Syria have suffered the most. Returnees swelled Jordan's population by 8.4 per cent and caused unemployment levels to rise above 20 per cent. Unemployment levels among Palestinians in the Gaza Strip and on the West Bank are among the highest in the world.

A dramatic exception to this gloomy trend comes from the countries of Asia and the Pacific, which have made great strides in job generation during the 1980s and are poised to continue expanding rapidly. The Newly Industrializing Economies (NIEs) – Hong Kong, South Korea, Singapore and Taiwan-China – are all facing severe labour shortages, with Malaysia, Thailand and Indonesia also moving in that direction. But other Asian countries continue to face major challenges in creating sufficient jobs for all. China has created a phenomenal 100 million new jobs since 1985 and continues to grow rapidly, but the country still has a pool of 130 million surplus rural workers. Joblessness in Chinese cities is projected to reach 5 million by the end of 1994. India needs to create at least 100 million new jobs in the next ten years in order to raise all its poor above the poverty line.

Factors Contributing to Rising Unemployment

Although the problem of unemployment is not new, a variety of factors have combined to aggravate the difficulties confronting most regions of the world in recent years.

- As a result of the decline of global military spending by one-third in real terms since 1988, employment in defence industries has fallen steeply and is expected to decline by at least 3 to 4 million jobs or roughly 25 per cent by 1998. In addition, 4.5 million military personnel will be demobilized during this period.

- The break-up of COMECON and the USSR have had a strongly negative impact on trade within Eastern Europe and with the industrialized West and developing countries.

- The relatively high interest rates in Europe, resulting in part from tight monetary policies pursued by Germany to offset the enormous costs of reunification, have had adverse effects on investment, growth and employment in the region. More recent rate increases in the US threaten to halt the declining trend in unemployment observed over the past year.

- The extreme disruption of the centrally planned economies of Eastern Europe during the early stages of their transition to market economies has led to high domestic unemployment in most cases.

- Slow recovery from the recent global recession has restrained the growth of foreign trade.

- Down-sizing by major corporations in response to intense competitive pressures has eliminated many jobs which are not being restored, even after the recession is over.

- Privatization and restructuring of public sector companies in response to fiscal pressures has had a similar effect. In the United Kingdom alone, an estimated 500,000 jobs will be lost for this reason in 1994.

- The impact of structural adjustments programmes has slowed economic growth and new job creation in a number of developing countries.

- Gains in productivity due to new technology, particularly delayed gains from the micro-computer revolution of the 1980s and the growth of factory automation, have slowed job growth in some industries.

- The increasing competitiveness of the NIEs of Asia and most recently China has displaced jobs in the West, primarily unskilled jobs.

The major impact of several of these factors has already been felt and is now beginning to subside. Some will continue for several more years. Still others may entirely reverse their direction and contribute to job growth later in the decade. Not one is an irreversibly negative factor that will continue to exert a downward pressure on job growth for the foreseeable future.

Job Creation during the Twentieth Century

A long-term, global perspective is needed to understand fully the employment problem and the prospects for eliminating it. Over the past four decades, the world economy has generated more than one billion jobs, more than were created during the previous four centuries. If past trends continue, it will create another 1.3 billion during the next 35 years. The current anxiety in the West is similar to that which the United States passed through in the 1890s when agricultural mechanization displaced 4.4 million farm workers, generating double digit unemployment and visions of a dismal future. Yet, since then, employment in the United States has expanded by nearly 100 million jobs or 400 per cent. Between 1990 and 2005, it is projected to increase by another 25 million. The same process of structural transition is repeating itself today and raising the same anxieties. Contrary to common belief, the US employment rate, the percentage of total population with jobs, has risen steadily throughout the century from 38 per cent to 46 per cent of the total population and is expected to reach 51 per cent by 2005.

This trend is true for the industrial nations as a whole. Between 1960 and 1992, total employment in OECD countries rose by 110 million jobs or 44 per cent, including a 22 per cent increase in the participation of women in the workforce. During this same period, unemployment rose by 23 million persons, representing a 259 per cent increase in the overall unemployment rate. More people are working than ever before, yet at the same time more people are unemployed, because a larger proportion of the population seek jobs. Growing anxiety about employment prospects in the West were aggravated by a sudden 50 per cent increase in unemployment after 1990, which displaced an additional 10 million workers in the OECD and was equalled only by the previous high of 1983. This increase is now showing signs of reversal.

These average figures disguise significant differences in performance of countries within the OECD. Since 1950, Japan's employment rate has risen from 43 per cent to around 50 per cent, while unemployment has remained in the 1 to 3 per cent range. The overall proportion of the population employed in the European Community has declined by 1 per cent since 1965 and is presently just under 41 per cent, but the percentage of the working age population employed has remained more or less constant over the past three decades, at 67 per cent, whereas in other OECD regions it has risen significantly – to exceed 75 per cent in North America, Scandinavia and Japan.

Europe's lower labour participation rate is attributable to a number of factors. A far higher percentage of the European workforce was engaged in agriculture 25 years ago and has since shifted to non-agricultural sectors, an adjustment that occurred in the United States during earlier decades. During the 1980s Europe chose a high-wage path to growth, passing on the benefits to the existing workforce but creating relatively few new jobs; whereas the United States, with a similar economic growth rate over the decade, showed lower income growth per worker, but a steadily rising employment rate. Europe is now confronted with the need for structural adjustment to compensate. In the United States, the extent of the unemployment problem is partially disguised in the form of low-wage jobs, which distribute total income over a larger number of workers. Twenty per cent of all full-time US workers have incomes that fall below the official poverty line for a family of four, though only a quarter of these live in households whose total income is below the poverty line. Real wages in the United States have not risen significantly over the last 20 years due to the dramatic increase in the supply of labour as a result of a 62 per cent increase in female participation since 1960 and the entrance of the baby-boom generation into the workforce. However, America's 'family living standard' has still risen by 40 per cent since 1970. *Within the next decade, the aging of the population is expected to reduce job pressures and even lead to labour shortages in some European countries.*

Job growth has been quite rapid in the developing countries over the last forty years, more than doubling total employment. The single most important factor behind rising numbers of unemployed persons and increasing absolute numbers of families below the poverty line in developing countries has been the 2.4-fold expansion of population in the Third World, and more than doubling of the economically active population since 1950, which have resulted in a 4 per cent decline in the overall employment rate. Population growth rates continue to fall steadily in most countries, with the exception of Africa, providing an opportunity for economic growth and job growth to catch up with the population explosion of recent decades.

Along with rapid quantitative job growth, the global economy has achieved dramatic qualitative gains in the nature of employment. During recent decades, there has also been a marked movement away from subsistence level manual occupations, primarily in agriculture, to more skilled and remunerative forms of employment. Worldwide, the percentage of the work force engaged in agriculture has fallen by 24 per cent since 1950, from 67 to 51 per cent.

Unemployment is of growing concern today primarily because population has expanded in recent decades even faster than job creation and because a larger percentage of the population, principally women, seek employment now than at any time in the past. The shortages of jobs and the resulting poverty represent the most pressing social problem in the world today. But viewed in historical perspective, it is clear that substantial progress has been made during the post-war period, making humanity as a whole more prosperous than at any previous period in recorded history. Over the past five decades, global GDP has multiplied seven-fold. In spite of unprecedented population growth, *per capita* income has more than tripled. Between 1965 and 1985, real *per capita* consumption in the developing world rose by 70 per cent. *Despite the paramount concern raised by the persistence of high rates of unemployment in recent years, available data do not confirm a long-term trend towards rising rates of global unemployment.*

Prognosis for Employment in the Twenty-First Century

Although it is difficult to make reliable employment projections based on past trends, we can say some things with a fair degree of certainty.

- In order to provide employment for every job seeker, the world needs to create approximately one billion new jobs during the next decade. This will require a job growth rate of more than 4 per cent per year compared to the less than 3 per cent achieved during the 1980s.

- About 95 per cent of the growth in the world labour force over the next 35 years will take place in developing countries. An additional 260 million people will enter the workforce during the 1990s.

- Employment in the East Asian economies is projected to grow by 37 per cent between 1990 and 2000, while the labour force will increase by only 17 per cent, leading to an increasing shortage of labour in the region.

- In contrast, employment growth is projected to lag behind labour force growth in South Asia, Latin America and sub-Saharan Africa.

- Although job growth has once again started in many OECD countries, economic growth alone will not be sufficient to bring down unemployment rates significantly, especially among youth and the long-term unemployed. Changes in values, attitudes, structures and policies will be necessary.

- Unless concerted action steps are taken, global unemployment will increase by 130 million during the 1990s.

Our thesis is that there is a great deal that can be done to prevent this outcome and even reverse the trend, leading to sharply reduced levels of unemployment and progressive eradication of poverty over the next decade.

How can we make such an optimistic prognosis in the face of the rising number of unemployed and rising concern of governments everywhere? Before presenting our case, it is necessary to challenge several basic concepts about job creation and unemployment.

Destroying Myths about Job Destruction

Two common, but pervasive, myths have gained ground that add an aura of scientific determinism to the fatalism regarding rising unemployment: the first relates to technology, the second to trade. The notion that science and technology will eventually eliminate the need and, consequently, the opportunity for human productive labour has been gaining ground since the early years of the Industrial Revolution, and, with the advent of automated production lines, computers and industrial robots, it has attained the status of accepted truth. Each generation welcomes with foreboding the advent of new technologies, attracted by their potential benefits and frightened by the immediate costs they impose. But contrary to popular conception and empirical observation, *there is little evidence to support the thesis that technological development is responsible for rising levels of unemployment in the medium to long term.*

In spite of widespread anxiety that machines are progressively replacing people in the workforce, *historically there has been a strong positive correlation between technological development and job creation.* It is certainly the case that the commercial application of each new phase of productive technologies displaces people from traditional occupations, reduces the number of workers required to carry out specific tasks, and can in the short term lead to fewer jobs in specific industries. In the process, a larger number of low-wage, unskilled jobs are replaced with a smaller number of higher-wage, more skilled jobs resulting in rising levels of worker productivity and rising personal incomes. But that is only the most direct initial impact of improved technology. Seen from a wider perspective and traced patiently along the course of its myriad consequences, the introduction of new technology acts as a catalyst that generates a positive ripple effect which, on average, results in the creation of many more jobs – more skilled, more productive and higher-wage jobs – than it destroys. The rising productivity made possible by technology reduces production costs and thereby lowers the price of products and services to customers and consumers. The lower prices result in increased demand, greater consumption, higher levels of production and even greater cost reductions due to economies of scale.

This represents only the first cycle of job creation. While jobs are being eliminated in low-skilled manual or assembly operations, simultaneously they are being created in industries that manufacture and service the more sophisticated machines, as well as in Research and Development (R & D) laboratories that develop the new machines, materials and manufacturing processes. The workers who operate the improved machines require higher levels of skill, which demands more education and training, thus creating demand for jobs in the service sector. The more productive and higher-paid industrial workers utilize their enhanced purchasing power to buy more goods and services than before – spending more on travel, consumer goods, housing, leisure, health and the education of offspring, and thus creating demand for more jobs in other industries. Rising incomes generate higher standards and expectations, bringing changes in lifestyle that create new needs and new commercial activities.

This process has led to enormous growth in new jobs. The best documented example of this process is the automotive industry. Inspired by the idea of making a car the working-class masses at the turn of the century could afford, Henry Ford adopted new manufacturing technology, the automated assembly line, to produce the first low-priced automobile. Ford's technology increased worker productivity more than seven-fold and reduced production costs by two-thirds. As an immediate result, thousands of small manufacturers of custom-built cars and horse-drawn carriages were put out of business. But the growing demand for low-cost vehicles generated explosive growth for the industry, creating tens of thousands of new jobs in the process. Globally, production rose from less than 250,000 vehicles in 1910 to 42 million in 1980. Nine decades later, the automotive industry is still the largest manufacturing industry in the world and the single largest source of jobs in the American economy. Every job created in automotive manufacturing has spawned roughly ten more in related occupations. Thus, about 9 per cent of the USA's entire workforce is employed in occupations directly related to automotive manufacture, sales and services, road construction and maintenance, and transport of freight and passengers. Globally, 7 to 9 million workers were employed in automotive manufacturing in 1980 and perhaps as many as 50 to 80 million in related occupations. In addition, the spread of automotive technology has had tremendous impact on the growth of other industries stimulated by the greater mobility of the public – retail trade, hotels, restaurants, tourism, recreation – and indirectly on agriculture, as well as every other service and manufacturing industry that benefits from lower cost and greater speed of passenger and freight transport.

Advances in technology provide society with greater conveniences and in the process endow the society with greater creative and productive abilities. Over time, these new abilities spur the creation of new activities in many different fields distantly related to the original point of innovation. The process results in improvements in health, which raise the level of physical energy; higher standards of education, which raise the level of mental energy and culture; and higher levels of social skills and organization, which raise the energy level of the entire society, making it ever more creative and productive. A comprehensive study of this wider process of job creation and destruction arising from technological innovation is needed to develop specific coefficients for measuring the impact of technological advances in different fields on total employment. Eventually, we may hope to dispel the widespread fear and sense of helplessness that this issue evokes.

The notion that there are a fixed or inherently limited number of jobs that can be created by the economy is a fiction. It is not just advances in technology that work in this fashion. Every major advance in social attitudes, institutions, values and lifestyles has a dual effect on employment, creating jobs in some areas and destroying them in others. Higher standards of education not only raise productivity, but also stimulate higher expectations that lead to greater consumption. Changing attitudes toward the environment have created entirely new industries and generated new jobs in every field where impact on the environment is of concern. New types of organization such as fast-food restaurants, franchising and hire purchase or leasing create new jobs by hastening the growth or expanding the activities of the society. Shifting attitudes toward marriage and the role of women create greater demand for jobs but also more opportunities for employment, because working women consume more and require additional services.

Anxiety regarding the impact of technological development on jobs has been aggravated by the belief – largely a hangover from the Industrial Age – that in the industrial nations automation is rapidly replacing high-wage manufacturing jobs with low-wage jobs in the service sector. Actually, services have had a dominant place in Western economies for most of the twentieth century. In the United States, they now account for 79 per cent of all jobs, 74 per cent of GDP, and generate a $56 billion trade surplus, compared to a $132 billion deficit for goods. Technological developments, such as advances in computers, telecommunications and medical technology, have played at least as great a role in the growth of the service sector as in manufacturing. New service jobs in banking, foreign trade, research, design and engineering, computer software, education, health, law, finance, business management, communications, transportation, media and entertainment demand higher levels of education and skills and offer higher pay. In 1992 the median manufacturing job in the US paid only $19 per week more than the median job in the service sector. The growth of technology is freeing workers from the drudgery of the production line, while providing consumers with a quality of life previously available only to the most wealthy.

The organization of production is also a major determinant of the number of jobs created. The Western pattern of mass production by monolithic corporations that emerged during the first 80 years of this century is no longer the inevitable or even the obvious pattern for either industrial or developing countries in the coming decades. Smaller, technology-intensive firms are faster at adapting new technology, more flexible in meeting specialized customer needs and generate more skilled, better-paying jobs. Recent experience, such as in the Prato region of Italy, indicates that proper blending of new technologies in existing productive sectors can be utilized to preserve a geographically decentralized, small-scale pattern of production and to enable small firms to match the competitiveness of countries with much lower labour costs. This offers an attractive alternative for preserving the small-scale decentralized pattern of production still prevalent in developing countries and for the future development of enterprises in new industries.

Each advance in attitudes, lifestyles, social institutions and forms of commercial organization has ultimately expanded the scope of economic activities and raised living standards substantially. Jobs are created by our innate human resourcefulness and ingenuity, expressed as invention, innovation and social imitation. The ultimate determinant of the number and quality of jobs in future will not be physical or even financial constraints, but − 'science, technology, values and social organization − in a word, the human imagination'.[2]

Trading Jobs

Those in the West who do not blame rising unemployment on technological advancement, usually blame it on trade. Business and economic literature is replete with articles stating that the high-wage industrial nations will suffer rising levels of unemployment due to the growth of imported goods from low-wage developing countries. The completion of the Uruguay round of GATT trade negotiations was delayed for years because this view fostered protectionist sentiment in the bastion of free trade Western nations. This issue elicits heated emotional debate that often overlooks obvious facts. For instance, increasing trade with East Asia and with low-wage developing countries is cited as a major cause of the fall in the wages of unskilled workers in the United States. As in the case of technology, there is evidence that free trade destroys jobs in some industries, especially unskilled or low-skilled jobs in high-wage economies. In some instances the devastating impact of increasing imports may justify a gradual approach to removing trade barriers. However, the overall impact of manufactured exports from developing countries has been vastly exaggerated. Exports by the Newly Industrializing Economies to the United States have risen from 1.1 to 2.1 per cent of US GNP over the past decade. America's share of trade with low-wage countries represents only 3 per cent of GDP, compared to 2 per cent in 1960. For the OECD as a whole, imports from

2   Harlan Cleveland, *Knowledge Executive: Leadership in an Information Society* (E.P. Dutton, New York, 1989), p. 190.

low-wage countries represent only 1.5 per cent of total expenditure on goods and services.

On the other hand, there is irrefutable evidence that expanding international trade *creates* large numbers of jobs, even in high-wage economies. The real issue, therefore, is whether the overall balance favours net job creation or net job destruction for each nation and for the global economy. On this issue the evidence is clear. Protectionism reduces overall economic welfare, often hurting those with the lowest incomes. In the long term greater international trade, like technology, expands overall employment opportunities substantially. Trade also counters the tendency of prices to increase along with incomes in more developed countries. Living standards rise as consumers benefit from the availability of lower-priced imported consumer goods.

One of the greatest barriers to solving the world's employment problem is the perception that trade destroys jobs. As in the case of technology, the interactions are complex and must be viewed in their entirety, rather than in isolated industries. The global economy is not a zero sum game in which increased production by one country must necessarily result in reduced production by another. Trade opens up new opportunities. It permits each country to specialize in industries where it possesses a 'comparative advantage'. This specialization enables it to evolve improved processes to achieve higher levels of quality and productivity, larger production volumes and lower costs. This results in higher incomes for its workers and makes their products more affordable in other countries, which in turn raises standards of living abroad. The resultant rise in real incomes domestically and overseas stimulates demand for more of these products as well as for other products that can be produced locally or imported from overseas.

Trade also tends to raise the quality of jobs in an economy. It forces higher-wage countries and their workers to specialize in technology-intensive and skill-intensive occupations that pay higher wages. At the same time, it also raises the wages of less-skilled jobs in low-wage countries by increasing the demand for workers to produce for overseas markets. The problem in the more developed countries is that the demand for low-skilled jobs declines and the gap in wages between skilled and unskilled jobs tends to increase, resulting in a decline in incomes and employment opportunities for lower levels of the population in these countries. This is a natural, healthy process of social development in which different sectors serve as engines for growth at different stages. The upward job displacement that earlier shifted job opportunities from agriculture to industry now shifts them to higher-skilled jobs in manufacturing and services. The negative side-effects of this process on some sections of the population alert us to areas where society must make special efforts to speed their development. As in the case of technology, research is needed to document this complex process across industries, between countries and over time. One product of these studies could be the development of specific job coefficients measuring the impact of growth in trade in different industries on overall employment.

Trade becomes of even greater potential benefit to industrial nations during the coming decade when economic growth in these countries is expected to be significantly slower than in the developing world. The pent-up demand generated by the destruction of Europe during the Second World War, the rapid expansion of population during the baby boom generation, and the explosion of new technologies in the past few decades, all generated strong internal demand in the OECD countries, resulting in steady economic growth. The slow growth of population and productivity in more recent years means that these factors cannot be expected to drive further economic expansion at the same rate. In contrast, average growth rates in developing countries are expected to be two to three times higher than in the industrial nations. The increase in the dollar output of developing countries was actually bigger than that of the most economically advanced nations in 1992 and 1993, and this trend is expected to continue. Measured in terms of purchasing power parity, developing countries now represent more than one-third of the world economy. More than 40 per cent of US exports now go to developing countries and two-thirds of the increase in US exports in recent years has gone to these nations.

The rising expectations and upward mobility of millions of people in developing countries represent a vast potential source of demand, higher incomes and jobs for the West. Increasing incomes among the poorest countries has the greatest multiplier effect on global aggregate demand, because even small increments in *per capita* income can lead to large increases in the number of households with incomes above the threshold for buying consumer goods. Asia is expected to generate half the growth in gross world product and world trade during the 1990s. This region will have one billion consumers of televisions, refrigerators and motor vehicles by the year 2000 and a rising appetite for both imported consumer and capital goods. East Asia alone, excluding Japan and China, will spend about $900 billion on infrastructure between 1992 and 2000. During this decade, China and India will add 21,000 megawatts of electricity generation every year and more telephone switching capacity than the United States and Japan combined. Latin America's annual requirements for investment in power, water and sewage, telecommunications and transport infrastructure are estimated at $60 billion. Rising incomes and increasing exports to the dynamic economies of Asia and Latin America could generate as many as 1.7 million jobs by the end of the decade in the United States alone.

The growth of the developing economies could provide the major impetus for economic expansion and job creation in both developed and developing countries. Government policies based on recognition of this fact can considerably improve the climate for development of these nations and correspondingly stimulate further growth in the West. Freer international trade will generate a flood of cheaper goods from the developing world that will give rise not only to greater purchasing power and higher standards of living for the Western consumer, but also to a 'demand boom' for sophisticated Western goods and services to improve infrastructure and meet the needs of billions of consumers in developing countries. *The vast inequalities in living standards that persist within both developing and industrial nations, and between the most and least economically developed countries, result in an enormous global loss of incomes and jobs. Accelerating the development of poorer nations and poorer sections of the population in each country is the most powerful instrument and the surest guarantee of continued growth of jobs and incomes for everyone in the next century.*

Strategies for Developing Countries

For the developing countries as a whole, the most critical question is how to create quickly hundreds of millions of jobs for the poor with limited purchasing power and limited capital for investment. The idea that most of these jobs could be created in the corporate sector or by government-sponsored activities has been put to rest. Currently, there are nearly one billion self-employed and unpaid family workers in the world, most of them self-employed farmers in developing countries. The self-employed represent 48 per cent of the workforce in low-income economies (less than $500 *per capita* GDP). For any strategy to be successful, it must give central importance to self-employment and entrepreneurship, with emphasis on agriculture, agro-industry and small firms in the informal sector. While a single approach will not be applicable to countries and regions of the world in different stages of development, a number of common principles and strategies are widely applicable.

Agriculture as an engine

Slightly more than half the world's workforce, of whom 30 per cent are women, are still engaged in agriculture. Agriculture will remain the largest single occupation for the foreseeable future. For too long this sector has been regarded by planners primarily as the source of essential food production. Historically, agriculture has also played a major role as an engine for economic growth and employment. The Industrial Revolution in nineteenth-century England was spawned by rising productivity and incomes in agriculture that increased demand for manufactured goods. In post-war Japan, South Korea, and more recently Thailand, rising agricultural productivity and a shift to commercial crops have been dynamic engines for economic growth, job creation, higher incomes and rural purchasing power, wider markets for produce, and the growth of downstream industries. In Taiwan, this was the result of a conscious strategy to utilize agriculture to stimulate job creation and domestic demand.

The vast technological gap between the levels of agricultural productivity achieved by most developing countries and the highest yields achieved globally represents an enormous untapped potential for stimulating economic growth and job creation. The reduction in agricultural subsidies to farmers in industrial nations called for in the recently signed GATT trade agreements will generate far higher international demand for agricultural exports from developing countries. In the next chapter, we argue strongly for an agriculture-led job creation strategy and cite evidence to show how it can generate sufficient jobs to eradicate poverty in many countries.

New deal for the self-employed

Excluding agriculture, there are 104 million self-employed and unpaid family workers in developing countries, representing 37 per cent of the non-agricultural workforce. Self-employed persons and the small firms which they establish have enormous potential for rapidly generating large numbers of new jobs and raising productivity to increase incomes, provided the right policy measures are in place to support them. Japan's economic growth has relied heavily on the proliferation of small rural enterprises. Today, 74 per cent of the Japanese workforce is employed by small and medium-sized firms. China created 101 million jobs between 1985 and 1991, 70 per cent in 'township and village enterprises', of which nearly half are privately owned. In many countries, a large proportion of small enterprises are established by women and employ predominately women. An appropriate mix of policies focusing on access to technology, training, credit, marketing and distribution channels can substantially accelerate self-employment, particularly in the informal sector and rural areas, and among women.

Expand services

The service sector represents only 25 per cent of the labour force in developing countries compared with more than 67 per cent in the industrial nations. Contrary to common conception, services can be a major contributor to job growth even in countries at earlier stages of development. This sector is as amenable to stimulation by government policies as agriculture or manufacturing, and it also provides impetus for the growth of other sectors. Supportive policies have enabled trade, transport and other services to generate more than 50 per cent of all jobs in Japan, Hong Kong, South Korea and Singapore. Services have produced more than half of all job growth in many other Asian nations, including private day-care centres, nursery schools and computer training institutes, which are multiplying rapidly in many countries, but can be expanded much further. India has adopted an innovative, low-cost, self-employment strategy to expand availability of long-distance telecommunications services by setting up small private telephone and fax centres throughout the country. Informal private service enterprises in construction, commerce, food catering, repair and transport have vast growth potential. Rapid expansion of education, training and public health, especially rural health and education, can also serve as a conscious strategy for employment generation.

Technology of organization

Much emphasis is placed on the widening gap in technology between North and South, but the gap in the technology of organization is even greater. Creation of new types of systems and organizations can create markets and jobs in many ways. The Dutch system of flower auction cooperatives is so successful that 68 per cent of the entire world's exports of cut flowers pass through markets in the Netherlands. The franchise system has led to a rapid proliferation of new businesses and new jobs in the West in such widely diverse fields as food services, home remodelling, dry cleaning and real estate. Industrial estates, export processing zones, export promotion councils, export insurance, warehouse receipts, quality standards, and thousands of other organizational innovations have been either created or borrowed by developing countries to accelerate social progress. A comprehensive study of successful systems and institutions that can be transferred and adapted to local conditions will document the enormous untapped potential for stimulating faster economic and job growth by inventing, imitating and further improving social systems.

Action Plan to Stimulate Employment in Developing Countries

Employment generation is a product of multiple factors that combine together. Stimulating job creation requires a comprehensive approach, rather than partial policies or piecemeal strategies. The achievements of the Newly Industrializing Economies (NIEs) of East Asia demonstrate that tremendous increases in employment generation can be achieved based on comprehensive strategies. While broad prescriptions should not be indiscriminately applied to the widely disparate situations confronting different countries, the availability of a number of tested methods underlines the fact that effective and proven policy measures can be formulated to meet the employment needs of every developing country. A number of the strategies briefly listed below are enlarged upon in subsequent chapters of the report, but listed here for the purpose of comprehensiveness.

Emphasize agriculture: Utilize agriculture as a source of economic growth and job creation by a shift to high value-added, commercial crops, supported by policy measures to upgrade technology, improve skills, raise productivity, ensure the supply of essential inputs, establish marketing and distribution channels, create linkages between agriculture and industry, and cater to export markets.

Promote small enterprises: Promote small enterprises by policies to make technology, training, credit, marketing and distribution channels more easily accessible to small business, and by forging linkages between universities, research institutes and small enterprises. The creation of micro-enterprise banks and credit unions specifically designed to cater to the needs of the self-employed and small firms can be especially effective. There are a growing number of these institutions targeting clients that lack access to commercial lending institutions, particularly women, providing unsubsidized loans, and achieving very low levels of default.

3 *Upgrade skills:* Absorbing new technology, raising productivity, improving the quality and competitiveness of exports – all depend on the skills of the workforce. Labour productivity has been increasing in East Asia by 10 per cent a year, half of which is attributable to investment in education and technical skills. Training institutions and programmes in most developing countries provide only a narrow range and low level of skill acquisition to a small portion of the population. Raise skills to increase productivity by vastly expanding the lower tiers of the agricultural, craft, technical and vocational training systems at the local level to provide practical training in job-related skills to the saturation point. Imbalances between supply and demand for skills exist at all levels in developing economies. Make a careful assessment of present supply and demand for key skills. Compare the density of different types and levels of skill in countries at the next higher stage of development and evolve programmes to raise the quantity and quality of skills to that level.

4 *Improve marketing:* The organization of marketing is typically one of the weakest links and, therefore, one of the greatest barriers to economic growth and job growth. Brazil set up a distribution system for the export of citrus fruits that has enabled it to become the world's largest exporter of this commodity. Improve distribution and marketing systems, especially for agricultural produce, by identifying missing links and establishing successful model programmes that bridge the gap between rural producers and urban or overseas markets.

5 *Expand services:* Actively encourage and support growth of the service sector through programmes similar to those utilized to support the expansion of small industry.

Develop exports: The new GATT treaty ensures that, contrary to earlier projections, export-led growth is far from over. After agriculture, the textile and clothing industry is one of the largest employment sectors in developing countries. The industry's global exports are $250 billion a year, of which Asian countries command 40 per cent. Trade in clothing is expected to rise by 60 per cent and textiles by 34 per cent over the next ten years. As labour costs have risen in East Asia, greater opportunities are emerging for lower-wage developing countries to take a larger share in growing international markets. In order to take advantage of the increasing opportunities opened up by liberalization of world trade, developing countries should accelerate steps to expand export-oriented markets by forging foreign collaborations and overseas subsidiaries, acquiring technology, creating an attractive commercial environment for foreign investment, and continuously building the skills of the labour force. **6**

Innovate organizationally: Significant improvements in the competitiveness and growth of businesses in developing countries can be achieved through raising organizational efficiency and dynamism through better internal management practices and better commercial systems in the marketplace. Conduct a comprehensive study of successful management practices, systems and institutions from both developing and developed countries that can be transferred and adapted to local conditions in order to accelerate development in each field of activity. Evolve new organizational patterns for existing industries based on adaptation of new technologies in small, geographically decentralized, labour-intensive production units in order to make these industries more responsive, flexible, efficient and competitive. **7**

Extend basic education: A distinguishing feature of the East Asian countries has been their emphasis during the early stage of industrialization on primary and secondary education, especially in rural areas. This strategy increases the productivity of the mass of the workforce, helps promote income equality, consumer spending power and broad support for high growth and pro-business policies. Raise the educational qualifications of the workforce to the **8** level pertaining in more economically advanced nations. Place particular emphasis on primary and secondary education, rural education and education of young girls.

9 *Disseminate information:* Encourage the establishment of new institutions, programmes and systems to speed and extend the dissemination of practically useful information as a powerful catalyst for more rapid social progress. Encourage a national climate of open-mindedness to foreign ideas, influences and success stories.

10 *Increase the velocity of money and other transactions:* Increase the speed of commercial transactions, especially money flows, in the economy by streamlining government and banking procedures, ensuring rapid utilization of funds by all government agencies, setting strict limits on the time taken for bank transfers, introducing agencies for credit verification and collection of unpaid bills, and improving the telecommunications infrastructure.

11 *Revamp higher education:* Educational systems which 'manu-facture graduates' compound the problem rather than alleviating it. The problem of the educated unemployed is not so much the amount of education they receive, but the type of knowledge and attitudes imparted. Reorient the educational curriculum at all levels, especially higher education, to impart the knowledge and attitudes needed to promote self-employment and entrepreneurship rather than salaried employment.

12 *Employment planning:* Studies of Japan and the NIEs indicate that conscious employment planning is an essential requirement for generating full employment. Place the employment objective high on the national agenda and evolve a comprehensive plan to achieve full employment by identifying untapped growth potentials in agriculture, industry, exports and services. Launch a nationwide pro-gramme to implement all employment-related strategies on a highest priority basis.

Comprehensive Strategies

While most of the prescriptions listed above are known to all, very few are systematically and efficiently applied. Africa can benefit enormously by applying strategies that have worked in Asia. The 'Prosperity 2000' programme evolved by ICPF for India and presented in the next chapter seeks to utilize a combination of these strategies to generate 100 million new jobs within a decade or less, which will be sufficient to raise 25 per cent of the world's poorest billion people above the poverty line. Given a comprehensive approach, the right mix of policies, good government and a conducive international environment for trade, technology transfer and investment, every nation has the capacity to develop and meet the employment needs of its people within the next one or two decades.

The Right to Employment

The transformation of social life in this century has drawn hundreds of millions of people away from a subsistence level existence in agriculture to urban areas and industrial employment. In the process it has brought about an unprecedented advancement in living standards around the world. But it has also engendered a way of life in which the livelihood of individuals is far more dependent than in the past on external conditions – the state of the national and global economy, trade policies, interest and exchange rates, levels of military spending and overall consumer demand. Modern society, even in the most liberal democracies, has become so structured that it leaves less and less freedom for truly independent individual initiative. Today, government intervenes in virtually every aspect of society's economic existence, restricting the freedom of the individual to seek his or her own livelihood and determining the type and number of job opportunities available. Employment opportunities are directly linked to government tax policy concerning capital gains, depreciation, energy, wages and salaries, as well as by policies governing minimum wage laws, interest rates, budget deficits, imports and exports, environmental regulations and restrictions, defence spending, immigration, industrial development, investment, licensing of practitioners, zoning laws and countless other public policy issues.

Without access to jobs, people lack the ability to ensure their own survival and support in modern society. As government has assured the right to education – indeed, compels it – it can and must also ensure the right of every person to gainful employment. Our very concept of the rights of the individual and the responsibilities of the society must undergo radical change. UN Secretary General Boutros Boutros-Ghali has called for a broader definition of human rights to include economic as well as political rights. The essential basis for meeting the world's employment needs is the realization that employment is an absolute necessity for survival in modern society and must be recognized as a fundamental right of every human being. Pragmatism as well as idealism compels this step. *Recognizing the right of every citizen to employment is the essential basis and the most effective strategy for generating the necessary political will to provide jobs for all.*

What is needed is not another job generation programme, but a change in social values that will accelerate the natural and inevitable evolution of society, from one in which labour is regarded as a dispensable resource to one based on full human rights and the enormous productive potential of the human being. The type and magnitude of change needed today is comparable to that embodied in President Roosevelt's New Deal for the American people during the Great Depression, at a time when 25 per cent of the workforce was unemployed: to the Indian government's decision to launch the Green Revolution in the mid-1960s to achieve self-sufficiency in foodgrains, at a time when the country was highly dependent on imported food to stave off famine: and to Mikhail Gorbachev's initiatives late in the 1980s to end the Cold War and transform Soviet society.

Is Full Employment Possible?

Few will argue with the compelling logic, justice and idealism of this view, but many will question the feasibility of practically implementing it. *As long as we continue to believe that society is truly helpless to manage job growth, there will be strong resistance to the full employment goal.* We must recognize that the present status and functioning of our economies is the result of specific choices that have been made in the past, based on priorities and values that were relevant or dominant at the time, but which we certainly are not obliged to live with indefinitely and, in fact, are continuously in the process of discarding in favour of new values and priorities. The rapid adoption of environmentally friendly policies around the world is positive proof of how quickly the rules, even economic rules, can change when there is a concerted will for a breakthrough. So too, the welfare policies of the European Union that have resulted in a 70 per cent rise in national income over the past two decades, but only a 9 per cent increase in the number of jobs, were due to conscious choices that favoured the employed over the unemployed, not the inevitability of the market.

Recent economic debate in the United States has brought this truth to the fore. At a time of historically low levels of inflation and high levels of unemployment, the US Federal Reserve has pursued a policy of raising interest rates in order to prevent a potential rise in inflation at some time in the future, which has had the immediate effect of dampening growth and slowing job creation, just at the time unemployment rates were beginning to fall towards normal levels. This has prompted some economists to question the notion of a 'natural' rate of unemployment. *The current high level of structural unemployment is the result of policies that can be changed.*

Every social condition is the result of current social values, attitudes and policies. The values, attitudes and policies underlying the present state of the US economy give highest priority to conserving the value of existing wealth, rather than creating new wealth through faster economic growth and higher rates of employment. The apparent obsession of central bankers supported by international financial institutions to raise interest rates in anticipation of rising prices, thereby sacrificing job growth in order to prevent even modest levels of inflation, illustrates negatively to what extent it is human *choices* – based on superstitious fear and a clinging to money value at the expense of human value – that prevent us from resolving this crucial problem. The current level of unemployment is one among several of its natural results. People's jobs are a variable being manipulated in the operation of economic policy. Through its acceptance of government policy, society has chosen the present system and, if it chooses, can alter it in preference for another.

The commitment to 'jobs for all' is also undermined by the false impression that the total employment available in society is inherently limited by the finite, material needs of the community. Modern economic history is witness to an ever-expanding growth in human needs to match the ever-increasing productive capacities of the post-industrial age. Creating more jobs is an expansive movement that generates more purchasing power, increases aggregate demand and consumption, stimulates further job creation, and moves the whole economy towards higher rates of growth. The expansion is not merely horizontal. It also involves the emergence of higher-order, non-material needs for education, health, recreation, entertainment, environmental protection and artistic fulfilment. The entry of women into the workforce has substantially increased the demand for day-care and house-care services, travel, recreation, automobiles, fashion and consumer goods. The raising of environmental consciousness has led to a rapid proliferation of new technologies, products and services.

A radical change in values, priorities and policies at countless points is required. It can only be done by the conscious initiative of government compelled by the expectations and demands of an electorate educated to understand the impact of government on economic life and the scope for increasing employment opportunities in a market economy. *If society decides that useful jobs must be created, then they will be created. Full employment can be achieved by any country that has the will and determination to achieve it.*

This does not mean that every country can accomplish the goal immediately. Nor does it mean that governments should try to spend their way out of unemployment by creating artificial jobs for all who seek them. But the high current costs of the unemployed certainly suggest that there are more constructive ways to spend available resources to solve the problem. Instead, a commitment to self-employment should lead the government to reexamine and where necessary alter the nature of its priorities and policies and the structure of its economic system in order to make achievement of this goal possible. The magnitude of the task and the prescription may vary, but the goal and determination can be shared by all.

Employment Strategies for the Industrial Nations

In the industrial countries, the phenomena of jobless growth coupled with persistently high rates of youth unemployment and of chronic unemployment among the poorer sections will not be eradicated by even the most optimistic rates of economic expansion or mere incremental adjustments within the context of present attitudes and policies. Although the problem has been aggravated by a variety of short- and medium-term factors whose effects will gradually dissipate over time – defence cuts, recession, East European economic crisis, German reunification, etc. – the present job crisis among Western nations is largely structural in nature. Although conditions vary from country to country, the crisis impacts most heavily on the unskilled, young people, urban poor, ethnic minorities and older workers. Specific programmes to effect structural changes will have to be introduced in order to ensure a fair opportunity to all, especially minority youth, to lead economically active lives. It is in this context that the European Union, the United

States and other Western governments have been considering ambitious proposals for addressing this issue. The Australian government has unveiled a $4.6 billion jobs package to reduce unemployment from 10 per cent to 5 per cent by the end of the decade by encouraging training for the young, the unskilled and the long-term unemployed. Recently the OECD has presented the main planks of an employment strategy to stimulate economic growth in the industrial nations, make labour markets more flexible, increase productivity, and revamp employment and unemployment security provisions.

The relative success of the US economy in creating jobs during the past decade has prompted other countries to emphasize the importance of policies to increase the flexibility of wage rates and bring down the price of labour by reductions in the statutory minimum wage. The main effect of this policy is likely to be a movement of jobs between nations, however, not a significant increase in the total number of jobs available. In fact, measures which reduce wage incomes could have the perverse effect of reducing aggregate purchasing power and employment.

Economic growth is recognized as an essential, though not sufficient, condition for higher rates of job growth – but fears of inflation constrain industrial countries from trying to stimulate faster expansion of their economies. The primary impact of moderate levels of inflation would be to encourage an outflow of investment to more stable currencies. However, if the industrial nations all agreed to relax their monetary policies, this effect could be minimized.

The real constraint on job creation in the industrial nations is not the price of labour, but the need for increased capital investment, partly to counter the effects of reduced military spending and the drastic fall in output and demand in Eastern Europe. Increasing public investment to stimulate employment is constrained by widespread concern about rising levels of public debt. Recent reports state that the gross debt of OECD countries has risen from 35 per cent of GDP in 1970 to 70 per cent in 1993. But this figure is of questionable significance. The gross debt includes the debt held by government departments and public agencies as well as by private institutions and individuals. When the government-held portion is deducted, the actual net debt of these countries is approximately half the gross debt, which means the net interest burden for servicing the debt is also only half. Furthermore, it is not clear that a comparison of debt to GDP is a very meaningful index. Debt is a cumulative measure of stock, while GDP is an annual measure of flow. When the total debt of OECD countries is compared to the total capital stock of these countries, the debt is equal to a relatively modest 15 per cent of the current capital stock of these nations.

In contrast to the recommendations made by the OECD, the Delors Plan for stimulating employment in Western Europe, which was recently rejected by member countries of the European Community, called for a large increase in public investment in expensive communication and transportation infrastructure projects as a means of creating more jobs in the near term and increasing the competitiveness of European economies by improving their infrastructure. Instead of investing in ambitious, high-tech projects whose future impact on job creation is unclear, the industrial nations should make substantial increases in public investment to improve the tools of the workforce by lending to promote small enterprises together with increased public investment in education and training, which will stimulate short-, medium- and long-term job growth.

The recommendations set forth in this report are based on the conviction that nothing less than a legal commitment of the society to guarantee employment is justified and nothing less will be sufficient to solve the problem. Only then can the requisite political will be generated to push through effective measures. We do not advocate a return to state socialism or expansion of the public sector. As in the case of the environment, the changes needed are in the priority given to achieving different social objectives in the formulation of government policy.

Recommendations to Achieve Full Employment in Industrial Nations

Earlier we noted long-term trends that suggest the recent rise in unemployment in the West does not necessarily forebode, and need not necessarily result in, chronically higher rates of unemployment in these countries. Granted that the necessary political and social commitment is forthcoming, there are a range of strategies which, taken in the proper measure and combination, can dramatically accelerate job growth and reduce unemployment. Each of these strategies has proved effective in stimulating employment, though none by itself may be sufficient to solve the problem. A comprehensive, total approach, rather than partial and half-way measures, is needed. No industrial country can claim that it systematically exploits all the potential benefits of the strategies in this list. This should be the highest priority of every Western government today.

Promote small businesses: All the publicity given to the impact of down-sizing by major corporations has obscured the fact that the top 500 US firms employ less than five per cent of the US workforce. It is also the smaller firms that are responsible for job growth. Businesses employing fewer than 20 workers presently account for 57 per cent of new job creation in Europe. Based upon the successful examples of many developing countries that have stimulated growth in this sector, there is vast scope for expanding services to support new enterprises through better access to management and employee training courses, credit and R & D facilities; by testing and certification for those who want to start businesses; and by establishing business incubators to provide work space and shared services as well as technical, financial and marketing expertise to start-up companies.

1

Reduce business failures: New businesses create most of the jobs, but they destroy most of them too, by going out of business. The failure rate of new businesses is extremely high in most industrial nations. In Italy, roughly 50 per cent fail in the first year. Of the more than 600,000 new business start-ups in the United States each year, 40 per cent close within 12 months, 80 per cent within five years, and 80 per cent of the remainder in the subsequent five years. Expanding programmes for management training, small business education and counselling, marketing assistance and financial management can bring down the failure rate dramatically.

2

Voluntary part-timism: Increasing the flexibility of working hours will serve the interests of both businesses and workers. Encouraging voluntary part-timism by removing the artificial barriers to job sharing created by employment laws, social security tax laws, administrative procedures and trade unions would raise the morale and productivity of those who prefer to work less, while creating openings for many who are now without jobs. In the Netherlands, voluntary part-timism has been identified as the biggest single potential for creating new jobs, capable of reducing

3

the country's unemployment by up to 50 per cent. Proportionately reducing working hours and salaries can spread the existing work more evenly over more people. Evidence suggests that reduced working time can raise productivity significantly. Extending vacation time and medical leave in the United States nearer to levels which the Europeans enjoy would create many more job openings. Work or job sharing is not an ultimate answer in itself, but it can have a beneficial short-term impact, allowing time for longer-term measures to take effect. As a minimum, governments should remove the artificial barriers to job-sharing created by employment laws, administrative procedures and trade unions. Social security tax systems should also be modified to remove the in-built bias that increases the taxes of those who hold multiple, part-time jobs, rather than one full-time job. Such constraints limited part-time jobs to around 10 per cent of the total in Belgium, France, Italy and Spain compared to around 25 per cent in Britain and Denmark.

4 *Modify tax policies:* The present income and payroll tax system raises the real cost of labour relative to other resources, such as capital and energy, and thereby discourages job creation. It heavily taxes people for working, which indirectly raises the cost of labour and reduces the number of jobs. At the same time the system provides investment and depreciation incentives that encourage industry to shift from labour-intensive to capital-intensive modes of production. Much of the shift from labour to capital might not be economically justified were it not for the in-built bias in this system. Low levels of taxation on the depletion of non-renewable energy resources in the United States is another distorting influence that makes machine-driven activity more cost-effective than it would otherwise be.

5 *Analyse job impact of government policies:* Almost every government policy has a direct or indirect impact on employment. Often the relationship is not recognized or intended. An analysis of the impact of major public policies on employment at the local, state and nation level can result in avoidance or removal of significant legislative and administrative roadblocks to job growth. Require employment assessment of new policy initiatives prior to adoption.

Re-orient social security programmes toward re-employment: **6**
OECD countries spend 2-3 per cent of GDP on labour
market policies, most of it to support the unemployed. The
United Kingdom spends nearly $14,000 a year on every
unemployed person. The United States spends three times
as much on welfare payments as it does on retraining the
unemployed. For three decades, Sweden achieved the
highest employment rate among OECD countries based on
'the passionate belief in full employment' and 'the right to
work' and on active policies to generate work for all, rather
than payments to the unemployed. Drawing lessons from
the Swedish model, introduce a comprehensive programme
of education and vocational preparedness for the unemployed, compulsory retraining for those who are unemployed for more than six months, and a strictly managed
penalty system for unemployed persons who refuse
successive job offers and do not seek retraining.

Improve labour market information and job placement systems: **7**
Labour markets are becoming more and more fluid. One in
ten jobs is now replaced in OECD countries every year. This
makes the strengthening of job placement systems a crucial
element in any full employment strategy. Lack of access to
information about job or training opportunities retards re-
employment. Sweden operates one of the most extensive
and efficient employment services, in close cooperation
with business, that is responsible for filling 60 per cent of
total job vacancies. Improve labour market information
systems within and between countries by increasing the
accuracy and comparability of data, requiring mandatory
reporting by businesses of all sizes, and freely exchanging
information between cities, states and countries on successful employment-generating strategies.

Raise minimum standards for education: Higher education **8**
increases productivity, raises personal expectations and
consumption, and generates additional jobs in education
and elsewhere. Lack of qualifications, inadequate and out-
dated skills commonly characterize the long-term unemployed. There is a strong positive correlation between
higher education and higher incomes. The employment rate
for college graduates in the United States is 75 per cent

versus 48 per cent for high school drop-outs; at the height of the recent recession, 3.2 per cent of college graduates were unemployed compared with 11.4 per cent of high school drop-outs. Only 57 per cent of 18-year-olds in the OECD countries are pursuing formal education. The Japanese built their highly competitive workforce by raising the educational attainments of the bottom half of their primary and secondary school population. Raising the minimum compulsory level of education, as Belgium did in the mid-1980s from 16 years to 18, slows the entrance of young people into the labour market, better equips them for employment and increases the demand for teachers. Extending compulsory education by two years or doubling the teacher–student ratio in the United States could generate several million additional jobs in teaching. *A national commitment to raise the minimum standard, the average level and the quality of education can act as a great medium-term stimulus to job creation.*

9 *Continuous training:* Technological development is dramatically speeding up the rate at which old skills become obsolete and new ones are needed. Education and training must become a life-long process for workers. In a number of countries, high levels of unemployment coexist with shortages of particular skills, reflecting significant mismatches between supply and demand for skills. The deficiencies in government-operated training programmes can be partially overcome by providing greater incentives to private firms to invest in training new and existing employees. Studies have found that a 10 per cent increase in expenditure on training can boost productivity by an average of 3 per cent over two years and by as much as 30 times the cost of training. Yet even today, only a relatively small number of companies conduct regular, ongoing training programmes. Launch a nationwide public educational programme on the tremendous potential gains in productivity from increased training. Support initiatives by providing incentives to intensify training programmes for all employees by every type of commercial and non-commercial institution in order systematically to upgrade the technical, vocational, organizational and managerial skills of the workforce.

School-to-work apprenticeship programmes: The transition
from school or college to work can be long and difficult.
Germany's apprenticeship programme equips nearly 70 per
cent of all teenagers with employable skills before they
enter the workforce. Two-thirds of the UK workforce have
no vocational or professional qualification, compared with
only 25 per cent in Germany. There is growing support in
the United States for establishment of a national youth
apprenticeship training programme that combines
classroom schooling with on-the-job skills training to
ensure a smooth transition to employment for those who do
not pursue higher education.

10

Link demilitarization to urban employment: The military possesses both the expertise and the physical infrastructure for
training large numbers of people in a wide range of technical, vocational and social skills. Building upon successful
US Defence Department programmes that re-deploy
soldiers to assist troubled inner city youth, closed military
bases can be converted into large training centres operated
by military teaching staff for instructing and housing urban
unemployed youth during an apprenticeship period.

11

Promote integrated urban development programmes: The Atlanta
Project is a bold attempt to evolve a new type of organization to address the problems of inner city poverty and unemployment. The inner city of Atlanta, Georgia, has been
divided into clusters in which members of the local community work closely with the staff of major corporations,
voluntary agencies, religious groups and a wide range of
government agencies to identify and promote employment
opportunities and other poverty-alleviation activities.

12

Promote organizational innovation: In recent years, large firms
have made significant strides in improving their speed,
efficiency and flexibility of response to changing market
conditions by restructuring operations into independent
companies and autonomous profit-centres. Small firms
need to develop new types of organizations to help them
acquire some of the benefits of larger size. An innovative
experiment has been launched by two dozen small
precision-manufacturing, defence contractors in the state of
Kansas, with the support of the US Defence Department, to

13

combine their technical, organizational and marketing resources for diversification into non-defence production. Initiatives of this type can help strengthen the 12,000 small tool and die-making companies in the United States as well as millions of other small companies in other industries and other countries.

14 *National service organizations:* National service programmes can be very successful vehicles for providing training and valuable work experience to youth before they enter the labour market. Service in activities designed to improve education, health and the environment can be of immense benefit to the country, while slowing the pace of new entrants to the workforce. The United States recently established AmeriCorps to strengthen and expand service and educational opportunities by providing educational grants to youth in exchange for community service in the fields of education, environment, human services and public safety. Participants receive a limited wage while serving, plus a post-service educational award for higher education.

15 *Pay the unemployed to work, rather than not work:* The high costs of welfare programmes, the negative incentives they provide to job seekers and the harmful psychological consequences of unemployment can be mitigated by modifying welfare programmes to require that the able-bodied unemployed either train or work in exchange for welfare payments. The type of work given may be varied depending on both the qualifications and the training needs of the individual – for example, as assistants in child education, or care for children and the elderly, or environmental protection. If properly administered, these programme have proved successful in reducing costs, imparting new skills and identifying false welfare claims. Redirect welfare expenses for creating jobs, rather than encouraging idleness, by paying welfare recipients to carry out public service activities in return for welfare payments. This requires the identification of employment-intensive programmes that provide clear benefit to the community without interfering with existing business, such as the US Civilian Conservation Corps that built the US National Parks system in the 1930s. Expanding or upgrading the educational system would be a priority area.

Make income distribution more equitable: The number of jobs available is directly related to patterns of income distribution. In Japan and other dynamic Asian economies, the ratio between the bottom and top pay is as much as 5 or 10 times lower than in the United States. A highly skewed income distribution results in lower levels of overall demand, growth and job creation. Lopsided income distribution fuels speculative investment, more and more of which goes overseas. The average wages for production workers in the United States are the lowest they have been since 1967, with 18 per cent of full-time workers not earning enough to keep a family of four out of poverty, up from 12 per cent in 1979. Income redistribution in the industrialized countries requires structural adjustments similar to those which the West has advocated for developing countries. A 'maximum wage' law can be introduced, requiring firms to pay taxes on exorbitant executive compensation.

Agenda for a Global Employment Programme

Employment is a global problem that cannot be fully solved by individual countries in isolation. Policy measures at the national level influence trade and investment flows and employment rates in other countries. Economic growth and expansion of employment in one country enhance employment opportunities in other countries as well. Therefore, coordination of policies is in the interests of the global community. A comprehensive and coordinated international effort is called for to improve the global climate for economic growth and job creation by evolving stable and supportive policies to regulate capital flows, foreign trade, debt, commodity pricing, immigration and labour movements, transfer of technology, investment, military spending and the arms trade. We set forth below a broad policy framework to stimulate global job growth with the aim of achieving full employment early in the twenty-first century.

1 *World Employment Programme:* Raising incomes and creating jobs in the developing countries is the best way to promote global economic growth and employment generation in the coming decades. The World Summit on Social Development should call for a comprehensive World Employment Programme to stimulate more rapid growth in developing countries as an engine for global economic expansion. The International Labour Organization has operated a programme for the past two decades, but solution of the employment problem requires an integrated approach that transcends the scope of any single international agency. The programme should establish specific objectives and coordinate efforts to stimulate international investment, increase labour market flexibility, promote productive skills, diffuse technology, eliminate protectionist trade policies that retard growth, increase trade between developing countries, and promote international cooperation on taxation systems to encourage more labour-oriented tax codes.

2 *Coordination of macro-economic policies:* The efforts of the industrial nations to achieve higher rates of economic growth and job creation are stymied by the need to maintain macro-economic stability at the same time. Due to the competition between OECD members to attract financial resources, rising interest rates or falling inflation rates in one country influence the inflow and outflow of financial resources from other members of the community. The efforts to curb inflation at the expense of slower economic growth and job creation need not be so rigorous, if OECD members more closely coordinated their policies to support macro-economic expansion. A modest, relatively uniform rise in inflation rates within the OECD would not then result in a significant movement of resources or fluctuation in exchange rates.

3 *Shift investment from defence to education and training:* Reduce global defence spending by an additional 50 per cent before the end of the decade to below a maximum threshold of $400 billion. Invest at least 10 per cent of the global savings from defence cuts in education and training.

Liberalize agricultural and textile exports: Utilize agriculture as an engine of industrialization, international trade and employment generation by reducing the barriers to a major expansion of agricultural production and exports from and between developing countries. More than two billion people in developing countries, representing about 35 per cent of the entire world's population, are dependent on agriculture as a primary source of livelihood. This compares with 45 million people in industrial countries, which represents less than 1 per cent of the world's population. Agriculture is the most heavily protected sector of world trade. In 1991 the industrial nations spent more than $180 billion on agricultural subsidies to support their farm populations, which is three times the total world overseas development assistance. These subsidies cost Western consumers another $135 billion annually in terms of higher food costs. Agricultural protectionism in the North not only places powerful constraints on exports from developing countries, but also directly interfere with the livelihood of one-third of the entire human race living in developing countries.

The elimination of the system of quotas and subsidies to Western farmers can dramatically reduce the budget deficits of industrial nations and bring down food prices, while stimulating large-scale expansion of agriculture, industrialization and job growth in developing countries. Existing trade barriers by the industrial nations to textile exports cost developing countries an estimated $50 billion annually. The complete elimination of these barriers could result in a doubling of textile exports by developing countries. This labour-intensive industry can be another engine for job creation in developing countries and rising demand for technology and capital goods from the industrial nations. *The progressive reduction, leading to the eventual elimination, of barriers to trade in agricultural products and textiles is an important step that can substantially improve the employment opportunities of people in developing countries.*

Improve access to markets: The most important structural change in the world economy over the past 35 years has been the five-fold increase in the world share of manufactured exports gained by the developing countries as a group, up from 4 per cent to 19 per cent, compared with a current market share of about 13 per cent each of the United States and for Japan. Although 54 per cent of these manufactures come from five top exporting countries, a large number of countries export more than $1 billion in this category annually. This has opened the door for self-reliant growth in many developing countries.

This growth could have been considerably more impressive but for constraints placed on it by both tariff and, particularly, non-tariff barriers. The latter have proliferated in recent decades and affected almost half of OECD imports during the 1980s. By the end of 1990, there were more than 200 export-constraint arrangements involving product groups of importance to developing countries. The incidence of anti-dumping cases against developing countries rose substantially in the late 1980s. The more recent effort by the industrial nations to impose 'fair labour standards' on exports from developing countries could well become another form of constraint, unless carefully formulated to focus on the basic rights of workers, rather than on arbitrary minimum wage levels. Efforts to accelerate the dismantling of both trade and non-trade barriers should be viewed as a central element of a global strategy to stimulate employment generation.

6 *Debt repayments:* The debt problem is a major obstacle to the development and welfare of at least 60 heavily indebted, developing countries, including two-thirds of the world's poorest nations. Most of these countries suffered a decline in *per capita* income over the past decade and are now in arrears with more than 20 per cent of their debt obligations. The debt burden discourages new foreign investment and lending to these countries and prevents them from stimulating economic growth through additional domestic savings and investment. International debt relief has helped ten, mostly middle-income, debtor countries significantly reduce their commercial debt. Past actions to relieve the debt burden on low-income countries have been relatively small in relation to the amount of debt, which has continued to rise under the combined impact of accumulated interest arrears on old loans, falling export commodity prices, and new compensatory loans, frequently given on expensive terms. Unrealistic pressure to repay debt undermines

debtors' capacity for constructive initiative. Past experience has shown that mere debt rescheduling in these countries does not solve the problem and may in fact aggravate it.

The extent of the problem is reflected in the heavily discounted prices of the debts of countries with low and lower-middle incomes in the secondary market and in negotiated buy-outs of the debt owed to commercial creditors. In 1993, the average market price of the debt was about 30 cents on the dollar. This market discount was a major factor in the decision to scale down the debt of Latin American countries by an average of 15 per cent and of Egypt and Poland by 50 per cent. The aggregate debt of the 61 debt-affected countries with low and lower-middle income is roughly equal to that of the half-dozen mostly middle-income countries assisted under the Brady Plan. Scaling down the debt of these poor countries by an average of 70 per cent would be appropriate in view of their economic plight, though the actual reduction would have to be negotiated on a case by case basis. In order to be of sufficient magnitude, debt reduction should be applied to all three major classes of creditors: bilateral official creditors, private sector lenders and international organizations. Debt reduction should be linked to each country's specific programmes for poverty eradication and meeting the minimum needs of the people.

Commodity prices: The problem of debt is closely linked to that of international commodity prices. The majority of developing countries are dependent on the export of primary products for their welfare and growth. These products account for 80–90 per cent of the exports of African countries, and 65 per cent in the case of Latin American nations. The extreme price volatility of commodity markets is especially damaging to low-income countries, which, regardless of the price, are forced to sell their products to meet minimum needs and pay debts. The obligation of the poorest developing countries to repay debts forces them to produce and export excessive quantities of basic commodities, which has been a principal cause of falling commodity prices. The more these countries export, the faster prices fall, making it impossible to generate sufficient funds for debt repayment by this means, which is often the only source of foreign exchange available to them. Distress sales by the poorest countries force even financially stronger countries to drop their prices in order to maintain market share, which encourages buyers to postpone purchases in expectation of still-lower prices.

The growth of agricultural incomes in developing countries is critically important to global job creation and economic growth. The expansion of agricultural exports under the new GATT agreement is likely to exacerbate the falling commodity price syndrome to the great detriment of the entire world economy, unless effective mechanisms are introduced to stabilize international commodity prices. Of the many efforts in the past, some were tried and failed, many were proposed but never implemented. The recent success of coffee-producing countries in lifting prices from a disastrously low level has been an exception to the rule. Collective and coordinated international action is essential to address this problem. Despite past failures, new efforts must be made to revive international commodity agreements, preferably covering both producing and consuming countries. This will be possible only if developing countries first arrive at a consensus approach among themselves, including the economic costs and benefits, and a financing plan. Financing for international commodity stocks could be supplied partly by producer countries in the form of building national stocks under collective supervision. Partly, it could come from bank commercial loans against commodity collateral, loans from regional development banks, the World Bank and IMF's Buffer Stock Facility, which has remained almost unused.

8 *Technology transfer:* Accelerate transfer of technology to and between developing countries. One or more profit-making commercial organizations should be established as a public sector joint venture of developing countries to promote the commercial transfer of technology to, within and between developing countries and to channel the profits from this activity toward research in these countries.

9 *Global employment model:* Our efforts to promote employment are constrained by a lack of detailed knowledge of how global labour markets actually work. We still do not understand the impact of technology, trade, macro-

economic policies, multinational corporations, shifting patterns of foreign investment and many other factors on job creation, and our ignorance severely hampers effective policy formulation and coordination. An international research programme should be organized under the ILO to construct a truly global employment model that monitors the impact of technological developments, expanding world trade, plant closings, movement of industry to low-wage countries, agriculture-led industrialization, economic growth, immigration policies, refugee movements and other factors affecting employment opportunities around the world.

Shift focus of technological development: The number of jobs created or destroyed by technology depends on the priority given to various objectives in the process of technological development. Presently, there is an in-built bias in technological R & D towards replacing human labour with capital and energy, even when similar levels of quality and efficiency could be achieved by alternative means. A conscious shift of focus could lead to the development of more labour-intensive production processes.

10

5

FOOD FOR ALL

The production of more food to meet the needs of a burgeoning population has been one of the outstanding global achievements of the post-war period. It has demonstrated the extraordinary capacity of humankind to meet a collective challenge of monumental proportions. It has harnessed the power of science and technology for the most cherished of purposes – preserving human lives. It has released the initiative and pride of long suppressed peoples to achieve self-sufficiency and determine their own destinies. It has finally lifted the suffocating blanket of pessimistic economic determinism that has stifled human hopes and aspirations for nearly 200 years since Thomas Malthus first set forth the thesis that human population will always outrun the growth of food production, thus ensuring the perpetual poverty of humankind. The remarkable achievements of countries such as India, which at a time when famine threatened to claim millions of lives launched a massive national programme that increased foodgrain production by three-quarters, and China, which nearly doubled food-grain production over the last two decades, are outstanding testaments to the accomplishments of people in many countries. Worldwide, production increases in major cereal crops are estimated to have provided enough food for more than a billion people.

Food has become a symbol of our collective human endeavour to create a better world for all. But the victory has been partial and neither the challenge nor the opportunity which food presents have been fully addressed. It is of crucial importance not only to the poor, but also to the peace and stability of global society that we complete the task of banishing famine and hunger once and for all. *Hunger anywhere threatens peace everywhere.* Hunger leads to political instability, social unrest, massive migrations, rebellions, civil war, crime and violence. Prosperity, which eliminates hunger, also tends to eliminate violence. Even in war-ravaged Africa, experience shows that where food is plentiful, war is avoided. The converse is also true. Historically, war and civil strife have been the single greatest cause of famines. In addition to destroying crops and food supplies, it disrupts food distribution through the use of sieges and blockades. In the past decade, war has had a greater impact on food supplies in Africa, particularly the Sahelian region, than have the severe droughts that periodically plague the continent.

Freedom from hunger and political freedom go hand in hand. As subsistence agriculture and periodic famine were the economic foundations of monarchy and feudalism, the generation of agricultural surpluses that stimulated commercialism, and later industrialization, have formed the basis for the rise of democratic institutions. Greater freedom for individual action and ownership both stimulate and are supported by greater productivity in agriculture. Authoritarian government is frequently either the result or the cause of food shortages – its use of force justified on the one hand to meet a crisis situation or necessitated on the other to restore order and initiate emergency measures. *Only under democracy is government compelled to pay attention to the needs of people at the lowest levels of society.* The dual pressures of a free press and electoral system have helped a free and democratic India to avoid famine for nearly 50 years, despite the recurring incidence of widespread famine in previous centuries, up to as recently as four years before the country gained independence. Even in China, which appears to be a blatant contradiction of this thesis, it was the liberalization of the agricultural sector and greater freedom given to the peasant community that were responsible for the remarkable increase in food production. For countries still at an early stage of political development, where government lacks even the force of authority to govern, the first essential steps may necessarily be toward greater centralized authority and control, a common stage in the political evolution of the nation state. But that central authority cannot release the full initiative of its farmers or tap the full potentials of agriculture without first instituting broader democratic measures. Recent events in Eastern Europe demonstrate that where states attempt to use authority as the lever for agricultural development, the achievements are likely to be limited and short-lived. The inability of the authoritarian system to produce enough food for its people was one of the major factors contributing to its downfall. *Democracy is the most potent fertilizer to ensure food security at the household level.*

ICPF was founded at a time when a consensus was emerging worldwide that drastic steps were needed to wipe out the hunger and famine that were ravaging parts of the developing world and afflicting to a lesser extent poorer sections of the industrial nations. Recognizing that the problem of food was inextricably intertwined with the problems of peace, political and social stability, and employment, and that no comprehensive solution to one was possible without substantial progress on the others, it was our hope and intention that this growing consensus on food could be harnessed to accelerate progress on arms control and disarmament. Ironically, events have unfolded in the reverse sequence. Rapid progress has been made during the intervening years to reduce international tensions, but little has yet been done effectively to address the food issue. Now that opportunity is before us and compels us to act, for without significant progress on abolishing hunger from the earth, our efforts at arms control and peace making may come to naught. Increasing the availability of food and jobs form essential components of a comprehensive strategy to eradicate hunger, poverty and violence from the world.

Food Security

Despite great achievements in the post-war period, we live in a world of persistent hunger amidst plenty. Presently, around 800 million people living in 46 countries are malnourished and 40,000 die every day of hunger and hunger-related diseases. Widespread famine currently threatens nine African countries, where the lives of 20 million people are at risk.

Hunger and famine are usually associated with a physical shortage of food. Yet, even where food supplies are adequate, absence of opportunities for gainful employment to generate the purchasing power needed to buy food can result in hunger. Lack of food and employment are the basis for the poverty that still afflicts one-fifth of humankind. When it comes to food there can be no justification or excuse – everyone must have enough to eat, and can have enough. A world dedicated to upholding the political rights and property rights of nations and individuals cannot fail to recognize and enforce the most fundamental of all human rights – the right to live.

Contrary to the fears raised in earlier centuries and revived in recent decades, today the world does possess the capacity to feed everyone, even at current levels of food production – subject as it is to disincentives, quotas, restrictions and trade barriers that food surplus countries impose to curtail food production, while other nations remain in perpetual deficit. In spite of a doubling of population in the developing countries since 1960, their average food supplies have increased from 1950 calories to 2475 calories *per capita* per day, or from an average of 90 per cent to 107 per cent of the minimum caloric requirement. During the past 12 years alone, *per capita* food production in developing countries has risen by 15 per cent. Overall, the proportion of people in developing countries suffering from hunger and malnutrition has dropped dramatically both in relative and absolute terms, from 941 million people constituting 36 per cent of the population of these nations in 1970 to 781 million constituting less than 20 per cent of the population in 1990.

Current projections indicate that the growth rate in world agricultural output will continue to exceed population growth over the next two decades. By 2010, foodgrain production is expected to reach four times the level in 1960. Increased production of other food crops is expected to raise *per capita* availability in the developing world to 2700 calories per day. *Per capita* meat production is expected to grow by 60 per cent and milk production by 20 per cent. During the same period, malnutrition is projected to decline to 640 million persons, constituting 11.6 per cent of the population of developing countries, a little over half the level in 1990.

Yet the achievements have not been uniform throughout the developing world. *Per capita* food production has actually declined in more than half of all developing countries over the past 15 years. In 18 countries with high rates of population growth, primarily in Africa, it has been deteriorating for the past three decades. While the Near East, North Africa, East Asia and Latin America/Caribbean regions are expected to achieve average food supplies of 3,000 calories per day by 2010, 200 million people will still be malnourished in South Asia and 300 million, or one-third of the population of sub-Saharan Africa, will suffer from severe food deficits. Due to rapidly expanding population, agricultural production in sub-Saharan Africa would have to grow at four per cent annually in order significantly to improve *per capita* availability of food. Thus far, only East Asia has sustained such high growth rates in agriculture, averaging 6.1 per cent from 1970 to 1990. This trend, if not halted and reversed, casts a renewed spell of gloom over the hopes of hundreds of millions of people to escape from hunger, and over all our hopes for peace in the twenty-first century.

The projection of future prospects based on past trends is especially questionable with regard to food. Not even some of the most prominent agricultural economists expected the gains in food production which have occurred in the past several decades. An international team of experts visiting India in 1963 projected a mere 10 per cent growth in foodgrain production by 1970, whereas growth actually achieved during this period was 50 per cent. Neither technological, nor financial nor natural resources pose insurmountable obstacles to achieving dramatically more over the next 15 years than is indicated by past trends or current projections.

The idea that hunger cannot be conquered because we are running out of land to support rapidly burgeoning populations is contradicted by the facts. Globally, there is no correlation between population density and hunger. China, with only half as much arable land *per capita* as India, produces 13 per cent more foodgrains *per capita*. Taiwan and South Korea have only half the farmland *per capita* of Bangladesh, yet they produce 40 per cent more food *per capita*. Tiny Netherlands, with the highest population density in the world, produces more than sufficient food to feed itself and remain a large net food exporter. Currently 11 per cent of the world's land surface is used for agricultural crops, just 4 per cent more than in 1960. A comprehensive theoretical study of soils, climate, vegetation and topography conducted in 1975[3] indicated that both land and water utilized for agriculture could be doubled, if necessary, and that the earth could support 36 times the 1975 level (18 times the 1990 level) of cereal production using the same share of cultivated land. There would be severe practical obstacles to such a vast expansion of croplands, but these findings suggest that physical limitations to food production are not the primary constraints. A more commonly accepted estimate indicates that the world's land and water used for agriculture could more than double.

Agriculture's Dual Role

Achieving food security necessitates increasing food production and employment opportunities. Agriculture plays a dual role in the abolition of hunger – it produces the food and it can also produce a great many of the jobs needed by households to buy food in developing countries. Since agriculture is the world's single largest employer, raising production and productivity in this sector can immediately place additional purchasing power in the hands of the rural poor, who will in turn utilize the additional income for purchasing more food, clothing and other basic consumer goods that will create more jobs and higher incomes for countless others. The increased agricultural produce becomes raw material for a wide range of agro-based industries and services that stimulate formation of new enterprises, and create downstream jobs as well as products for further processing, domestic sale or export. This is the rationale behind the Prosperity 2000 strategy

3   Buringh, van Heemst and Staring. See *World Food Outlook 1993* (World Bank), p. 48.

for India, which forms a viable model for many other countries to emulate.

Promoting job creation in agriculture appears at first glance to contradict the global trend of the past hundred years, in which employment in this sector has declined steadily from historic highs of more than 70 per cent in the industrial nations to the point where, today, only 2 per cent of the workforce in the UK, 3 per cent in the USA and 4 per cent in Germany are directly engaged in farm operations, although a much larger percentage of the workforce in these countries work in businesses and industries linked to agriculture. Nevertheless, this strategy follows a natural course of development that has occurred in many countries which now have a relatively small portion of their workforce in agriculture. *Agricultural surpluses and rising farm incomes are preconditions and stimuli to economic growth and industrialization.* For most developing countries with the vast majority of people still residing in rural areas, the most cost-effective and practical strategy to generate more jobs and raise personal incomes is through agriculture. *Today, more than 1.1 billion people in developing countries, constituting 58 per cent of the economically active population, work in agriculture. The decline in proportion of the workforce in this sector must necessarily be gradual. An employment strategy which generates a large number of new jobs in the non-farm rural sector could contribute substantially to diversification of rural employment opportunities.*

A similar strategy has proved highly effective as an engine for growth in a number of East Asian countries, which employed crop-intensive and labour-intensive technologies to achieve increasing levels of employment and productivity in agriculture. *Empirical evidence from these countries confirms that wherever agriculture becomes prosperous, labour becomes scarce.* Between 1952 and 1968, land reform in Taiwan increased the number of cultivators five-fold, leading to dramatic increases in output and productivity, a shift from foodgrains to higher value-added fruit and vegetable crops, and the creation of more than 100,000 jobs in post-harvest and processing activities. These changes in employment led to enhanced rural incomes and purchasing power, growing domestic demand for goods and services, including manufactured goods, and further job growth. Land reform in South Korea during the early 1950s increased the number of owner cultivators from 50 per cent to 90 per cent and led to a 4.7 per cent annual growth in labour productivity per hectare over a 15-year period. Then, as agricultural technology improved and industrialization gained momentum, the proportion of South Korea's workforce engaged in agriculture fell from 55 per cent to under 16 per cent over the following three decades. Thailand, which has had the fastest growth of the East Asian economies in recent years and still employs 70 per cent of its workforce in agriculture, has also attained high rates of production and employment in the rural sector through diversification in agriculture from traditional cultivation of rice and rubber to high-value crops and agro-based industries.

Economic Potential of Increasing Demand for Food and Agricultural Products

There are powerful social forces active in the world today that can stimulate significantly greater growth in both food demand and food production. Liberalization of world trade, especially trade in agricultural products; emphasis on aggressive strategies to expand employment opportunities in developing and developed countries; advances in technology for agricultural production, food processing and dissemination of information; rising levels of education, which spur rising expectations; and the energizing impact of democratization – all these factors can substantially raise growth rates in supply and demand for food above those currently projected for the next two decades. Current projections, made at a time when Eastern Europe was in the depth of its transition crisis, would also prove too conservative if demand were to recover more rapidly in some of these countries. Already Russia's cocoa imports have risen to four times the level in 1991.

The gap between the availability of food in industrial nations and in developing countries remains large. Food supplies *per capita* for all developing countries, measured in terms of total calories available, are only 72 per cent of the levels in the industrial countries. The availability of protein for consumption is 40 per cent lower in developing countries than in industrial nations. Viewed from another perspective, this gap represents a huge potential for the growth of agriculture, and through it for more rapid industrialization and job creation in developing countries, with rising exports from industrial nations. Rising incomes are accompanied by a diversification in diet which generates greater demand for wheat, meat and dairy products, fish, vegetables, fruits and processed foods. Projections for the year 2010 anticipate a 60 per cent increase in cereal consumption in developing countries, a 52 per cent increase in meat consumption, and a 69 per cent increase in milk consumption. Meat consumption in China has tripled since 1978 and is expected to more than double again over the next two decades. Sugar consumption in developing countries is currently less than half the average of industrial nations. In India, sugar consumption is projected to rise from 13 kg to more than 25 kg, generating a demand for a 100 per cent increase in sugar cane production, the establishment of 300 to 400 new sugar mills in the country and the creation of 3 to 4 million new jobs in this industry alone. Worldwide, raising the average level of sugar consumption in developing countries could generate tens of millions of additional jobs in agriculture, industry and services.

Viewing the future demand for food from this perspective reveals a tremendous opportunity. Vast sections of humanity now aspire to the higher quantity, wider variety and greater nutritional content of food once consumed only by the wealthy. An effort to raise nutritional standards in the developing countries nearer to the levels prevalent among industrial countries will not only eradicate hunger, but also dramatically spur economic growth, employment, and purchasing power among the rural poor, stimulating growth of production and jobs in industry and services, as well as increasing exports and imports. Raising the entire world population to the level of the prosperous nations would require a 72 per cent increase in total world food production, measured in terms of calories. In order to meet the people's nutritional requirements for fruit and vegetables, India's production of these crops needs to double within the next decade. Achieving that high level will generate more than six million new jobs in the country.

Broadening the scope to include other agricultural products, particularly textiles, the potential for accelerating global economic growth by an agriculture-led strategy is even greater. Cotton is a crop with a very high income and employment multiplier effect. *Per capita* cotton consumption in poorer developing countries such as India is less than half the level in China and less than a third the level in industrial nations.

Measures of the gap between the prevailing levels of nutrition in developing countries and the levels achieved in the West reveal a huge potential for increasing demand for agricultural production, which can serve as an engine to drive the growth of the world economy. Extrapolation from ICPF's studies of the employment potential of expanding agricultural production in India suggests that more than one billion jobs can be created worldwide through a strategy that focuses on raising agricultural productivity as an engine for improving diets, employment and industrialization.

Challenges in Agriculture

The ratio of growth of foodgrain production to population growth has entered into a period of decline over the past decade – increasing at just one per cent per year compared to three per cent during the previous two decades. There is a similar trend for other staple crops and meat. For fish, there has actually been a net decline of seven per cent in *per capita* world production. To a large extent, this slowdown is the result of slower growth in demand, especially in industrial countries, underlining the fact that food security is predominantly an economic problem rather than a technological one. But the decline in the growth of global agricultural productivity over the past decade is also attributable to a variety of political, economic and environmental factors.

Political priority

After the Second World War, developing countries that had suffered from recurring famine in early periods struggled to increase food production as an urgent national priority to keep up with surging population growth and spiralling demand for food. India's Green Revolution was spurred by the imminent threat of severe famine in the mid-1960s. China was compelled to produce more food by the loss of perhaps as many as 30 or 40 million lives to famine in the late 1950s. But the very motive which stimulated these achievements moderated them as well. For while these governments took concerted steps to meet the minimum needs of the population for food, they tended to overlook the equally great potential to utilize agriculture as an engine for economic growth and job creation. Once minimum food needs were met, attention was diverted to other sectors of the economy. Politically, the elimination of the famine threat arising from food shortages is one of the reasons for slower growth in agricultural productivity in recent years. This has resulted in a marked decline in investment by developing countries in government-sponsored agricultural research and rural techno-infrastructure. This tendency has been compounded by the false notion that in order to achieve economic growth, new jobs must be created in industry and services.

Economic policy

The resurgence of faith in the free market and liberalized trade has placed developing countries under increasing pressure from donors and international financial institutions to abandon special types of economic assistance to the agricultural sector in the form of subsidies for supply of critical inputs such as fertilizer and seeds and price supports for marketable crops. This pressure has recently been aggravated by the impact of structural adjustment programmes that usually involve drastic reduction in government subsidies. In Ghana, for instance, the cost of fertilizer as a percentage of total cultivation cost has risen ten-fold in recent years. The impact of macro-economic reforms on agriculture has been most severe in the countries of Eastern and Central Europe, where production in this sector has fallen drastically over the past few years.

Technology

Slower growth in productivity can be attributed to a slowdown in the development of improved hybrid varieties, shortages of quality seeds and fertilizers, and the absence of techno-infrastructure facilities needed for storage and processing, expansion of markets, transport and distribution.

Environment

A number of factors are posing serious obstacles to productivity growth and threaten even current levels of production. Of the poor, 80 per cent in Latin America, 60 per cent in Asia and 50 per cent in Africa live on marginal land of low productivity and high susceptibility to environmental degradation. Raising productivity on these lands can be extremely difficult. Quality farm lands are being lost at an astonishing rate to diversion for non-farm uses, desertification, deforestation, soil erosion, and the depletion and pollution of water resources. These factors have resulted in the degradation of nearly one billion hectares worldwide since the Second World War. In addition, climatic changes resulting from the increased emission of carbon dioxide into the atmosphere are expected to exert additional negative impact over the long term, the extent of which is difficult to assess.

Opportunities in Agriculture

Rapid and sustained expansion of food and agricultural production cannot be achieved without concerted efforts to address these factors. At the same time there are a number of positive factors that offer opportunities to increase productivity significantly in the near to middle term.

Closing the productivity gap

A survey comparing the levels of productivity for major crops between countries reveals a wide disparity between proven technological potentials and actual field results for every crop. Cereal yields in Western Europe and North America average 4.5 tons per hectare, compared to three tons in Asia, 2.3 tons in Eastern Europe and the former Soviet Union, two tons in Latin America and slightly more than one ton in Africa. The Food and Agriculture Organization (FAO) projects a 40 per cent increase in wheat yields in 92 developing countries, excluding China, by 2010. In rice, countries with widely differing climatic conditions, such as Australia, Korea, Egypt, Spain, Japan and Italy, achieve average yields nearly double the world average and two to three times the yields achieved in countries such as India, Malaysia, the Philippines and Thailand. Total rice yields in 92 developing countries are expected to rise to 37 per cent by 2010. Maize yields in Greece, Chile, Austria, Italy and Germany average more than double the world average, and five to six times the averages achieved in large maize-producing countries such as India. Even comparing areas under irrigated maize, average yields range from 1.5 to 8.4 tons per hectare. New varieties of maize are under development that yield 30 per cent more grain in a drought season than conventional varieties. They could be especially effective in lowland tropics, including much of Africa. Potato yields in Belgium and the Netherlands are roughly three times the world average. This productivity gap between what is routinely achieved by different countries represents a vast immediate potential for improving yields that does not require significant additional investment of time or money in R & D. The world already possesses the knowledge, technology and organizational capacities to raise considerably average world yields in major crops.

Emphasizing cultivation practices

The phenomenal increases in productivity achieved over the past three decades through the development of improved and hybrid varieties of seeds have overshadowed and distracted attention from the equally great potential of raising yields through improvements in methods of cultivation. This is especially true since much of the slowdown in productivity growth is attributable to depletion of soil and water resources, which can be partially rectified or offset by improved practices. Growing environmental concerns in the West have generated pressure for reducing fertilizer consumption in developing countries, when in most instances fertilizer application levels are lower than those in Western Europe by a factor of five or ten times. Increased, rather than reduced, use of chemical fertilizers will be essential to the expansion of agriculture in these countries and can considerably increase crop yields. Total fertilizer consumption by developing countries is expected to double by 2010. Furthermore, replacing macro-nutrients lost during intensive cultivation does not compensate for the depletion of more than a dozen micro-nutrients that also determine the quantity and quality of crops. Even in such agriculturally diverse countries as the United States and India, it has been demonstrated that better management of micro-nutrients can raise productivity substantially – in some intensively cultivated areas by as much as 50 to 100 per cent or more in a wide variety of crops – without significant changes in the structure or method of cultivation. Greater attention is needed to conserving and applying organic sources of manure and raising nitrogen-fixing crops, as well as to the use of bio-fertilizers. Unlike the creation of new irrigated lands, the application of such environmentally sustainable field practices is neither very costly nor technology-intensive, and can be widely propagated through improvements in agricultural training and extension.

Increasing exports

Over the next six years, the agreements reached during the Uruguay Round of GATT negotiations are expected to reduce the tariffs levied by the industrial nations on agricultural products by 37 per cent and on tropical food exports by 43 per cent. Developing countries will cut agricultural tariffs by an average of 24 per cent. In addition, North American and Western European countries have agreed to cut agricultural subsidies by one-third. Together these cuts are expected to result in a 20 per cent rise in exports of agricultural and processed foods by 2005. The share of developing countries in this increase has been estimated at $20 billion to $60 billion annually. Increased trade can act as a strong stimulus to the growth of agricultural, agro-industrial and rural employment, provided that these countries respond dynamically to the opportunity by raising productivity and strengthening rural infrastructure for storage, processing and distribution. However, *rising demand within developing countries themselves will limit overall growth of exports, and increasing exports will push up domestic food prices, unless much greater priority is given to matching production with opportunities for home and external trade.*

Increased private investment

The modernization of the farm sector greatly needs the investment, technology, professional management and marketing expertise which private firms can bring. Wherever land reforms have resulted in the division of farms into small parcels, farmers need to be supported by well-organized services, particularly for post-harvest handling, provided either by companies or cooperatives. Economic liberalization offers expanded opportunities for private enterprise to work with small producers in a wide range of agro-industries to combine the social benefits of small holdings with the economies and marketing expertise of corporate management. The contract system of agricultural production introduced in backward regions of Thailand has enabled small farmers to work closely with private businesses to produce labour-intensive, value-added crops, with technology, training and marketing provided by the companies, resulting in a rapid rise of farm incomes and job opportunities. Developing countries possess significant advantages in terms of climate, year-round production and low labour costs that are conducive to foreign investment. With private capital flows on the rise, there is an opportunity for developing countries to upgrade technology and obtain direct access to foreign markets by providing a conducive atmosphere for foreign investments and collaborations in agri-business ventures, such as hybrid seed production, flowers, processed fruit and vegetables, fresh and salt water aquaculture, and sericulture.

Shift from commodity-based to resource-based planning

The responsibility of governments to achieve dramatic increases in foodgrain production to keep pace with population growth naturally led to a commodity-based approach to agricultural development in many developing countries. Governments projected demand, set production targets for specific crops, and instituted programmes to help farmers produce the food needed to meet the minimum needs of the population. But once shortages are eliminated, the focus on specific commodities becomes a barrier to further agricultural development, because it retards diversification into more profitable commercial crops. Contrary to free market theory, farmers in many countries have tended to continue production of traditional crops, even when prices have fallen in response to increased supplies.

There is still a need for government to educate and encourage farmers to adopt resource-based planning, oriented to national and international market potentials and based on principles of economics, employment and ecology. Resource-based planning examines how the available land and water resources can best be utilized to achieve maximum and sustainable economic return to the farmer, which is only rarely the priority of governments in developing countries that tend to focus on production targets for specific commodities. This shift can lead to diversification into commercial crops, such as fruit and vegetables, that generate significant increases in on-farm employment and incomes and act as a stimulus to downstream agro-industries.

From minimum needs to maximum potentials

The factors which have perpetuated commodity-based planning in agriculture have also fostered an emphasis on minimum targets, rather than maximum goals. Often government has perceived that its responsibility was to ensure sufficient food to prevent famine, not maximum output and profitability. Government machinery has proved effective in forcing through radical measures to disseminate new technology, seed and production methods in the face of crisis, but it usually lacks the driving impetus to work for the highest benefit of individual farmers. The shift needed is for planners to study the potentials of the agricultural sector to serve as an engine for job creation and higher incomes, and as a stimulus to industrialization and exports, and then to formulate national goals to maximize exploitation of these potentials.

Integration of agriculture, marketing and processing

Conscious efforts can be made to foster the natural linkage between agricultural and industrial development by placing emphasis on crops that have the greatest potential for stimulating the growth of agro-industries, services and exports. Filling in the missing links in the chain of processing and distribution, such as pre-cooling for fruit and vegetables, can enable small farmers to produce for national and export markets; it also results in higher at-farm prices and creates alternative forms of rural employment.

Empowerment of women

The vast majority of women living in rural areas are engaged in agriculture. Therefore, upgrading productivity, skills and incomes in this sector is the single most effective means of improving the livelihood of women in developing countries. Skill development programmes in areas such as hybrid seed production, floriculture, inland aquaculture, vegetables and poultry can be particularly beneficial. Promotion of micro-level credit institutions and savings programmes can generate capital for the establishment by women of small rural enterprises.

FOOD SECURITY IN AFRICA

The present prognosis for Africa resembles the pessimistic assessment of Asia in the 1960s that projected most Asians would face starvation in the 1970s. Over the past two decades, total food production in Africa has grown at exactly the same rate as for the world as a whole, but high levels of population growth have resulted in declining availability of food *per capita* in many countries, particularly in the sub-Saharan region. This suggests that a grim outcome is not inevitable, if concerted action is taken now.

Several factors have impeded achievement of higher agricultural growth rates in the region: political instability and civil unrest, poor macro-economic and agricultural policies, drought, and physical difficulties in farming in some areas. The ravages of war have had the most devastating effect, but inadequate and counter-productive policies have also had a major impact. Low mandated prices for agricultural products have acted as a disincentive to producers. State control of farm support systems, including marketing, transportation and input supply, is highly bureaucratic, inefficient, and, often, corrupt. Overvalued exchange rates encourage the import of low-priced farm products, depress local farm incomes, and make exports uncompetitive. Underdeveloped infrastructure results in high transport and marketing costs. The slow rate of technological development and diffusion have slowed growth in agricultural productivity. Irrigation potential is underdeveloped and poorly managed.

A major international commitment is needed to reverse the trends and end the famine threat in Africa. The region possesses considerable potential that could be converted into higher rates of growth. Africa has the world's largest reserve of arable land, one billion hectares, of which only 20 per cent is presently cultivated. Fertilizer use in sub-Saharan Africa is very low relative to other developing countries. Per hectare consumption averages just 13 per cent of the level in India and 3.5 per cent of the level in China. Recent studies indicate that the area under irrigated crops could be expanded four to five times, primarily through small, private irrigation systems. Improved farm systems have demonstrated that they can raise the yields of most crops in the region. Changes in agricultural policy can improve the efficiency in factor and output markets, raise the incentives of private small farmers, and improve technology generation and dissemination. Institutional reform can improve marketing and distribution services. Investment in infrastructure can significantly lower marketing costs. Indigenous technological capacities can be strengthened to develop location-specific technologies, rather than relying on direct material transfer of crop varieties unsuited to local conditions. Greater emphasis on the training of local manpower can significantly improve the effectiveness of agricultural extension systems and integrated rural development projects.

Special Status of Agriculture

The obvious limitations of government-directed agricultural development, coupled with the resurgent popularity of free-market policies following the collapse of communism in Eastern Europe and the successful completion of the GATT negotiations, raise fundamental issues about the status of agriculture and the role of government in this sector. Advocates of private enterprise contrast the failures of Eastern European agriculture with the achievements of the industrial nations as ample evidence of the free market's superior capacity to achieve high levels of agricultural productivity. Recently, international and bilateral financial institutions have promoted the market as the most effective instrument for managing agriculture throughout the world.

This view leaves two questions unanswered. First, if the market is so effective, why is it that every major capitalist economy utilizes such a vast array of subsidies, incentives, controls, production quotas and fixed pricing mechanisms to govern production and trade in agricultural products? Even after GATT, protection for this sector by industrial nations will remain high. Second, granted that the market works effectively for mature capitalist societies with high levels of technology, education, productivity, living standards and food surpluses, and relatively small portions of the workforce dependent on agriculture, is the same necessarily true for countries at an earlier stage of development, in which (1) a majority of the workforce is dependent on agriculture for sustenance, (2) levels of education, productivity and incomes are low, and (3) any increase in food prices can have a devastating impact on food consumption levels in the country? The answers to these questions are relevant both to the countries presently making the transition from centrally planned to market economies in Eastern Europe and to poorer developing countries striving to achieve food security.

Nations accord special status to their agricultural sector for several reasons. Continuous supplies of food are absolutely essential to the welfare of the population. Food prices are extremely sensitive to changes in the supply of foodstuffs. Even a small increase or decrease in supply can lead to a very wide fluctuation in prices. A bumper harvest can depress prices to the point of bankrupting large numbers of farmers. A poor harvest can send food prices soaring beyond the purchasing power of large numbers of people. Buffer stocks, subsidies and incentives are used to protect agriculture from sharp price fluctuations. Although the principles of free trade argue that countries should produce only those items in which they possess a competitive advantage and procure the rest from overseas, few nations are willing to entrust their food supply entirely or even substantially to foreign parties. For decades Japan maintained trade barriers to keep the price of rice at more than six times the international level in order to protect and preserve domestic rice producers; the US government exports subsidized wheat; and the European Community sells subsidized milk powder and butter internationally at prices up to one-third below the domestic level.

The debate over the legitimate role of government in protection of the agricultural economy is partially a question of timing. Market institutions and competitive strengths are normally built up over decades. Advanced nations with highly mechanized and efficient agricultural sectors are in a much better position to withstand the impact of foreign competition than countries at an earlier stage of development. Countries suffering from food deficits and those in the midst of radical economic reforms are ill-advised to make a sudden, wholesale shift to market mechanisms to stimulate growth of this sector.

ICPF strongly favours a movement towards the liberalization of world trade in agricultural products because it can be of immense benefit to job creation, industrialization, and economic growth in developing countries, and thereby act as a driving force for growth and employment generation in the industrial world as well. The liberalization of domestic policies for this sector is also needed in developing countries where government controls and populist policies have often retarded growth of agriculture. However, the timing and extent of these measures should be dictated by the relative strengths and needs of each particular country, not by strict adherence to any economic doctrine.

Role of Government

Agricultural subsidies and protection are subsets of a larger issue – the role of government in agricultural development. The experience of the past four decades strongly supports the view that government can play a vital role in stimulating agriculture up to the stage where the rural economy demonstrates the dynamism needed to take off on its own. Although the Green Revolution has been widely heralded as an achievement of modern technology, the hybrid seeds and chemical-based cultivation practices that formed the technological basis for the breakthrough in foodgrain production constitute only one part of a comprehensive, integrated development strategy in which government played a central and crucial role. This strategy included massive, country-wide demonstration programmes to introduce farmers to new technology, the establishment of new public sector agencies for rapid multiplication and distribution of seeds, assured markets and guaranteed floor prices for foodgrains to eliminate fear that higher production would result in crashing prices, construction of additional storage capacity to house the increased production, import or manufacture of fertilizers, and, most importantly, for transport, distribution and marketing of surplus grains in food deficit areas. Few developing countries – perhaps few countries at any stage of development – could have marshalled resources on such a massive scale and instituted such widespread changes so rapidly without heavy reliance on the government for both planning and execution. *In the majority of developing countries, government is still the most organized and efficient agency and the only one capable of such significant initiative. In formulating strategies, it is essential to take fully into account both the stages and steps of the development process. At this stage in their development, it is highly unlikely that food-deficit African nations can make rapid progress toward food self-sufficiency without strong government support and investment to improve technology, training, techno-infrastructure and trade.*

Once the rural sector begins to exhibit its own dynamism, as in the majority of developing countries, there is strong justification for a shift in the role of government from that of prime mover, planner and controller of development to that of catalyst and pioneer. Government agencies can tap the potentials of agriculture, identifying new commercial opportunities, educating farmers, demonstrating new potentials, assisting in the transfer and dissemination of new technology, and promoting the establishment of effective organizations – preferably privately or cooperatively owned by farmers or at least with their participation – to process, distribute and market what is produced.

Coping with the environmental problems to preserve the ecological foundations essential for sustainable agriculture is an area in which government has special responsibilities and must play a leading role on an ongoing basis. Regulating the diversion of prime farm land for non-farm uses, expansion of irrigation capacity, control of groundwater exploitation, major programmes for reforestation and to prevent or reverse desertification, and regulation of pesticide use can only be effectively planned, monitored and regulated by governments.

Comprehensive Strategies

In this and previous chapters, we have tried to present an integrated perspective of the political, economic and technological factors that need to be taken into account in formulating a comprehensive approach to the issues of peace, food and employment. In an effort to illustrate the potential efficacy of this approach in a country representing nearly 25 per cent of the world's poor, ICPF conducted an in-depth country level study in India to evolve a strategy for stimulating massive increases in job growth and food production (see box pp. 122–24).

PROSPERITY 2000 STRATEGY FOR INDIA

The potential for accelerating job creation and increasing food production through a mix of the strategies discussed in this report is illustrated by the strategy which ICPF has proposed to achieve full employment in India and thereby to raise the entire population above the poverty line by generating additional employment opportunities for 100 million persons in the coming decade. This strategy utilizes agriculture as an engine for growth by accelerating the development of commercial agriculture, agro-industry and agro-exports. It calls for a shift in thinking concerning agriculture from production for survival and subsistence to production for maximum and sustainable profit, from emphasis on meeting minimum needs to realizing maximum potentials, from commodity-based to resource-based planning. It seeks to tap the country's competitive advantage in labour-intensive agricultural crops and allied industries to double agricultural production – raising the annual growth rate to 4 per cent (versus 2.3 per cent in the 1980s) – achieve complete nutritional self-sufficiency, raise rural incomes and double India's total exports.

Creating new jobs through this low-cost strategy can be accomplished entirely with the country's own resources, though foreign firms will find investment in India's agro-industrial sector very attractive. Initially, about half of the new jobs will be generated on farms by raising productivity through methods to improve management of micro-nutrients and water, expanding the total irrigated area by more complete utilization of the substantial additional capacity that has already been created, emphasis on more labour-intensive commercial crops such as sugar, cotton, fruit, flowers, and vegetables, sericulture, inland and coastal aquaculture, reclamation of wastelands for forestry and fodder, and increasing subsidiary incomes from animal husbandry and poultry.

➡

The expansion and intensification of cultivation of these products will raise agricultural output by $25 billion and generate approximately 45 million equivalent full-time unskilled and semi-skilled jobs in agriculture for unemployed and under-employed farmers and landless labour.

The additional agricultural production will form raw material for expansion of rural industrialization and non-farm employment. Another 10 million jobs will be created in downstream agro-industries located in rural areas – in sugar mills, cotton and textile mills, processing units for fruit, fish and silk, and in marketing and distribution – thus serving as a counter-magnet to urban migration. Growth of agro-industry will stimulate demand for industrial machinery and services. The multiplier effect of skyrocketing rural demand will stimulate demand in a broad range of consumer industries and create an estimated 45 million rural and urban jobs in industry and services.

Funding for the strategy would come from a mix of public sector and private sector investment. The funding requirements are within the range of current five-year projections: 84 per cent of additional planned investment in agriculture and 25 per cent of additional planned expenditure in industry. The average cost per additional job is less than $1,000, roughly one-tenth the average cost of jobs in India's private sector and one-hundredth the cost of new jobs in the public sector.

Implementation of the strategy will require a substantial investment in training of both on-farm and industrial workers, but the plan is based on the recognition that enhancing the skills of the nation's rural work-force will take time and must be done incrementally. As the programme gains momentum and rural incomes rise, the demand for industrial products and services will grow, resulting in a shift to greater farm mechanization and gradual movement of more and more workers to non-farm employment.

Organization is a crucial issue in a country of more than 90 million small farmers. The strategy envisions the establishment of several new types of organization to bring together small farmers for processing, marketing and distribution and to promote more active linkages between farmers and the private industrial sector, both Indian and foreign.

In order to implement such a massive strategy within a ten-year period, government must play a central role as catalyst and pioneer, rather than owner or manager, to generate widespread public awareness about the technological and commercial opportunities, identify optimal and sustainable resource-based potentials for specific regions, facilitate the transfer and dissemination of technology, provide training and

➡

demonstration, invest in the techno-infrastructure needed for transport, storage and distribution, offer management education to rural enterprises, and promote the establishment of new organizations.

The Prosperity 2000 strategy has been adopted by the Indian government and incorporated in India's Eighth Five Year Plan. A Small Farmer's Agri-Business Consortium, a specialized agency for implementation of the strategy, has been established by the government to coordinate implementation. In order to evolve a detailed methodology for implementation and to demonstrate the feasibility of the strategy model, district programmes are being organized in 12 districts around the country. A detailed study of Pune District in the State of Maharashtra has documented the potential for creating 750,000 jobs through this strategy. Extrapolation of these results suggests that the 100 million jobs that India needs to create and the 1 billion needed in the developing world are, indeed, achievable, provided that industrial countries adopt trade policies on agricultural products designed to enhance export opportunities for developing nations.

International Agenda for Food Security

The crucial importance of food security to world peace and economic development demands that the international community take collective responsibility and initiative to eradicate hunger and famine on a global basis as a complement to the initiatives of individual countries to deal with the problem domestically. The growth of food production in developing countries can be accelerated dramatically by the application of resource-based, location-specific strategies that incorporate a proper blending of traditional and frontier technologies and integrate all the links in the chain of production, processing, transport and distribution. Conditions vary too widely from country to country for detailed recommendations to be broadly applied. However, a number of strategies are relevant to the majority of developing countries. Some of the components of an Action Plan designed to achieve this goal are given below.

Elimination of agricultural trade barriers by industrial nations. **1**
The agreements reached for liberalizing agricultural trade in the Uruguay Round of GATT are an important step forward, but they will not release the full dynamism of the agricultural sector, which is so critical for more rapid growth of incomes and employment in both developing and developed countries. In the previous chapter, we have called for rapid reduction leading to a complete elimination of agricultural subsidies and other trade barriers by industrial nations, which can generate a positive multiplier effect. It has been estimated that complete liberalization of trade in agricultural commodities would yield an annual gain (in 1992 dollars) of about $25 billion for OECD countries and $22 billion for developing and formerly centrally planned countries. Actual gains could be very much higher. These subsidies cost Western consumers several hundred billion dollars annually. In addition, they lead to dumping of surplus sugar, cereal, milk and beef in developing countries, often pushing down the prices which farmers in these countries receive for their produce to far below their production cost. The benefits of eliminating these subsidies would be multiple. For instance, eliminating subsidies to sugar-beet growers and dairy farmers in Europe would stimulate greater demand, not only for imported sugar from developing countries, but also for cocoa, which combined with sugar and milk is the basis for the chocolate industry. Measures of this type will result in substantially increased demand for agricultural products from developing countries, the first step in an upward spiral of global economic growth that will stimulate industrial exports and job growth in both East and West.

Global, environmentally sustainable Green Revolution. The term **2**
'Green Revolution' has been praised for its positive impact on crop productivity and criticized for its likely adverse effects on the environment and social equity. It is often overlooked that one of the most beneficial consequences of the Green Revolution has been its 'forest-saving' nature. If agricultural production had not been increased through higher productivity, more forest land would have been diverted to annual cropping. India alone would have needed at least 50 million hectares of additional land to

produce the wheat and rice it now produces, if average yields had remained at pre-Green Revolution levels. It is, therefore, important that the concept of higher productivity per unit of land, water, time, energy, labour and capital be extended to all farming systems and all regions. Most developing countries will have no option but to produce more food and agricultural commodities from less land and water in the twenty-first century. The challenge lies in accomplishing this in an environmentally and socially sustainable manner. The FAO should launch a coordinated international effort to extend the principles and strategies of the Green Revolution to eradicate global food shortages within a decade. The Green Revolution was originally applied to improving productivity of wheat and rice in high potential areas. After the first rounds of phenomenal success, the effort to extend it to other agricultural regions and other crops lost momentum, because the urgent necessity had been eliminated. Recognizing the importance of agricultural surplus to rural employment, industrialization and exports, renewed efforts are called for to apply the comprehensive, integrated approach of the Green Revolution to high potential commercial crops and to all regions. With the knowledge gained over the past 30 years, greater emphasis can be placed on ensuring that the productivity improvements are not only economically viable but also ecologically sustainable. Region-specific strategies should be adopted for mountain areas, high rainfall tropics, uplands and irrigated plains. The crops covered should include foodgrains and oil seeds, cotton and jute, sugar cane, fruit, vegetables, dairy, meat, medicinal plants, spices, and agro-forestry for fodder, fuel and industrial raw materials.

3 *UN development force for food deficit regions.* The complex task of planning, managing and executing nationwide programmes to eradicate food shortages may be beyond the political, administrative and management capacities of some governments, hampered by the absence of training and experience, political instability or social strife. The slowest member country retards the progress of the whole world. The interests of global peace, political stability and basic human rights justify and may necessitate external

assistance to help countries establish viable food security systems. In countries that are unable either to produce sufficient food or to initiate coordinated programmes to overcome present deficits, the international development force proposed earlier in this report can act in a trusteeship role to assist in designing and implementing integrated programmes to upgrade food production and distribution. UNDP can undertake the role of coordinating the activities of all UN agencies in this effort. Emphasis should be placed on sustainable production and distribution – not just relief operations – through the introduction of effective systems for planning, administration, education, demonstration and implementation.

Model districts. The potential benefits of applying a resource-based, location-specific approach to agriculture can best be demonstrated by the establishment of model programmes in different agro-climatic regions. The models should be large enough geographically to serve as a viable index of national-level potentials and of economic and ecological sustainability. Although the concept may vary from place to place, the central approach is to examine in detail the current usage of both land and water resources and then formulate a district level plan for utilizing available physical, technological, human, managerial and financial resources in a sustainable manner to optimize, over time, production, productivity, farm incomes and employment, non-farm occupations, self-employment opportunities, agro-industrial development, exports and expansion of the service sector. This analysis is likely to identify a wide gap between present and potential achievements, which can form the basis for creating an alternative district development plan. Government can seek the assistance of farmers' organizations, private enterprise, educational and research institutes, and voluntary agencies for gathering information, analysis and plan formulation. Implementation of the plan should be primarily through activities that facilitate more efficient operation of market forces, such as assisting farmers to identify and transfer improved technology, establishing commercial organizations of small farmers and linkages between farms and industry, disseminating information on markets and technology, demonstration, education, training and incentives to stimulate rapid multiplication. The UN development force can undertake to assist countries in the design and implementation of model district programmes in food deficit countries, and to transfer the expertise needed for replication in other parts of each country.

5 *World food model.* The actual structure and dynamics of the development of global agriculture and its relationship to industrialization, employment and trade needs to be fully understood in order to plan for, and achieve, a world free of hunger. Although national and international institutions maintain a variety of data bases and models to track the impact of production, trade and prices in agriculture, these models are too limited in scope and detail to construct a working global model of the agricultural sector, which could serve as a valuable tool in projecting the medium- and long-term interactions of changes in food production, consumption, employment, trade, productivity, technology and environmental factors. A world food model, which forms the essential basis for evolving a global strategic plan, can help eliminate both food deficits and surpluses.

6 *On-farm training.* The massive demonstration programmes, conducted in farmers' own fields by countries such as India to propagate the Green Revolution technology, proved that even uneducated, traditional peasant farmers in developing countries will rush to adopt new technology when its application and benefits are clearly demonstrated. The slow dissemination of new technologies that still hampers agriculture in these countries is largely due to the ineffectiveness of more traditional types of extension and farmer education conducted on a relatively limited scale by agricultural colleges, technical institutes and research stations. This gap in the agricultural education system can be closed by expanding the agricultural training network to the village level. The establishment of farm schools in villages, on land temporarily leased from local farmers, can combine the advantages of both formal training and demonstration on farmers' fields, with emphasis on economic viability and ecological sustainability. This is a low cost strategy that requires prior training of a large number of

village level instructors, but little investment in infrastructure. The schools can demonstrate the economic benefits of new and improved crops and cultivation practices, engaging local farmers as both students and staff, and covering most of the cost of training in the form of sale proceeds from the farm schools' production.

Water conservation. The inefficient and negligent use of water in agriculture is one of the most serious barriers to a sustainable expansion of agricultural production. Public policy regarding the cost of water supplied by major irrigation projects and low-cost or free distribution of power for pumping underground water aggravate the problem. Technologically, the solutions to water depletion are largely in hand. What is needed is a massive effort in public education and demonstration, coupled with incentives to encourage their adoption. In monsoon regions it has been demonstrated that recharging underground aquifers by reverse pumping during rain-surplus seasons can restore ten years of water depletion in one rainy season. Proven methods are available and have been commercially applied with great success, as the achievements of Israel so dramatically demonstrate, radically to reduce water consumption by as much as five- to ten-fold, while at the same time significantly increasing crop yields. The most productive of these methods, involving the construction of greenhouses, is too capital-intensive for immediate widespread adoption in developing countries. Drip and sprinkler irrigation are far more moderate in cost and still result in enormous savings of water. The cost of adopting these methods can be further reduced by more widely popularizing them, so as to achieve increasing economies of scale in their manufacture.

Low-input sustainable agriculture. While we have argued against pressure on food-deficit developing countries to reduce their comparatively low-level usage of mineral fertilizers and chemical pesticides, empirical studies sponsored by the National Academy of Sciences and the Department of Agriculture in the USA found strong evidence, long resisted by scientists and commercial farmers in the West, that chemical-free farming can be as productive and cost-effective as chemical-based methods. Industrial countries that offer subsidies to encourage chemical usage should modify their policies to provide active incentives for the use of chemical-free methods instead. During the last ten years, Indonesia has succeeded in bringing down the consumption of chemical pesticides without adversely affecting grain production through the nationwide adoption of integrated pest management systems for food crop protection. India has launched a massive national training programme to popularize biological methods of pest control, which can reduce the consumption and cost of chemical pesticides by 50 to 75 per cent. Public education programmes of this type are needed at the national and international level to disseminate information about chemical-free methods to producers and to educate consumers in developed and developing countries about both the health and environmental benefits of organically grown produce.

9 *Inland aquaculture.* Depletion of deep sea fishery resources has resulted in a significant decline in world harvests from the sea. Proven technology is available for substantially replacing sea-grown fish with fresh or salt water pond-grown varieties. The new intensive and semi-intensive methods of cultivation can generate yields 10 to 100 times higher than traditional extensive methods. Due to the warmer climate and lower labour costs of the developing world, inland aquaculture can become a major stimulus to rural employment, incomes, processing industries and exports.

10 *Micro-level indicators of food security.* Development initiatives have been severely limited by the absence of accurate and sensitive measures to assess the impact of national-level policies and programmes on food security at community and household level. New indices, such as the Sustainable Livelihood Security Index now under development in India, need to be evolved and applied; they should combine measures of income and employment; food and nutritional status, including the availability of safe drinking water and sanitation facilities; ownership of productive assets; and education and productive skills.

6
TRANSITION TOWARDS WHAT?
Strategies for Rapid Social Transformation

The pace of human development continues to accelerate. The world has changed more during the present century than in the previous nineteen centuries combined – economically, socially, politically, scientifically and technologically. In recent decades humankind has been buffeted by a bewildering array and intensity of transforming powers – democratization, decolonization, demilitarization, globalization, universal education, scientific advances, information, successive technological revolutions brought about by the automobile, telephone, radio, television, jet aircraft, computers, satellite communications and genetic engineering. Coping with such rapid change has not been easy. It has brought in its wake a broad array of problems – a widening gap between the most advanced and least developed sections both within and between nations, a disequilibrium between growth of population and economic growth, rising unemployment, alienated youth, increasing violence and crime, depletion of natural resources, degradation of the environment, overcrowded cities, mass migrations of talent from South to North, displacement of millions of political and economic refugees, the breakdown of the family and the erosion of traditional social institutions.

Although much has been learned about the various stages of social and economic development, much less is known about the actual process itself by which societies transit from one stage or level or form to another. As a result, our efforts to speed the transition are often haphazard, stumbling and fraught with difficulty. Today former colonial nations such as Vietnam and Zimbabwe strive to catch up with countries that have never been subject to foreign rule. The tribal nations of central Africa struggle at great cost to transform themselves into modern states. Even within the prosperous West, the speed and extent of progress is uneven, leading to the emergence of 'developing countries' within developed nations, of poverty-stricken families in inner cities with rates of chronic unemployment as high as 50 per cent or more.

Nothing is of greater value to humanity's quest for progress than an understanding of the development process and the means for consciously directing it more effectively. The tremendous economic achievements of Japan during the post-war period, followed during the last two decades by other East Asian economic powers and most recently by China, suggest that the time required for transition can be substantially abridged and the fruits of development achieved much sooner than has been accomplished by nations in the past. The rising expectations of people around the globe and the potential risks of failing to heed their call have added a greater sense of urgency to the quest for this knowledge.

Eastern Europe

The challenges posed by extremely rapid transition are nowhere more graphically depicted than in the current transition of the countries of Eastern Europe after the collapse of the Berlin Wall, the end of the Cold War and the break-up of the USSR. Although this transition is often described in political and economic terms, it is far broader and deeper in its implications. These nations are in the midst of a simultaneous multi-dimensional transformation – politically, from authoritarian to democratic forms of government; economically, from a centrally planned command system to free market economies; industrially, from defence-oriented to consumer-oriented production; administratively, from highly centralized to decentralized systems; structurally, from state ownership of property to multiple forms of ownership in all spheres; socially, from closed and isolated to open and internationally integrated societies; culturally, from almost exclusive emphasis on values of equity and collective security to strong emphasis on the values of freedom and individual responsibility.

The transformation of Eastern Europe and the former USSR is of vital concern to all of us. Never before in human history has such massive change been carried out as an essentially peaceful revolution. The end of apartheid in South Africa and recent progress in the Middle East show that this process continues to have beneficial repercussions around the world. At the same time, this incredible advance has been accompanied by events that have destabilized the political and economic systems of the entire region, led to the break-up of the USSR, war in Bosnia, the collapse of the Warsaw Pact and the COMECON trade system, a massive brain drain and the threat of huge waves of economic refugees. These changes, too, have had implications for all nations within the region and beyond – severely affecting trade around the world, from the tea estates of Sri Lanka and India to the wheat fields of the United States, Australia and Argentina.

So, too, the further course of this transition will have a profound impact on all nations, both developed and developing. The future of world peace, the world political system and the world economy hang in the balance. A successful rapid transition will open up new markets to stimulate a new round of growth for the sluggish economies of the West, much as the Marshall Plan stimulated American prosperity in the 1950s. It will equally present economic opportunities for developing countries unable as yet to meet the quality requirements of highly competitive Western markets. Failure of the transition holds the danger of economic collapse and political instability within Eastern Europe, which could even lead to renewed political tensions and another economically devastating arms race. Already ongoing wars are being fought in the Balkans, the Caucasus and several other regions of the former Soviet Union. Crime is on the rise. Ominous signs have appeared that the authoritarian past is not yet fully buried and could once again arise, if the forward momentum of the transition process does not quickly improve the lives of people within the region. The whole world has an immense stake in the successful outcome of the transition in Eastern Europe.

Initial Results of Reform

The pre-existent conditions, the starting point of the transition, the timing, speed and extent of the reforms introduced during the past five years varied considerably among the 25 nations of Eastern Europe and Central Asia. But, with few exceptions, they were founded on the same general principles and on the policy recommendations of Western proponents of rapid transformation to total free-market liberal capitalism, based on a simultaneous shock strategy encompassing macroeconomic stabilization, prices and property rights. Western governments and the international financial institutions, led by the IMF, strongly advocated this approach and linked financial assistance to its adoption. The strategy called for rapid deregulation of prices, privatization of farms and industry, introduction of a convertible currency, and balancing the budget to reduce the high fiscal deficits, primarily by reducing military expenditure and subsidies to producers and consumers. The assumption was that a programme with these elements would result in a significant increase in production, efficiency and the availability of consumer goods within a short time.

The actual results were quite contrary to the expectations of these countries' Western economic advisers, as well as to the governments and people of the region. The initial phase of reforms had a disastrous impact on the economies, on the people and in some countries on peace and political stability. From 1990 to 1993 production in all 25 nations declined drastically, from a minimum of 10 per cent in Poland, 20 per cent in Hungary and 22 per cent in the Czech Republic to a maximum of 45 per cent in Russia, 57 per cent in Latvia and 75 per cent in Armenia. Investment fell by an average rate of 13–14 per cent per year from 1990 to 1992, and by a three-year total of more than 50 per cent in Russia. The fall in real incomes followed that of output, and the impact was made even more severe, especially for pensioners, by the simultaneous dismantling of the vast social support system and dramatic increase in the cost of essential consumer goods. The drastic decline in living standards for the vast majority has been accompanied by the emergence of a new class of instantaneous millionaires, some on the basis of their ability in combining factors of production in new circumstances and others due to hoarding of goods under inflation, loopholes in newly enacted legislation on privatization, and personal influence with those in power.

Inflation in most of these countries gained tremendous momentum as the reforms proceeded. In 1993 alone, consumer prices rose by more than 100 per cent in 15 countries, out of which 11 former republics of the USSR reported increases of more than 300 per cent. This was accompanied by a sharp rise in unemployment from extremely low historical levels prior to 1989 up to an average of 17 per cent in 1994.

The tremendous physical and psychological stress experienced by people in the region as a result of the economic collapse is reflected in the sharp fall in birth rates and the steep rise in death rates. Since 1989, the birth rate has fallen by more than 20 per cent in Poland, 25 per cent in Bulgaria, 30 per cent in Estonia and Romania, 35 per cent in Russia and more than 60 per cent in Eastern Germany. Such abrupt changes have been observed previously in industrial societies only during times of war. Infant mortality is rising in many of the countries. Not surprisingly, there have been increasing indications of public discontent and voter dissatisfaction with the course of the reforms in the vast majority of countries.

Simultaneous Shocks

The collapse of the East European and Central Asian economies from 1990 to 1994 resulted from their exposure to a series of simultaneous shocks.

1   *Stabilization and adjustments:* The majority of countries, having suffered from inflation and balance of payments problems in the 1980s, applied sharp stabilization and adjustment programmes in the early 1990s to stop inflation, balance budgets, and close balance of payments gaps, while at the same time liberalizing prices in order to correct major price distortions. These deflationary policies led, in most cases, to sharp declines in output.

2   *Resource allocation:* Sudden dismantling of the central planning machinery responsible for the allocation of materials for current production and allocation of funds and materials for investment in these countries was another shock. It proved impossible in the majority of countries to create and organize, overnight, commodity and financial markets of sufficient depth and flexibility to substitute effectively for the planning machinery.

3   *Import liberalization:* Drastic import liberalization led to the inflow of better-quality, lower-priced foreign goods that depressed demand for domestically produced goods. The shock impact of imports was aggravated by the fact that farmers in the region were forced to compete in some cases with subsidized agricultural products from the West.

4   *Privatization:* Although the actual progress of privatization has been relatively slow in most instances, the uncertainty regarding the future status and ownership of enterprises and property has inhibited investment, slowed up current production, and led to widespread plunder of state property.

5   *Trade:* As the socialist structure of these countries began to change and the political influence of the Soviet Union diminished, there was a huge drop in the trade between countries of the region, and, following the break-up of the USSR, between the republics of the Soviet Union as well.

Not all countries in the region experienced all five shocks. Those that were spared proved better able to sustain output and real incomes. Czechoslovakia had not suffered from inflation and was largely free of external debt. Hungary, which had decentralized its economy and had introduced significant elements of the market in production and investment before 1989, was not subject to the sudden shocks due to import liberalization and termination of planning.

Lessons from the Reform

The failure of the transition strategy to produce the anticipated results has given rise to extreme hardship, growing anxiety, frustration and anger within these countries. Internationally, it has generated intense debate about the reasons for the failure, the efficacy of 'shock therapy', and the appropriateness and adequacy of Western assistance. These questions reflect an inadequate understanding, both within and outside the region, of the stages and process and essential conditions for an effective transition under the circumstances prevalent in Eastern Europe at the time. Understanding of this failure holds the key not only to the rapid revitalization of the former Soviet and other Eastern European republics, but also to meeting the challenges of present and future transitions in Africa, Asia and the West. This understanding can be summarized in the form of several lessons that can be derived from the general experience of countries in the region.

1 *Multi-dimensional transitions cannot be brought about by uni-dimensional strategies:* The economic dimension of transition cannot be viewed and acted upon in isolation from its political and social dimensions. The reform programme was developed and guided by domestic and foreign economists who viewed the transition much like a change of clothing – the casting off of one set of economic principles and the adoption of another – ignoring the critical importance of social and political factors. This view could be summed up in the often expressed attitude, 'Good economics makes good politics!'

Transition is the process by which society moves from one form or level of activities to another. While social scientists conveniently divide social activity into several categories – political, economic, social, educational, religious, cultural – in practice these dis-tinctions are at best only partially true. Economic activities in any society take place on the foundation of the political system, social values and customs, and the psychological aspirations and attitudes of the people. During normal periods of slow and gradual change, the impact or role of other dimensions operates below the surface and appears minimal. Economists studying the results of economic variables tend to overlook the influence of factors from other fields on the assumption that non-economic factors are constant. Under relatively stable and static conditions, these economics principles can be employed to predict changes in economic variables to a considerable extent. But under circumstances in which underlying economic, social and political conditions are undergoing radical change, the relevance and predictive capacity of purely economic concepts is quite limited. This was the situation confronting the states of the region at the beginning of the transition period, and the reason why the actual results of the reform differed so drastically from what had been anticipated.

The situation in Eastern and Central Europe was further complicated by the disproportionately large size and importance of the defence sector in the economy. This necessitates, not only a change from one economic system to another, but also a restructuring of the entire economy from a defence orientation to a consumer orientation. This change in structure could not be brought about by reliance on macro-economic policy.

2   *Political and social consensus is essential for rapid social change:* In a democratic society, the market cannot be instituted by decrees or authoritarian methods which belong to the old system. In the new political climate, reforms will be successful only in the measure that they are understood and accepted by the population. The vitality of the market depends on releasing the initiative of people to act in their own perceived best interests by producing and distributing goods and services for consumption by others. This initiative cannot be ordered, it can only be encouraged. Economic policy recommendations failed adequately to anticipate either the impact of the programme on the people or their reaction to it. In the early stages of reform, the public exhibited an incredible degree of patience, tolerance and endurance under conditions of growing hardship. Gradually public resentment and personal suffering (especially for the aged, children and new entrants to the workforce) became so severe in some countries that no government could have sustained the programme without facing political upheaval or violent revolution.

There is some truth in the argument that 'shock therapy' did not fail in Russia and other countries, because it was never actually implemented. At each crucial juncture either the central bank or the government pulled back from enforcing the necessary fiscal discipline. But it is equally true that 'shock therapy' never could have been implemented by a democratic government, when it imposed such enormous hardship on the people and generated a polarization and fragmentation of political forces within the country. Where similar strategies have succeeded in other parts of the world, it has usually been under authoritarian governments, such as in Chile.

Where force is not possible, the only viable alternative is to build social consensus in support of the reform strategy. Ultimately, the success of the reform measures will be determined by one factor – the extent to which the people understand, accept and are motivated to act under the new system. Before introducing any new measure, maximum effort should be made to communicate its purpose and nature to the people and win their understanding and approval. *Public education is the most powerful policy instrument.* With public opinion widely divided over the best course of action, it is necessary to win back the understanding, support and endorsement of the population for an alternative programme which the major parties and social groups can back. This requires educating the public to understand both the costs and benefits involved in any reform strategy, the trade-offs between immediate advantages and immediate sacrifices required to establish a new and stable equilibrium.

3   *Economic strategy must be balanced:* A market economy can be introduced gradually or step-wise, but it cannot be introduced in a fragmentary or piecemeal manner. Deregulation of prices was the most prominent feature of the strategy in most countries, because it was the easiest to implement. But under conditions of shortages in economies dominated by huge monopolistic enterprises, price deregulation led to skyrocketing prices and spiralling inflation. A market flourishes only when several essential conditions are met – freedom of pricing, freedom of entry and exit from industry, free flow of information, unrestricted movement of goods and services, competition between enterprises, control of monopolies, and private ownership of property. The entire package of free market practices must be implemented hand in hand, otherwise it does not work. Freeing pricing without first regulating or dismantling monopolies, promoting privatization of land and enterprises, ensuring free flow of goods, and establishing wholesale markets and multiple distribution outlets lead to speculation, soaring prices, hoarding and falling production. Historically, the free market evolved over centuries in conditions of surplus production

and stable currency, neither of which exist in Eastern Europe today. Efforts to accelerate the development of the market will have first of all to meet the political, legal, social and economic conditions historically required for its creation. And these conditions must be met simultaneously.

4   *Macro-economic stability is a precondition for increasing production:* It is extremely difficult to increase production in a context of general macro-economic instability and hyperinflation. The rapidly falling value of local currencies minimized their utility as a medium of exchange. Agricultural as well as industrial enterprises seeking a stable medium in which to hold their wealth increasingly resorted to hoarding marketable, non-perishable commodities such as food-grains or converting local currency into foreign money wherever possible. This was particularly devastating for agriculture, where higher production was desperately needed to meet consumer demand and reduce dependence on food imports. The breakdown of the local currency as an effective medium of exchange was accompanied by an unfavourable shift in the terms of trade between agriculture and industry, resulting from the near-mono-polistic position both of the suppliers of farm inputs, especially fertilizers and farm machinery, and the processing units that pur-chased farm produce, such as dairies and meat processing plants. Together, these factors precipitated a rapid fall in farm production and food availability. There can be no solution to the food problem without first establishing a stable medium of exchange.

5   *Macro-level policy must be complemented by micro-level change:* Putting in place the right macro-level policies may be necessary, but it is far from sufficient to create a functioning market. The governments of the region have been so preoccupied with 're-engineering' their economic and political systems and with meeting the conditions to attract foreign aid and investment that they have tended to over-look the many essential and practical steps needed to implement the reforms on the ground. Even if governments had been able to get all the laws and economic policies 'right' the first time, there is no assurance that the actual impact on the people would have been less harsh than it has been.

   The so-called 'shock therapy' strategy pursued by these countries has been widely criticized for its severity and seeming indifference to social costs. But debates regarding the appropriate speed and social cost of reforms divert attention from a more fundamental problem with this approach. The essence of shock therapy is a reliance on macro-economic factors to bring about a radical restructuring of the economy and a radical change in the behaviour of individuals and enterprises. While monetary policy may prove useful for dealing with short-term adjustment problems within a relatively stable environment, there is no evidence to support its use as the principle instrument for social transition. Monetary variables are indicators of the functioning of an economy, but the essential factors which determine the strength and health of an economy are the productivity of its enterprises and its workforce and the material resources of the country. Tight monetary policy can generate intense short-term pressure for change in behaviour, but this pressure is applied indiscriminately and often with unexpected and unanticipated results. The primary result of premature liberalization of prices was to encourage trade and speculation while discouraging production and investment. It distracted attention from fundamental changes in institutions and social attitudes needed for the transition to be successful.

Macro-level policy measures have to be complemented and supported by parallel micro-level efforts to educate the population about the new economic system, to generate a free flow of information – not just freedom, but the actual exchange of information, which is still severely limited in these countries – to develop new distribution systems, to impart appropriate business and managerial skills, to provide access to credit, to build up new social institutions and to encourage and promote new enterprises. In most cities of the former Soviet Union, for instance, there is not a single wholesale market for food. There are no systems for consumer credit, no agencies in charge of promoting small business development. In the absence of these and other essential micro-level conditions, even the right macro-level strategy will not evoke the anticipated response.

6   *Government regulation is essential for a free market:* A free market does not mean an unregulated one. Quite understandably, decades of totalitarian government had generated such powerful resentment against strong government that by way of reaction the society sought for solutions which did not require government to take a highly visible, leading role. The reform programme was based on the implicit assumption that the market is a self-regulating mechanism which can substitute for regulation by government. This notion is contradicted by the experience and practice of every major market economy in the world. Government plays a critically important role in defining and protecting property rights, ensuring

competitive conditions, controlling monopolies, regulating foreign trade, establishing and enforcing quality standards, safeguarding the rights of investors and consumers, preserving the environment from over-exploitation and pollution, encouraging investment, and upholding the rights of employees to minimum wages, safe working conditions and social security in the case of lay-offs. The policies that have made possible the most successful recent development initiatives of nations around the world, especially in Japan and the newly industrialized nations of the Pacific Rim, do not support the argument for unregulated free market forces. These countries combined freedom for entrepreneurial initiative, private property and market prices with carefully crafted industrial policies and tightly controlled foreign trade and investment practices to nurture and protect nascent industries and restrict foreign investment. At the same time, they organized the importation of foreign technology on a massive scale. They utilized import tariffs, export incentives, tax relief and other mechanisms to guide development of their domestic economies.

The reform programme involved the dismantling of most of the administrative mechanisms by which an economy can be monitored and controlled by government. In place of free market conditions, organized crime and corruption became rampant. In seeking to reject thoroughly the authoritarian form of government that suppressed the rights of the people, many of these countries allowed the power and authority of their central governments to decline to the point where they could no longer enforce conditions needed for operation of either a command economy or a free market system. The power of government in the West may be veiled by the fact that its laws are usually obeyed without the need for exercise of force, but the threat of enforcement is as real for tax evaders in North America as it was for free marketers under the communist regime in USSR. Regardless of the system, strong government is a prerequisite for a strong economy.

The experience of the past few years has clearly demonstrated that the state must play a very active role in order to bring about a smooth and rapid transition and this role cannot be limited purely to regulation of the market. Intervention will also be necessary in the form of central planning and industrial policy, at least during the transition period. The radical restructuring of entire industries – defence, agriculture, aluminium, steel – is too complex and massive an undertaking to be made the responsibility of market forces and individual firms.

7   *Agriculture has to be given a special status:* For reasons discussed in the previous chapter, the state has an especially important role in the regulation of agriculture. After the collapse of communism in Eastern Europe, the rise of free market and free trade polemics generated considerable confusion regarding the necessity and legitimacy of state regulation and intervention in protecting and preserving agriculture, which is the beneficiary of innumerable subsidies and supports in virtually every industrialized nation. It is ironic that advice coming from overseas almost invariably recommended eliminating supports to this critical sector of the economy. In the midst of radical economic revolution, the economy, especially the agricultural economy, is in no position to adapt simultaneously to the dual stresses of internal reorganization and external competition.

8   *New institutions and systems are needed to create a market economy:* The establishment of a free market system is retarded by the absence of many basic commercial institutions and systems. The market economy has given birth to a vast array of institutions by which, and through which, it operates – stock and commodity exchanges, systems for mass production, just-in-time inventory management, commercial insurance, franchises, mail order catalogues, courier services, feeder airlines, producers' and consumers' cooperatives, marketing boards, export promotion agencies, leasing, venture capital and mutual funds, credit and collection agencies, commodity brokers, real estate agents, trade unions, industrial associations, industrial estates, exclusive export processing zones and countless others. Our knowledge of transitions will be complete and our capacity to abridge the time and costs of change will be full only when we have come to understand the role of these institutions and have found ways to develop them rapidly.

The need for new institutions in Eastern Europe is apparent in all fields of commercial activity. It is particularly acute in agriculture. Hoarding, speculation by traders, regional shortages and price variations have been aggravated by the absence of alternative systems of distribution to replace the old centralized food procurement system. Privately operated commodity exchanges have sprung up to handle wholesale transactions. But unfamiliarity with such institutions, and the lack of a firm legal basis for enforcement of contracts and a system of grading and inspection to guarantee the quality of produce traded, have kept most buyers and sellers away. A mechanism is needed to insure distribution of food to deficit areas, to guarantee farmers an indexed floor price for foodgrains under conditions of unstable, soaring prices, and to establish and maintain a national buffer stock against emergency. The Indian Food Corporation and Indian National Dairy Development Board, the autonomous marketing boards in the UK, and the US Commodity Credit Corporation are model institutions from which the Eastern Europeans need to borrow, adapt and innovate to suit the conditions of vast food-deficit nations.

Simple commercial systems need to be created to support commerce and industry as well – even such basic systems as telephone listings of sources of products and services that are found in every telephone directory in the West. If trade is to develop between private enterprises, credit checking agencies and collection agencies need to be established. For enterprises which do not qualify or cannot compete for limited bank resources, financial institutions offering hire purchase or leasing of industrial and consumer goods are necessary. The market reforms were expected to lead to a rapid proliferation of new small enterprises, but most of those created so far are engaged only in trading and retail sales. Small business development centres, business incubators, industrial estates, and venture capital funds are needed to encourage entrepreneurship. Some large industrial enterprises have begun leasing portions of their space and equipment to groups of employees who form small businesses for production of equipment and components. This practice should be encouraged and popularized as a natural step towards privatization.

9   *Information is a stimulant and fuel for transition:* The shortage of reliable information and of institutions to disseminate it are major constraints on the development of the market. In a command economy, a few people at the top receive most of the information and take most of the decisions, while the rest of the population carries them out. In contrast, the market is based on millions of decisions taken every day by millions of individuals in fields, factories and retail stores around the country. All these decision makers require timely access to reliable sources of information. Information is needed to make sound business decisions, such as the production of or demand for different commodities or variations in price by region or over time. Easy access, maximum dissemination, full disclosure, precise accuracy and credibility are imperative. Creating these conditions will require the establishment of new institutions and substantial investment in infra-

structure. In many of these countries, the press has freed itself from being solely an instrument of government, but television is still largely under state control. In the entire former USSR today there is no adequate agricultural extension service to transmit research findings from the laboratory to the field, especially to small private farmers. Poor communications systems are incapable of handling the large volume of telephone, fax, telex and computerized messages needed for commercial linkages with other countries.

10 *Catalytic initiatives can release social dynamism:* Social change is facilitated and accelerated by initiatives to introduce or demonstrate new patterns of activity and behaviour appropriate to the goals of the transition. One of the most successful initiatives of the Russian government in recent years has been the distribution of millions of small private agricultural plots to urban and rural households. Since a food shortage in the urban areas was the most pressing problem and greatest source of anxiety for the population, the government took steps to distribute more than 16 million small private plots to urban and rural families, so that highly vulnerable households could produce at least a portion of their own food requirements. These plots now account for more than 50 per cent of vegetable production and 80 per cent of potato and fruit production in Russia. Transitions require changes in behaviour and the private plots became an activity in which millions of people could participate in order to augment their own living standards and alleviate national food shortages. Similar catalytic efforts are needed in other fields to engage the population actively in new and improved activities.

11 *Reduce reliance on foreign aid:* The prospect or lure of foreign aid has itself become an impediment to successful transition. In order to qualify for foreign assistance, these countries have overlooked the vast under-utilized resources available domestically, rejected the knowledge and advice of their own most experienced people in favour of foreign advice, sacrificed their most cherished social values, discarded even successful institutions and systems, and taken steps which, it was painfully obvious to many within these countries, could not possibly lead to the intended results under the prevalent conditions. In the 1950s, the Soviet Union managed to recover from the horrendous destruction it suffered during the Second World War and to embark on a period of rapid industrial growth without any external assistance. But today, without having passed through the ravages of war, the republics desperately seek

foreign support and feel helpless without it. It is right that the world community should generously support the successful completion of the reform process in this region that is so vital for world peace. But it is also right that these countries should recognize the enormous untapped potentials which they possess – human, natural and productive – rather than be distracted by the prospect of a large influx of foreign capital.

ALTERNATIVE STRATEGY IN YUGOSLAVIA

The extreme damage wrought by the economic reform programme in these countries over the past half decade necessitates an urgent search for more viable alternatives, a search that has been retarded until now by the widely held view that none exists. Very recent events in Yugoslavia suggest that even in the limited area of economic stabilization and adjustment, an alternative strategy can be more successful. Although the long-term impact of the Yugoslav experiment is as yet unknown, its remarkably positive initial results merit serious consideration.

The economic disorder that accompanied recent political developments in Yugoslavia resulted in an explosive increase in prices of more than 100 per cent per month in 1992. Despite efforts to control monetary expansion, hyperinflation exceeded three million per cent in 1993 – far higher than the inflation rate reached in Germany following the First World War and, quite probably, the highest rate in recorded history. The price spiral was accompanied by a steep fall in real purchasing power by as much as 75 per cent. The budget deficit increased rapidly as the value of government tax revenues fell further and further behind the rising cost in current terms of its expenditures, due to the time lag between tax declaration, collection and expenditure in a period of very rapid price increases.

In January 1994, the government embarked on a comprehensive monetary reconstruction programme to achieve price and exchange rate stability; to remove administrative controls over production, investment, prices, salaries, and interest rates; to re-establish the role of the central bank in monetary stability; to reorganize public finances through an efficient tax system, including more efficient tax collection and better coverage of the large 'grey' economy; to reduce government administrative and defence expenditure to the maximum possible extent; to maintain price supports for important agricultural commodities as an incentive for production; to stimulate economic activities of private, cooperative and public sector enterprises through equal access to credit and government facilities; and to

➡

encourage the takeover of sick firms by stronger, more efficient companies. At the same time, the programme was intended to mitigate the harsher effects of shock therapy programmes on the working class and fixed-income pensioners by providing free scope for collective bargaining, enforcement of a minimum wage policy and a social safety net for the unemployed.

It was recognized from the outset that stability of the currency was an absolute precondition for the success of the reform programme, which depended in turn on the firmness and consistency with which it was implemented. The central element of the programme was the introduction of a new currency, the 'superdinar', in parallel to the existing currency, but without demonetizing or confiscating it. Inspired by an experiment in the Soviet Union during the 1920s, the value of the new currency was tied to that of the Deutsche Mark and made fully convertible without restriction. Based on the country's very limited foreign currency reserves, new issues of the currency were to be utilized primarily to inject real purchasing power into the economy, revive demand and stimulate production, while covering the government's budget deficit during an initial six-month period needed for sufficient recovery. In this way the foreign currency and gold reserves were used as a buffer to moderate contraction of the money supply and avoid the shock usually accompanying such efforts. Issuing of the old dinar was stopped, but it remained in circulation as legal tender. An interest rate of six per cent was established for the superdinar – the first real, positive interest rate in years – to make holding the new currency an attractive alternative to hoarding goods or foreign exchange. It had been widely anticipated by foreign experts that this strategy would result in an immediate run on the country's foreign reserves and thereby a collapse of the new currency's foundation.

Contrary to expectations, the initial months of the programme have yielded spectacular results. Inflation fell to zero per cent in the first week after the issue of the new currency and remained below one per cent during the first five months. Instead of a massive outflow of foreign currency through conversion of superdinars, people have rushed to cash in their foreign currency, resulting in a 60 per cent increase in the nation's reserves during the first three months. One of the most significant features of the programme has been its fair distribution of benefits and low social cost to the population. In contrast with the widespread outrage felt by Russian citizens over repeated episodes of demonetization and confiscation of household savings, the Yugoslav people have enthusiastically accepted the new currency as representative of a new deal for the poor and the working class. In addition, instead of the severe contraction of output experienced elsewhere, production rose by more than 100 per cent during the first five months, stimulating an increase in employment and demand for new investment. Real tax revenues have increased significantly.

➡

The astonishing initial success of the programme can be attributed to its balance and comprehensiveness, and to the following specific features: the government's recognition that stabilization was absolutely essential to economic recovery; the widespread public support for the programme, which was in large part due to the efforts to protect weaker sections from its harshest effects; the simultaneous relaxation of controls on industry; support for a natural rather than a forced process of privatization, based on the specific circumstances of each firm rather than on ideology; continued price supports for agriculture and a minimum wage for labour, which are crucial for maintaining food supplies and social stability; and rejection of import liberalization in order to protect domestic manufacturing against a major shock during the initial period of recovery. *Possibly the greatest strength of the Yugoslav programme is that it was of necessity conceived by people within the country rather than by foreign experts, and depended entirely on domestic resources and capabilities for its accomplishment, rather than on pleas for foreign assistance. Self-reliance released the creativity, generated the determination and mobilized all available resources to make the transition successful.*

It is too early to predict the eventual outcome in Yugoslavia, subject as it is to extraordinary external constraints on public policy. However, the initial evidence is sufficient to demonstrate that alternative approaches can and must be fashioned which are more comprehensive in scope, more balanced in implementation, more pragmatic in conception and less influenced by extreme ideological viewpoints. It is likely that further study of the Yugoslav model will reveal important applications not only for countries suffering from hyperinflation or the effects of radical transition, but for those carrying out more modest programmes of economic reform.

Recommendations for Accelerating Transition in the East

Conditions within the 25 nations of Eastern Europe and Central Asia vary significantly enough to limit the scope for broad generalizations on strategy beyond the statement of principles presented in this chapter. However, there are a number of specific recommendations applicable to all or most of these countries that can be applied to accelerate the pace and ease the pain of transition.

1 *Generate consensus for the transition programme:* The transition should be an expression of the will of the society for change and it should help generate greater unity and harmony within the society. Further attempts to put through any macro-economic reform package will meet with strong political and social resistance unless a national consensus on the strategy is arrived at beforehand. Any programme involves a set of choices regarding which are the most acceptable costs and important benefits. Before launching new initiatives, governments should conduct public inquiries and debate alternative packages of policies and practices. The inquiry should realistically access the expected costs and benefits of each package. After educating the public about the need for choice and the necessary costs involved, the final selection of the most acceptable package should be made by the people themselves through a national referendum.

2 *Establish macro-economic stability:* The errors in earlier efforts at adjustment and stabilization have led some to argue for a series of compromise programmes that do not seriously address the imminent dangers of hyperinflation and economic collapse. No transition strategy can be successful without first creating stable conditions for economic growth. No effort to improve agricultural production or the availability of food will be successful so long as the currency is not accepted as a stable means of exchange. This is the ultimate justification for the insistence of the international lending community on harsh measures to stabilize the economy. If the previous stabilization programmes have not proved politically viable, socially acceptable or economically effective, alternative programmes similar to the Yugoslav strategy must be attempted without further delay, backed by the full commitment of government. In some cases, it may be necessary to temporarily reintroduce controls on wages and prices as an interim measure to stop the free fall of the currency. But whatever the method, it is essential that this effort be combined with simultaneous implementation of other essential policies.

3 *Eliminate crop losses:* In Russia and the other republics of the former USSR, highest priority in agriculture must be given to efforts that will increase the availability of food and reduce the huge crop losses and massive food imports. These losses vary by crop and region but average between 25 and 50 per cent of total field production for major crops. A reduction in crop losses could completely eliminate millions of tons of grain imports. The reasons for such enormous losses include poor quality of seeds and planting material, the lack of sufficient local storage capacity, inefficient and inappropriate equipment for planting, harvesting, storage and processing, poorly motivated farm workers and shortage of labour at harvest time. Demonstration projects have proved that potato losses can be reduced from 35 per cent to under 5 per cent in one year. A viable solution requires concerted and coordinated activity by government, industry and agriculture at a time when each is operating in isolation from the others.

The main elements of a viable plan to reduce losses for foodgrains, vegetables and potatoes have been proposed by a Dutch cooperative agri-business firm. The aim of the plan is to reduce food imports to zero and eliminate food shortages within three to five years. The plan requires acquisition of foreign production and storage technology, but depends only marginally on import of equipment, most of which can be manufactured in domestic defence facilities. The hard currency requirement is minimal. But the plan does require a leading role by government and financial assistance to farms. In order to be effective, it needs to be supported by a massive public education campaign on use of new technology to eradicate crop losses combined with demonstration plots on both large-scale and small private farms throughout the country. The Commission recommends immediate implementation of the plan with the objective of improving the agricultural economy, increasing the food supply and completely eliminating dependence on food imports .

Study benefits of economic union: Of the estimated 50 per cent fall in GDP among the republics of the former Soviet Union, approximately half can be attributed to the break-up of the economic union. Restoration of a common economic space – which is being criticized internationally as a surrender of sovereignty to Russia at a time when both Western Europe and North America are striving for closer economic union –

4

could immediately restore most of that lost output. The advantages of cooperation between republics needs to be carefully examined. A study should be conducted by a credible institution to estimate the economic losses incurred by the break-up of the common economic space between the former Soviet republics and to assess the benefits of restoring an economic union in some form. It should estimate overall economic growth and living standards for each republic over the next five years operating within and outside the economic union. This study can serve as a powerful argument for closer cooperation among the republics. The study can be undertaken at very low cost by a consortium of researchers from different research institutes within the Commonwealth of Independent States.

5 *Privatize and develop road transport:* Transportation is a major bottleneck to development of a market economy in much of the region. Under the centrally planned system, most freight was hauled by trains over main routes to large cities for distribution in bulk by huge government procurement agencies. Under a market system, millions of small producers and consumers must be free to buy or sell wherever the price is most attractive. This requires a vast proliferation of small goods transporters in the private sector, which are rare in many countries today. The large freight transport monopolies have to be replaced by entrepreneurial companies with small fleets competing for freight business. Immediate steps are needed to expand capacity and introduce competition in this vital sector by promoting the development of private road transport companies at the national, regional and local level. Special loan and leasing programmes should be established to enable small firms and individuals to purchase vehicles and pay for them out of the revenues generated from use.

6 *Regional models and pilot programmes:* Pioneering initiatives need to be encouraged to act as demonstrations and catalysts for new types of activities in the country. In a region as vast and diverse as this and in countries such as Russia, which extends over eleven time zones, no single model or pattern will be widely applicable. Therefore, several areas in each country representing different economic

and social conditions should be selected for establishment of model transition programmes. In each area, a study should be conducted of resources and economic potentials, existing institutions and infrastructure, current levels of skill and social attitudes regarding the market system. Detailed strategies should be devised to educate the public about untapped opportunities, strengthen the institutional infrastructure, impart needed skills, establish catalytic demonstrations and encourage multiplication of successful new activities. A plan should be adopted at the forthcoming UN Social Summit for establishing model district programmes in Eastern and Central European countries. Plans for transition should cover all of the factors listed above, providing trained personnel to assist in the establishment and initial operation of new institutions and systems.

Plan for institutional development: An assessment of the type and functioning of existing institutions and economic systems should be compiled to identify missing links that need to be provided to support the transition. Based on this study, a master plan should be drawn up for establishing the necessary institutions and systems in each country. In order to prepare a cadre of managers for private sector industry and institutions, specialized institutes of management should be set up in each country. **7**

Launch a massive programme to impart new skills and attitudes to the population: In countries where private enterprise was extinguished for decades, entrepreneurial, financial and marketing skills can be extremely limited. An analysis should be undertaken of the types and levels of skills needed for transition to a market system, covering areas such as entrepreneurship, management, national and international marketing, strategic business planning, finance, quality control, product development, production technology, design, and human resource development. Experience in former colonial nations where entrepreneurship was also stifled for a long period indicates that a profound change in attitude is necessary before people will risk leaving or forego seeking salaried and pensioned jobs in favour of self-employment, even when the salaried jobs are scarce or unavailable. Such a basic change of attitude, **8** which normally requires a change of generation, can be accelerated by a massive programme of public information, education and demonstration spanning several years.

9 *Study the benefits of economic recovery on world trade:* Recessionary trends are affecting many parts of the world today. The prognosis in the West, especially in the European Union, is for slow growth during the 1990s. The progress of developing countries is impeded by slow growth in the industrialized nations and the collapse of Eastern Europe. What would be the impact on the world economy of a rapid recovery and economic expansion in the countries of the region? What would be the result elsewhere of further decline in Eastern Europe? These questions are of vital relevance to the entire world. A detailed study should be conducted under the auspices of the United Nations, OECD or the European Commission to quantify the potential gains or losses to the global economy of rapid or slow progress of the transition in Eastern Europe and Central Asia.

10 *Scientific resources:* Science has been one of the greatest casualties of the reform programme. Severe fiscal constraints have forced governments to reduce drastically budgetary allocations to research institutions, leaving most of these institutions with little or no source of revenues to support their activities. High priority must be given to developing a detailed plan for preservation of the scientific research infrastructure during the difficult transition period and for restructuring it so that it can be integrated effectively into the emerging market system. The drain of talents must be stopped by a concerted national effort to exploit each country's competitive advantage in science by marketing these capabilities internationally, and particularly by linking up with other countries in the region and with developing countries that can most benefit from the region's scientific and technological capabilities.

Search for a New Model

Ironically, despite all the international debate about transition, thus far the actual goal of the transition process has never been clearly spelled out. It is widely presumed to be to some form of capitalist system, but which variety – the Swedish? The Japanese? The American? Although the ostensible goal of transition has been to economies based on private ownership, three years after the initiation of transition programmes, very little privatization has actually taken place in most countries of the region. It is widely believed that acceleration of this process will lead to rising unemployment and a widening gap between the rich and the poor, leading to the creation of a huge underclass that had been virtually eradicated in previous decades. Is this result really the best these countries can hope for in the foreseeable future?

The events in Eastern Europe have been widely hailed as a victory for democratic capitalism over authoritarian communism. The obvious failure of the latter has been used to support the claim of the former to be the sole political and economic heir to the next millennium. This view has been applied to justify the imposition of radical shock therapy on the unsuspecting and unprepared populations of Eastern Europe and stringent structural adjustment programmes on many developing countries. But the claim itself is based on a limited and superficial interpretation of history.

The fall of the Berlin Wall marks the end of a confrontation between two divergent systems that have been struggling toward reconciliation throughout the present century – one based on the human right to freedom and the determinism of the free market, the other based on the right to basic economic security and the determinism of the state. One has made people subservient to the needs of the state, the other has left them subject to the whims of the market. True communism has never existed. What lived and has finally died in Eastern Europe is not communism, but statism, the domination of the state and use of state authority to govern the life of the nation, in practice reducing people to forced labour. True capitalism, which regards people as a factor of production, passed away more than half a century ago, when the challenge of communism prompted Western societies to incorporate socialist principles and measures to mitigate the blind justice of the free market. There are no true capitalist societies in the world. There are no free markets. The free market system is highly regulated and controlled by the very state over which it claims victory. But although in reality both systems are dead, the ideology of the capitalist system lives on and casts an illusory impression of supremacy.

Rather than searching for a victor and vanquished, the urgent need is to find a successor that combines and synthesizes the enlightened values of both systems – freedom and equality, liberty and security. It has been amply proved that the authoritarian state is incapable of exerting a benevolent authority over the people without imposing severe restrictions on freedom, stifling human energy and creativity, leading sooner or later to rising discontent and a loss of social vitality. It is also abundantly clear that money as an institution operating through the free pricing mechanism of the market system – although it does succeed in generating high levels of energy, creativity and productivity – regards people as a purchasable commodity or a potential market, but is otherwise indifferent to human values and welfare. Neither the determinism of the state nor the determinism of the market can be adequate in themselves to achieve the goals of peace and prosperity that we strive after.

It has been generally assumed that the transition now taking place in Eastern Europe will sooner or later lead these countries to adopt forms of government and economy identical to those prevalent in the West. But for those raised in a society that offered a great measure of social security, the poverty and insecurity of the Western system are gross inadequacies. While it is clear that these new democracies have rejected the authoritarian statist system, it is not yet clear what finally they will accept, discover or invent as a more acceptable alternative. The creativity and inventiveness they have exhibited in seeking an alternative in the past may quite possibly lead them to discover that better social system which both East and West are in need of.

Viewed from an evolutionary perspective, we may surmise the general direction and likely destination of that quest. The requirements of the state and the market must eventually give way to the needs of people. The values of authority and money must be supplanted by acceptance of the fundamental value of the human being. Human welfare and well-being must become the central determinants of social policy, in place of the compulsions of the centrally controlled state bureaucracy and the decentralized market pricing mechanism. *The first essential step in that direction is a commitment by market economies to guarantee the right of every citizen to employment.* Neither the mechanism of state planning and control nor the mechanism of market prices can accomplish this on their own. A blending of their values and methods – freed from the blinkers of dogma and the determinism of limited imagination – can lead us to the answer.

Wider Perspective on Transitions

The outcome of all great social transformations – of which the present instance ranks in magnitude and importance with that of the French Revolution and the movement which freed India and so many other former colonies from imperialism, economic exploitation and cultural domination – depends on the degree to which individuals and institutions within the society have been prepared to understand, accept and respond to the new environment ushered in by the transition. Two hundred years ago the people of France were ready to overthrow the old order but ill-prepared to create anything new, with the result that the old soon re-established itself and lived on for another century. It took India's leaders more than four decades to prepare their people for freedom and it has taken another four to overcome the vestiges of colonial rule that prevented the country from releasing its energies for prosperity. Long after the foreign conquerors had left, colonialism lived on in the institutions of government and in the attitudes of the population. Decades of freedom and education were needed for the country to outgrow a sense of inferiority, a seeking for security, a feeling of submissiveness and complacency, and to acquire a sense of pride, ambition, high aspirations and expectations, a seeking for achievement, and a spirit of adventure and enterprise – and still the task is not complete.

Development is like a chemical reaction that is determined by the variety and quantity of elements present and the conditions under which they are put together. If one essential element or condition is missing, a social transition like a chemical reaction may not take place at all. The absence of peace in war-torn Africa or democratic freedoms in former colonial nations, the absence of social stability or an entrepreneurial class, the absence of a functioning banking or educational system, the absence of the minimum necessary infrastructure for transportation and communication – any one of these may be enough to prevent transition until the deficit is made up. If even an inessential element or condition is missing, the process of transition may take much longer than would otherwise be necessary. Lack of information, lack of education, lack of necessary skills, lack of supportive laws or incentives or protection against losses – insufficiency in any of these areas may be enough to slow or delay the process of change by years or even decades.

The world needs a coherent intellectual framework for understanding and dealing with radical transitions. High priority should be given to developing a fresh conceptual approach that is not encumbered by allegiance to existing theories and systems. Transitions should be regarded as social transformations which depend on and result in corresponding changes in the political, economic and other spheres. Efforts to guide a multi-dimensional social transition through uni-dimensional strategies, particularly those limited to manipulation of macro-economic policy, are unlikely to yield the anticipated results. Even those transitions which are apparently confined to economic activities within a stable political context necessarily depend on changes in social attitudes and in social institutions which can be dealt with most effectively by assuming a wider perspective of the process. Clear visualization of the before and after states of transition, the existing system, the goals to be sought after, and a detailed picture of the changes that need to occur in behaviour, attitudes and institutions are necessary for deriving the most effective transition strategies.

With the knowledge the world possesses today, with the example of many successful nations over the last four decades, and with its highly educated and motivated people, surely the nations of Eastern Europe and Central Asia can abridge the time required and the hardship of lessons learned by trial and error to a few years. But this cannot be accomplished by sweeping remedies or hastened by over-eagerness or impatience. It will require application of a profound understanding of the process of development and transition. *We believe that a properly conceived effort to draw on the best available knowledge and experience of other countries can generate a transition strategy that avoids the dangers and pitfalls of the initial approach to reform and puts in place the essential foundations for the new system to function effectively and generate benefits for the people before the dawn of the new century.*

7

Developing Human Resourcefulness

In the preceding chapters we have tried to draw attention to the uncommon opportunities that the world presents at the dawn of a new millennium for the abolition of war and the eradication of poverty. None will question the desirability of achieving peace, democratic freedoms and prosperity for all. But many may doubt the practical feasibility of accomplishing these necessary goals. Every great endeavour requires a proportionate investment of energy and resources for its accomplishment. The realization of peace and prosperity is no exception. What, then, are the resources required for this achievement and where are we to find them?

The history of civilization is the process of humankind discovering greater and greater resources and learning how to utilize them to acquire higher and higher levels of physical security, productive power and comfort. In the earliest phase, these resources were almost exclusively material. The next phase brought the discovery of tools and instruments that made the material resources far more productive and valuable than before. Gradually, society discovered rudimentary organizational resources – the capacity to organize productive activities in a more effective manner. The organization of farming utilized the tree to make a plough with which to cultivate repeatedly the same land, giving birth to sedentary societies. The organization of crafts, commerce, armies, governments – constructed from a fabric of customs, rules, systems and laws – each made use of the material resources for greater productivity, power and achievement. At each stage of this evolution, society discovered the power of knowledge to increase further the productivity of the material, technological and organizational resources at its disposal. A knowledge of weather patterns boosted productivity in agriculture. A knowledge of astronomy enabled sea-worthy vessels to travel across the oceans to distant lands. This led to the invention of systematic education as a method to pass on acquired knowledge and skills to the next generation and thereby continuously increase them.

The Ultimate Resource

These rich and varied discoveries came as the result of a careful observation and analysis of the external world around us, an infinite exploration and experimentation with things, an endless trial and error blending of minerals and plants to forge metals and produce medicines. *As a result, for millennia we have tended to overlook or, at best, grossly underestimate the greatest of all resources and the true source of all the discoveries, inventions, creativity and productive power found in nature – the resource that has made minerals into ships that sail the skies, fashioned grains of sand into tiny electronic brains, released the energy of the sun from the atom, modified the genetic code of plants to increase their vigour and productivity – the ultimate resource, the human being.* World Food Prize recipient and father of India's milk revolution, Dr V. Kurien, has decried the tendency to credit external factors for the accomplishment of people. 'It is the farmer that has produced this miracle, not the cow.' And so it can be said of the Industrial Revolution and the Green Revolution.

Looked at from a different perspective, the entire evolution of civilization is a progressive act of humanity's self-discovery. At each stage of external observation and exploration, people have discovered more of their own inner capacity for resourcefulness. The material, technological, political, economic and social development of the world over countless centuries is an external expression of the growing discovery by humanity of the unlimited creative power of mental ideas, emotional aspirations, physical skills and higher values. The real process of creation and development is from the immaterial to the material, from the inner to the outer, from idea to invention, from aspiration to achievement, from the lofty value of freedom and the ideal of self-determination to the founding of democratic nations, from the soaring emotions of an emperor's love to the beauty and grandeur of the Taj Mahal, from the urge for adventure to the discovery of a new continent, from the technician's joy in expressing perfect skill to the marvellous powers of a microprocessor. All begin as an inner urge that expresses externally in life.

Leadership in Thought

In times of crisis, great leaders rise to remind us that the true resource is ourselves. Thus, Winston Churchill inspired the tiny British nation with the courage to stand and fight fascism when all the rest of Europe had surrendered; thus, Franklin Roosevelt halted the collapse of the US banking system during the 1930s by convincing the people that fear was their greatest enemy and that the basic economic strength of the nation was intact; thus, Gandhi inspired whole generations to fight against colonialism, apartheid and other forms of oppression in a non-violent manner; thus, Gorbachev broke down the psychological barriers to peace and human understanding that had divided the world into two opposing armed camps for four decades; and thus, Deng Xiaoping committed the Chinese nation to provide food and clothing for all its citizens, launching a period of phenomenal economic progress for one-fifth of the world's inhabitants. These great acts of leadership were fundamentally acts of leadership in thought, of leaders who knew the power of human creativity and determination to achieve what few believed possible.

It has been our objective to show that now is a time of unprecedented opportunity, provided that we shed the artificial fetters that limit our ideas, attitudes and actions. *When we rely on external resources, we achieve the minimum because our achievement is based on what we see before us. When we rely on the inner resources, we achieve the maximum because we are constantly led to discover more of our own unlimited capacities.* Why should we wait before acting until we are compelled by the irresistible force of the rising expectations of the world's masses, by the explosion of violence in our cities, or by the complete breakdown of our economic systems because of spiralling unemployment? Why should we not act now to prevent these outcomes and reverse the trends that threaten to make them a reality? All the resources necessary are within our reach, within ourselves. We need the courage to think and say that it is time to abolish weapons of mass destruction and call a halt to the use of war for settlement of disputes, that it is time to insist that all people enjoy the most basic democratic freedoms, that there can and must be enough food produced to feed everyone, and that every person must be guaranteed the right to gainful employment.

The barriers to these achievements are not material or technological. It takes money, materials and technology to make war, not to stop it. That requires a determination and insistence, an intolerance of violence, which must start with a commitment of the world's leaders and the total empowerment of the UN to enforce peace. It takes material resources and technology to suppress people, not to make them free. That requires an acceptance of basic human rights as a non-negotiable minimum requirement for each nation to participate in the international community, which must start with a voluntary abdication by the great powers of the principle of rule by might that governs the present structure of the UN. Renunciation of the veto power, expansion of the Security Council and democratization of UN decision-making processes will forge an institution capable of meeting the challenges of the future, rather than living in the shadow of the past. Why should we wait for these things to happen inevitably after a lapse of decades or centuries when we are amply capable of attaining those beneficial results now, to the great advantage of everyone?

Many will argue that, when it comes to food and jobs, the external resources are the real constraints. We disagree. It has been amply demonstrated that the main cause of famines is not inadequate production or supply of food. In the modern day, famine is primarily an economic problem of entitlement, not a physical problem of shortage. The world possesses enough technology to double or triple the food supply in a decade, if only the world's poorest two billion people have the purchasing power to consume it.

So, too, the problem of employment. Humankind has employed itself ever since the dawn of civilization. So long as people have wants and are willing to work to fulfil them, there need not be a shortage of jobs for all who seek them. The problem today is not a shortage of money or technology. The problem is that we have constructed a hermetically sealed economic system that does not permit all people to express that willingness. Even if we reached the advanced stage of technological development that enabled one-tenth of the world's population to produce all the goods and services to which all humanity could ever aspire, what would prevent us from distributing that work in such a manner as to provide everyone with the opportunity to acquire the purchasing power to consume their share of that over-abundance? The main limit on the production of sufficient goods to create prosperity for all is not material, financial, or technological. It is the inefficiency and arbitrariness of the present economic system that fails to take advantage of the vast latent market potential of nearly half the human race. Give these people the chance to work and they will create the markets to provide jobs and higher incomes for everyone. The single act of removing the artificial subsidies and import barriers for agricultural products in industrial nations that protect the jobs of so few in the West, and deny jobs to so many in developing countries, can help realign global labour markets, creating vast scope for employment generation in the South that will act as an engine for industrial exports and full employment in the North.

Ultimately, the achievement of peace and prosperity for all does require an enormous investment of resources, but the resources demanded are human resources that dwell within ourselves, waiting to be tapped. These resources can never be exhausted because the more they are drawn upon, the more they grow. *The real challenge of development is developing people – not only in the external sense of providing them with food, clothing, good health and fresh water, but also in the inner sense of developing their awareness, attitudes, skills and values to make them more enlightened, productive and contented human beings. What we need today is fresh leadership in thought by our leaders to educate themselves and then the world about the opportunities of the third millennium, and then to take the actions to convert these possibilities into actualities. Developing our human resourcefulness is the single greatest need and opportunity of our time.*

Tapping Unutilized Resources

Economic and social development strategies emphasize the strengthening of social capacity by building up physical infrastructure, production facilities and commercial organizations, and by creating a conducive environment for increasing economic activity through appropriate laws, fiscal, monetary and trade policies. Human development strategies focus on improving the welfare and capacities of the individual through better health, education, political choice and economic opportunity. Together they encompass the two basic components of all development – personal and institutional, individual and collective. The challenge is to develop simultaneously both individual and social capacities and utilize their potentials in a complementary manner. For the individual, development involves acquisition of greater knowledge, more progressive attitudes, improved skills and higher values. For the collective, development involves establishment of more useful and productive institutions, systems, organizations and cultural values.

The conventional view that development is essentially a function of scarce economic inputs must give way to the perception that the opportunities and potentials for rapid development far exceed actual achievements in every country. Looking back over the past few decades, we realize that the speed of social progress could certainly have been much greater than it was. The tremendous potential for accelerating development is most easily illustrated by instances in which actual achievements substantially excelled expectations, such as the enormous leap in world agriculture during the 1960s and 1970s and the phenomenal growth of incomes, employment and exports in East Asia during the last ten years. These unforeseen accomplishments reflect the magnitude of potentials that these countries possessed but had not previously utilized.

The untapped resources of the society can be categorized under several headings:

- *Knowledge* of the process of development and the factors that stimulate it.

- *Education* that imparts progressive social values and practically useful perspectives.

- *Information* that creates awareness of opportunities.

- *Values* that foster productivity, organization and social cohesion.

- *Skills* that improve quality and productivity.

- Successful *systems* that improve efficiency and expand activities.

- *Organizations* that promote cooperation, coordination and broaden the sphere of activity.

- Environmentally friendly *technologies* that can be widely adopted.

- Social *attitudes* that foster self-confidence, individual initiative, and positive responses to new opportunities.

- Development-oriented *laws*, *policies* and *programmes* that can be more fully implemented.

A huge surge in development can be achieved if every socially available resource and potential is fully utilized by the people – if every capable youth, male and female, continues education up to the level of his or her highest aptitude; if every family employs all the health care knowledge and best practices known by the society; if every government self-employment programme and training programme is fully utilized; if all known technology for improving agriculture is widely publicized and put into practice; if every successful system and institution is replicated and applied to full advantage. The highest priority must be to evolve strategies for utilizing these vast social resources more effectively.

The magnitude of this potential is illustrated by the enormous gap, referred to earlier, between average yields on major food crops achieved by poor developing countries in Asia and Africa and the yields obtained by the world's most productive producers. Proven technology already exists that is capable of raising low yields well above the world averages. The real limiting factors are inadequate dissemination of information about best practices and success stories, inadequate skills in employing these methods, inadequate organizational arrangements for marketing and processing, as well as outmoded policies and attitudes about food self-sufficiency and the role of agriculture in the national economy. Developing these individual and institutional resources should be our highest priority.

Theory of Development

A greater knowledge of the process of development that we seek to accelerate is the first essential resource needed for achieving the goals set forth in this report. The UN Secretary General has rightly drawn attention to the worldwide crisis in development economics and called the need for new thinking on development 'the most important intellectual challenge of the coming years'. Until now development has been largely a haphazard, subconscious or half-conscious process of trial and error experimentation, an application of partial strategies, a confusing mixture of productive and counter-productive initiatives, an unscientific and often superstitious clinging to half-truths or old-truths that no longer have any relevance.

Development is not merely a set of goals or programmes. It is a social process by which human beings become mentally aware of new opportunities and challenges, conceive of ideas, create inventions, release their energy and enthusiasm for achievement, and acquire the skills and organizational capacities for action. A better understanding of that process will enable us to avoid the errors and tardiness of past efforts and accomplish in the next few decades what might otherwise take centuries.

The world possesses sufficient experience and information to formulate a comprehensive and integrated theory of development as a social process. The theory should explain the process by which human society has developed to where it is today, the forces which propel its growth, and the stages of its past and future progress. It should be based on the perception that the political, economic and social life of humankind is a single, inseparable whole and, therefore, that comprehensive, total strategies must be applied to resolve our problems, because partial strategies lead to partial solutions which disturb the harmony of the whole, generating unwanted side-effects.

This knowledge should be utilized to formulate a model of development that is based on the internal dynamics of the process rather than on its external manifestations or extrapolation of future trends from past data. This model should become so precise that we can anticipate the impact of peace, more education, greater political freedom, rising social expectations, and high values such as guaranteed employment on the progress of society. This conceptual knowledge should enable us to understand and replicate fully the conditions responsible for the post-war achievements of Japan, China's recent 20 per cent growth rate or Yugoslavia's remarkable conquest of hyperinflation. A comprehensive approach will enable us to anticipate the imbalances and side-effects generated by partial initiatives and to evolve total strategies to avoid them.

The comprehensive conceptual model needs to be complemented by the development of models for employment, food, education, trade and other fields that go beyond the national or sectoral approach to show the impact of the complex interactions that are key determinants of the development process – for instance, the impact of democracy on agriculture and of increasing agricultural productivity on employment, industrialization and trade, the impact of rising education on democratization, social tolerance for diversity, personal expectations and social stability. Once formulated, these conceptual models need to be applied under a variety of conditions to test their validity and demonstrate the value of a comprehensive approach to development. Therefore, we have proposed that the UN adopt a number of districts in different regions of the world, including crime-ridden inner cities or impoverished rural areas in industrial countries, to evolve and apply strategies for their rapid transition to a higher level of development.

Six Goals in Education

Once formulated, this knowledge needs to be imparted through education. Education is the greatest known civilizing force and the single most powerful lever for human development. Training imparts skills, but education increases the capacity of the individual at a more basic level, making the mind more active and alert, converting physical energy into mental energy, training us to see things from a wider perspective, to question and challenge the *status quo*, to think and imagine, to innovate and invent, to make decisions for ourselves and to act on our own initiative. *Education is the process by which society passes on the accumulated knowledge and experience of countless centuries to new generations in a systematic, concentrated and abridged form, so that today's young people can start their lives at the high point of knowledge and wisdom attained by preceding generations.* Education replaces the slow, subconscious process of trial and error learning with a swift, conscious process. This accumulated knowledge is a great power that can be utilized to accelerate human development and abridge the time needed for society to arrive at progressively higher levels of material, social and psychological fulfilment.

Despite the massive efforts of international institutions to create awareness of the vital role of education in peace, democracy, economic development, population control and environmental protection, progress on extending the benefits of education to all humankind is still grossly inadequate. In 1990, 948 million people or about 20 per cent of the entire world population lacked even basic literacy skills. Adult literacy rates in the least developed nations still average less than 50 per cent and are less than half that in a number of countries. Unless more intensive efforts are made, worldwide the absolute number of the illiterate will decline only marginally by the year 2000. Illiteracy is likely to increase by 10 per cent in South Asia – home to more than 40 per cent of the world's illiterate – and by nearly 7 per cent in sub-Saharan Africa.

Although universal primary education has been a goal for decades and primary education has been made compulsory in most countries, 128 million children living in remote rural areas, urban slums and refugee camps – representing 20 per cent of the total school-age population – are still excluded from primary education. Unless greater measures are introduced, this number may rise to more than 160 million by the turn of the century. Achieving true universality of primary education by the year 2000 will require a massive investment in school buildings, teachers and instructional materials for an additional 230 million school-age children. An additional 4 million teachers will be required, 20 per cent more than in 1990. In sub-Saharan Africa, gross primary enrolment will have to double before year 2000 to achieve this goal.

In addition to the quantitative deficiency in educational enrolment and achievements, the quality of teaching facilities, materials and staff is severely deficient in many countries. Most developing countries hire teachers with only a secondary school certificate and a minimum of teachers' training. This contributes to the high rate of primary school drop-outs and grade repetition. Only 71 per cent of first-grade entrants complete primary school in developing countries.

Addressing these challenges will require a substantial increase in financial resources devoted to education. In most regions, public expenditure on education has risen in recent years. In 1990, the world average was 13.5 per cent of total government expenditure, or 4.8 per cent of GNP. More than one-third of the countries in the world still spend more on the military than on education. Efforts to improve education must go hand in hand with efforts to promote peace and disarmament and drastically curtail military spending. Mechanisms should be put in place to insure that a significant portion of reduced military spending is invested in education and training.

The very highest social priority should be given to six educational goals in both developing and developed countries. First, there must be a massive effort to achieve UNESCO's goal of *eradicating illiteracy* worldwide by the year 2000. The problem can only be banished by an all-out commitment of every national government to eliminate the huge backlog of illiteracy, while at the same time insuring that every child is taught to read and write. National youth service corps and military personnel can be utilized to help provide the necessary manpower.

Second, every possible step must be taken to provide *education for female children,* an essential requirement for social equity and quality of life improvement. Nearly two-thirds of the world's illiterate are women. In the poorest developing countries, literacy rates among females are 40 per cent below rates for males and the average number of years of schooling for females is 60 per cent lower. But perceptible progress has been made. Between 1980 and 1990, female primary school enrolment rose from 44 per cent to 47 per cent of total enrolment, although it actually declined in the Arab states and remained virtually unchanged in South Asia. Uneducated females represent a huge reservoir of untapped human potential that must be given every opportunity and full assistance to develop their innate capacities. This will call for accelerated efforts to establish crèche and child-care facilities, abolish child labour, and remove gender bias from text books and educational institutions. The cost of raising female educational levels up to that of males worldwide has been estimated at $2.5 billion, a small amount for an initiative that could have such wide-ranging benefits.

Third, literacy must be complemented by *techniracy,* education that imparts basic technical information and skills to the population through a variety of teaching methods suited to the educational level of the recipients. Detailed recommendations are presented in the next section of this chapter. At the other end of the spectrum, comparable efforts must be made to raise scientific literacy, which is essential for the continued growth of technology, productivity and employment in modern society. The pervasive influence of science in society requires that we bridge the gap that presently divides the sciences and humanities and evolve an educational system in which science is no longer regarded as a specialized field of study.

Fourth, radical changes are needed in the content of school curricula at all levels to make education relevant to the real needs of the students and the development of the country. The society whose system of education is integrated with the social aspirations of the country will develop most rapidly. The system of education prevalent in most developing countries is oriented toward the outer form – acquiring a degree or qualifying certificate – rather than the inner content of knowledge. Educated unemployment is a direct result of a system that fosters obedience and rote learning rather than individual initiative and creative thinking. A new system of *development education* needs to be introduced at all levels to equip the student with an understanding of his/her society, its achievements and potentials, and the opportunities open to each individual to participate in its future growth. The index of its success will be the extent to which students of this curriculum seek self-employment rather than salaried jobs.

Fifth, *minimum and average educational levels should be raised in all countries.* Two centuries ago education was a luxury of the rich and it was simply inconceivable that every member of the population in any country could receive even a minimum level of education. Few of the industrial nations fully meet their own present minimum standards for every citizen. These minimums are arbitrary, not optimal. Raising the minimum levels of achievement further in all countries may be the most important initiative that governments can render to prepare their citizens for a more productive, prosperous and peaceful future.

Sixth, new educational systems must be evolved to prepare people for life in the twenty-first century. Education imparts knowledge of the past and the general ability to deal with the future, but this ability is only in potential. It is not fully developed in the form of practically useful knowledge. An educational system that endows the individual with the capacity for physical accomplishment, psychological fulfilment and original thinking would enable society consciously to abridge the development process and accomplish goals within one or a few decades that would otherwise take place over the span of a century or more.

We believe that it is possible to fashion a system that directly prepares students for life in the twenty-first century, because the necessary knowledge already exists subconsciously in society and consciously in a few stray individuals or social groups. Materially, the world already possesses the knowledge needed to produce sufficient food and other necessities to eradicate poverty from the earth, but this knowledge is not yet a conscious possession of humanity as a whole that is passed on to every individual, even in the most advanced nations. Socially, every culture possesses the knowledge of the essential qualities necessary for lasting success. This knowledge, if consciously formulated, can be systematically imparted to the entire population through formal education. Psychologically, the right attitudes, values and motives enable the individual to attain a self-existent happiness and inner harmony which nothing can disturb. This knowledge too can be consciously formulated and communicated through the educational system of the twenty-first century. Mentally, our knowledge is partial, biased and largely dependent on social status and opinion, rather than purely rational criteria. True mental objectivity can be taught. Human fulfilment in the twenty-first century depends on our ability to provide an education that imparts not only material facts, but also the mental perspectives, psychological attitudes, personal values, individual skills and organizational abilities needed for the full blossoming of human resourcefulness and accomplishment.

Developing Skills

Improving the quality and quantity of productive skills is essential to implementing the strategies for peace, democratization, food security, economic growth and full employment set forth in this report. The phenomenal growth of East Asian countries is the direct result of their massive investments in upgrading the skills of the workforce. Rather than generating excess workers, rising productivity has generated greater demand for labour. Labour productivity in South Korea rose 11 per cent per year between 1963 and 1979, mostly due to investment in education and skills. This increase has been accompanied by a growing shortage of labour, equivalent to 1 per cent of the workforce in 1991. Investment in education and training helped Thailand raise labour productivity by 63 per cent during 1980–5. It, too, is moving from a labour surplus to a labour shortage economy.

An enormous range and depth of physical, technical, organizational, managerial and social skills are needed in order to utilize constructively the freedom which democracy provides, the productive power of new technologies, and the efficiency of modern institutions and systems to achieve greater developmental results. These skills admit of constant and continuous improvement without limit, in the same way that technology and organization can always be further improved. A comparative survey of the level and quality of skills in any country with those of countries above and below it on scales of economic and human development will reveal the crucial role of skills in development. A scale of progression on key skills can help every country identify its relative position, assess the scope for further progress and evolve strategies to fill the gap. *Raising the skills of society to those of countries higher up on the scale will enable the country to move to that higher level.*

Despite enormous expansion of educational and training institutions, most developing countries suffer from a shortage of quality vocational skills among the huge number of people at lower levels of the society who seek desperately to raise their standard of living. This shortage retards the growth in productivity and quality needed to meet domestic needs and achieve international competitiveness. The technical training infrastructure in these countries should be expanded by the establishment of craft and vocational training institutes at the local level in every community to impart a wide range of basic technical skills. A massive programme of basic vocational and skills training should be launched on a parallel with the 100 per cent literacy programmes that are now being promoted by many governments to wipe out rural illiteracy. The military in many developing countries possesses the organizational capabilities and experience with intensive training to assist with this task. An institutional gap exists in agricultural training systems. In most developing countries, agricultural colleges, universities and polytechnics train researchers, government, bank employees and extension officers, but not farmers. Producing more food with less water, less chemicals and less soil erosion requires high levels of skill. The chain of agricultural training needs to be filled out at the lower level by establishing thousands of village-level farm schools as proposed in the chapter on food security.

The switch from centrally planned to market-oriented economic systems in Eastern Europe cannot be successful until the population has acquired the skills needed to function effectively in the new economic environment. Under the communist system, emphasis was placed on education and training in technical subjects with little attention to marketing, organizational, commercial and interpersonal skills, which are essential requirements for functioning in a market economy. A detailed inventory should be compiled of the types and levels of skills needed for transition to the market, covering areas such as entrepreneurship, management, national and international marketing, strategic business planning, finance, quality control, product development, production technology, design, and human resource development. Intensive training programmes need to be introduced to impart these skills on a massive scale.

Even in the most advanced industrial nations there is vast scope for upgrading skills to improve productivity and to keep pace with rapid technological development. Inadequate skills are a major impediment to the assimilation of new technologies. The increasing demands of global competitiveness place pressure on workers in these countries to continuously improve their skills. The mismatch between the skills of the workforce and the evolving needs of industry aggravates unemployment. Studies of the return on investment from training programmes document the enormous benefits of continuously upgrading the skills of the workforce. Private sector investment in training will prove inadequate unless it is encouraged by incentives or complemented by greater public investment in this sector.

Information Superhighways

Information promotes political freedom, economic development and social justice. The transforming power of information under *glasnost* opened up Soviet society to events in the outer world and created widespread awareness of the alternative approaches and achievements of other nations. Information brought down the Berlin Wall, ended the Cold War and ushered the world into a new era. Information about economic opportunities and potentials is an essential ingredient, a catalyst, of the development process. In the past, development strategies have tended to place too little emphasis on the power of public awareness to release people's energies and initiative on a massive scale. The vast accumulation of knowledge and new technology for rapid dissemination of information that the world possesses today can be utilized to increase the speed of change, eliminate many false starts and wrong turns and much unnecessary suffering. *The goals and strategies recommended in this report aim to accelerate the process of political, social and economic development by creating greater public awareness of desirable and achievable objectives and releasing the initiative of individuals and institutions to pursue them more vigorously. Information is the most powerful catalyst for this process.*

The speed and extent of knowledge transfer are far from optimal between and within nations – even within industrially advanced nations – due to lack of information, out-dated attitudes and beliefs, lingering superstitions, and conventional wisdom. Ignorance and scepticism about new opportunities are characteristic of development at each stage and in every field of activity. Information about success stories helps overcome this resistance and spurs people to action. Enormous potentials are waiting to catch the attention of the society and take off at this moment. Proven technology exists in many fields that await application because people do not know or do not believe that it can be employed successfully. Imitation of intensive aquaculture methods commonly employed by farmers in Taiwan and Singapore can raise average fish yields in South Asian, African and Latin American countries 25-fold. Advanced methods for micro-nutrient management can double or quadruple fruit and vegetable yields in most developing countries. A complete list of proven but untapped technologies and commercial opportunities should be compiled for each country, each region and local area. Programmes should be initiated to publicize information about commercialization of agriculture, stimulating industrialization, encouraging self-employment and new business start-ups, improving management practices, etc.

Role of the media

Free and well-developed media are vital to democratization and development. For this very reason, the dissemination of information by the media carries with it a great responsibility that cannot be effectively shouldered where private profit is the sole motive, or government control limits freedom of expression. The media can play an invaluable role in disseminating relevant information to the public, but the type and quality of information being carried in most developing countries must be radically improved. The worldwide tendency to focus on the immediate and dramatic at the expense of that which could make a substantial and lasting contribution to development requires greater efforts to creatively present socially useful information in an easily accessible and interesting form.

Information in developing countries

In the industrial democracies there are usually multiple sources of independent information available to the public on most issues. The same is not the case in developing countries, where very often the sole source of information is government – which lacks credibility because the quality of information is poor or it is politically motivated – or academic institutions that are insulated from practical, especially commercial, realities. The need is especially great for broadcasting value-added information at the local level.

Specialized agencies should be established in developing countries in the form of public foundations or independent research institutions to provide a credible, unbiased source of information by identifying critical gaps in public awareness needed to stimulate development in various fields; conducting studies to document proven practices in agriculture, business, education, health, government, media; disseminating information on new opportunities; commissioning films, novels, short stories and syndicated columns to communicate developmental information; supporting pioneering examples of new or improved activities in different fields; encouraging others to imitate successful pioneers; recognizing and rewarding high achievers. *A modest investment in new institutions to disseminate information can have an impact comparable to that of the information superhighways being heralded in the most industrially advanced nations – accelerating adoption of new activities, magnifying response to government programmes, and doubling the total developmental achievements of a country over the next five years.*

Information as a stimulus to transition

The people of Eastern Europe and the former Soviet Union are highly educated, but long deprived of free access to information. Recent economic reforms have dramatically increased the importance of information in the functioning of the economy. The breakdown of the command system necessitates the establishment of new channels for the dissemination of information about economic principles, commercial opportunities and successful practices within and outside the country. The macro-economic reforms introduced to free prices and legalize private property cannot generate the desired results, unless the population is also given easy access and exposure to a very wide range of essential information on new technologies, legal reforms, trade potentials, self-employment opportunities and modern management practices. The plethora of new laws, regulations and deregulations being enacted in these countries have left the population baffled and bewildered regarding what is now legal or illegal, acceptable or not permissible. The transition of these nations can be significantly accelerated by systematic dissemination of important information to the population regarding potentials in agriculture, industry, technology, commerce, management and law, as well as in politics, public administration, international relations, education, social institutions and health.

Information needs of industrial nations

Even in the information-rich West, where the average citizen is overwhelmed by a continuous barrage of ideas, opinions and so-called 'facts' of varying accuracy and credibility from myriad sources, there is a need for more reliable information. This superabundance conceals gaping holes of ignorance. American foreign policy toward the USSR in the 1980s was certainly influenced by the fact that, as recently as 1988, more than 50 per cent of Americans believed the Soviets fought against the United States in the Second World War. The irrational alarm which economists sounded in the late 1970s about the impact of inflation on the poor in the US overshadowed compelling evidence published by a leading economic institution that poorer Americans were actually better off and it was primarily the rich who were less advantaged by the price rise. The importance of continuous investment in training is not fully understood by all but the most advanced corporations. There is considerable scope for increasing awareness in areas such as self-employment opportunities, the linkage between education and career development, management practices, and foreign trade opportunities. Ignorance and superstition concerning drugs, crime, ethnic and race relations, the environment, health, education, child care, and the life of the elderly demoralize the population and make effective social action difficult in these areas. These problems can be minimized by educating the public to understand the changes taking place and to adopt appropriate new behaviours.

Raising awareness internationally

Public opinion is an even more important determinant at the international level, since the authority of global institutions is still quite limited. Rising ethnic and nationalistic sentiments threaten the integrity of states and impede progress toward regional cooperation and global governance in many countries, because their populations lack reliable information regarding the enormous costs of political and economic fragmentation. The global debate over the Uruguay Round of GATT has been obscured by lack of clear information regarding its impact on the countries involved. International negotiations on debt, aid and the environment are complicated by lack of awareness about the opportunities that greater economic integration will generate for all nations. International institutions, non-governmental agencies and the international media play an important role in providing information to the world community, but there are still huge gaps to be filled in all fields. A conscious and systematic effort is required at the international level to put in place both the institutions and the technology for information superhighways needed to support peace, democracy and sustainable development in the twenty-first century.

Building Social Organization for Development

The achievement of peace, food security and full employment cannot be accomplished without more fully utilizing one of the most creative and productive of all human resources – organization. The march of humanity is marked by the development of larger-scale, more complex and more efficient types of organizations to serve higher and wider social needs. Advances in the technology of organization, as much as advances in the technology of production, have been responsible for global progress during the present century and, especially, during the post-war period.

We have argued earlier that establishment of effective and lasting peace requires a radical restructuring of the existing institutions for global governance. Unless and until the UN comes to embody in its own functioning the principles of representative democracy, it cannot hope to play a leading role in maintaining peace and freedom in the world. As government and political leaders know only too well, an organization with responsibility but without authority is doomed to failure. Unless UN member states invest international institutions with the necessary authority and meet their financial commitments to support them, the world will continue to drift and flounder, powerless to oppose petty dictators and ruthless aggression. Unless a cooperative world military force comes into existence, every country will continue to be burdened with the enormous expense and insecurity characteristic of the old system.

Perhaps more than any other institution, the military has understood and demonstrated the enormous power of organization to accomplish a goal. The Gulf War was a dramatic illustration of the importance of reliable information, perfect planning, logistical support systems, effective chains of command and swift responsiveness to changing situations. *If humankind could mobilize and apply the same efficiency to the war on poverty and unemployment that it has exhibited in preparing for and waging military wars against each other, very soon there would be no more poverty or unemployment to fight.* During the Second World War Ford Motors converted from manufacture of cars for the masses to making trucks and airplanes for the military, producing B-24 bombers at the rate of one per hour from a single production plant. If conversion from civilian to military production could be carried out by so many countries within one or two years, it must be possible to convert the military from war-based to peace-based applications, and defence industries from military to civilian production, within half a decade. That requires human resourcefulness in organizational innovation.

Organization is the means by which people work together cooperatively to achieve common goals and, in the process, to serve society in a wide range of functions. The achievement of food security and full employment depends on the establishment of new types of public and private organizations – commercial, financial, industrial, export, research, educational and training. These institutions are needed to encourage, support, standardize, regulate and control development activities. New institutions lie behind the success of most major development achievements. India's Green Revolution was as much a product of new quasi-governmental organizations created for supplying inputs, warehousing and marketing as it was of new farm technology. India's revolution in milk production was propelled by the rapid proliferation of producer cooperatives. Thirty years ago government was the only agency capable of setting up and managing activities on so massive a scale. Today the society is more developed and many of these functions can be handled more efficiently in the private sector. In either case, organization must play a central role.

Wherever countries fail to live up to their natural potential, some institutional gap will be found that prevents new activities from taking off. In examining the potentials of commercial agriculture and agro-exports in India, ICPF identified critical missing links in the organization of production, transfer of technology, training, and the storage, processing, marketing and distribution of perishable commodities. Extension of proven systems can significantly accelerate development. The establishment of a new type of institution – the township and village industries – in China, and the unique system for linking them with scientific institutions, made possible the country's phenomenal achievements in rural enterprise and employment generation. These enterprises now represent 16.5 per cent of all businesses in China and employ 22 per cent of the workforce. Institutional innovations of this type are possible in every state and every country. A comparative study of institutions and systems in more and less developed regions and countries for every major sector will make it possible to construct accurate scales and reliable road maps for more rapid development.

In the countries of Eastern Europe and the former Soviet Union, the social institutions that served under the centralized command system need to be transformed out of recognition, or entirely replaced, in order to support a market-oriented system. Attempts at economic reform that focus primarily on changing laws and public policy without creating the necessary institutional infrastructure cannot succeed. Thousands of systems that have been fashioned by human resourcefulness are needed to support economic activity in different fields. The system of warehouse receipts enables American grain traders to purchase unseen crops with full confidence in their quality. The absence of this simple system retards trade on the recently established commodity markets in Russia and other CIS countries. A complete listing of essential institutions, small and large, should be compiled, based on the experience of other nations, and plans drawn up for introducing them.

Thus far, the development of social organizations, like the development of technologies, has been partial, piecemeal and sectoral, leaving large gaps between parallel and interrelated activities and institutions. This is especially evident at the international level where the organization of the collective social life of humanity is rudimentary and fragmentary, though far more complete than it was a few decades ago. In spite of the phenomenal growth in global communications, transportation, commerce, finance and tourism, it is still more difficult to carry out most activities internationally than it is domestically, because the international activities are not as well organized. For instance, transfer of technology still involves a process that is largely trial and error. Firms in developing countries seeking to acquire the best available technology for importation or acquisition have to search at considerable expenditure of time and money to discover what is available within their own country as well as overseas. The process of identifying and commercially transferring technology can be vastly simplified and accelerated by the establishment of international technology transfer corporations, sponsored by UN agencies such as UNESCO and UNIDO, specializing in all major fields of technology. These corporations should be operated on a commercial, for-profit basis, though governments of developing countries could become shareholders in order to promote their formation. Each corporation could undertake a detailed study of available technologies in its field and offer to assist corporate customers in developing countries in selecting the most appropriate technology to meet their needs. The corporations could also acquire the rights to important technologies with large-scale applications and then market them widely.

Velocity of social forces

Speed is a powerful engine for development and an important index of organizational efficiency and effectiveness. The higher the level of organization and development, the faster everything moves. The more developed the society, the faster it communicates new ideas and new information, develops new technologies and products, establishes new systems and institutions, adopts new policies and laws, transports goods, delivers services and carries out activities. Money, information, education, technology, public opinion, training, administrative decisions, transport, and communication are powerful social forces and resources. Their productivity can be increased by increasing the speed with which they are employed, in the same way that land productivity can be raised by increasing cultivation from one to two cropping seasons per year.

In the most industrially advanced nations, the velocity of money is roughly 2.5 to 3 times higher than in the average developing country. Removing administrative red tape and inefficiencies in the banking system can multiply the use value and productivity of real money, because the same money can be utilized for more transactions. The same is true for information, technology, training, transport and other factors. Increasing the speed of dissemination of information and new technology can accelerate the creation of new businesses and new jobs. In many developing countries, inefficient bureaucracies are slow to take decisions, issue licences, review applications, sanction loans, and amend legislation. This inefficiency directly impacts on the pace of development. Streamlining and expediting decision making and the movement of other social resources is a highly effective strategy for spurring development. *Comparative scales need to be created to measure the movement of each of these social forces within and between nations. Strategies can be evolved to stimulate more rapid overall development by directly acting to increase the velocity of these forces up to ten-fold or even more.*

Progressive Attitudes

The world we live in today is an external expression of our inner attitudes. The world we aspire towards can be realized only by acquiring the attitudes corresponding to those achievements. Every political leader knows the power of attitudes. Great leaders possess the power to change them. Many of those who frankly acknowledge that external limitations such as money and technology are not insurmountable barriers to changing the world erect an alternative myth of inner determinism by insisting that the attitudes of people, and especially their leaders, cannot be changed.

In contrast, we view attitudes as one of the greatest of human resources, one that possesses a remarkable capacity for adaptation. Over the past two decades, we have witnessed and been parties to a radical change in attitudes of people, leaders and nations around the world regarding preservation of the environment. It would have been difficult to conceive in 1970 that, in spite of the myriad technological difficulties and powerful economic interests at stake, the entire world would make such a dramatic shift of attitude so quickly. This change was not brought about from above by enlightened leadership, but rather from below in response to a swelling tide of public awareness and concern, growing as a result of the work of countless individuals, voluntary agencies and research institutions projected through the media, confirmed by the findings of the UN World Commission on Environment and Development, embodied in the specific resolutions of the Earth Summit and in the growing body of environmental laws being adopted by every country, and now commonly incorporated in the educational curricula at every level.

The changes called for in this report require changes of attitude of this magnitude. But no longer is it necessary for a great visionary leader to espouse a new attitude. The higher general levels of public education, the worldwide extension of the media and the active initiative of literally thousands of institutions serving the public interest can exert a powerful force for change, which sooner or later political leaders will accept and espouse.

What is the shift in attitudes demanded to achieve global peace and prosperity?

- From a competitive, egocentric, state-centred attitude toward national security, that seeks to enhance security for some nations at the expense of the rest of the world, to an attitude of true global co-operation for collective human security.

- From demanding that other nations grant democratic rights to their people to a willingness to extend democratic principles to the governance of international institutions.

- From preoccupation with problems and limitations to an appreciation of the opportunities for more rapid development.

- From wanting to meet people's minimum needs to wanting to help them realize their maximum potentials.

- From the attitude that everything is determined by external constraints – money, other nations, political leaders, the general public – to the attitude that everything is determined by our inner resourcefulness and that there are no limits to what it can accomplish.

- From viewing the developing world as a problem or a burden to viewing it as a vast untapped potential for global progress.

- From feeling that those who cannot find jobs must be paid social welfare to the attitude that everyone must be offered opportunities for gainful employment.

Cultural Values and Development

The growing violence, more and more visible disparities between rich and poor, and large-scale destruction of the environment cited in this report have raised widespread concern that the present course of development is undermining the cultural as well as the natural environment for human development. A careful analysis of the relationship between culture and development reveals that cultural values are the essential foundation for all lasting social achievement.

The security, stability, productivity, growth and sustainability of society are determined by its values. This report calls upon nations and the international community to make a conscious shift to values that can generate greater domestic and international security, higher rates of sustainable growth, and more equitable distribution of benefits for all. The insistence on immediate abolition of war, eradication of poverty, democratic human rights and full employment expresses a commitment to the pre-eminent values of human life, social and economic as well as political freedom, and the development of the full potential of the individual. The achievement of these high human values also requires the achievement of a large number of physical, organizational, social and psychological values: higher productivity, better quality, more efficient utilization of resources, faster speed, more systematic functioning, improved coordination and cooperation, punctuality, cleanliness, open-mindedness, tolerance, harmony and a host of other values essential for high achievement in any field. Therefore, we have stressed repeatedly the importance of the value of integration in the formulation of strategies, of maximum utilization of human and social as well as material and technological resources, of greater speed and organization, and other values.

Values are a powerful instrument to spur development. They are goals or standards that set the direction and mobilize the collective cultural energies of the society for great accomplishment. They prompt us to strive for the maximum that is conceivable, rather than the minimum that is achievable. Values form the basis for the tremendous developmental achievements of the past two hundred years, such as the Japanese commitment to teamwork and consensus, the American devotion to enterprise and innovation, the German dedication to quality, and the Dutch commitment to partnership with other people, rather than exploitation. Development is retarded by the slow pace at which new values are acquired, which normally requires a change of generation. But values can also be consciously transmitted through education in order to abridge the time needed for transition. The efforts over the last ten years to implement the value of environmental security illustrate the range of knowledge, information, attitudes, institutions, systems, and skills needed to achieve any high value in life. The recommendations presented in this report are intended to form a basis for identifying and providing the values, attitudes, organizations and skills needed to achieve peace and prosperity at the dawn of the third millennium.

It is well known that societies which are able to harness their cultural energies for development tend to progress very rapidly. Yet at the same time, we know that cultural factors can also be a barrier to rapid progress. Clinging to the external forms and norms of behaviour which distinguish one culture from another generates resistance to progress, whereas the inner content of culture is a powerful engine for collective achievement. Customs are the external form of culture, values are the inner content. The customs vary widely, but the values are universal.

The controversy over the relationship between culture and development is complicated by the fact that development both creates and destroys cultural forms and values. Every developmental achievement results in an abandonment of old behaviours and attitudes, and the acceptance of new ones. Development destroys survival-based, traditional values and creates achievement-oriented, progressive values. Over the last two centuries in countries around the world development has strengthened expansive values that encourage greater freedom, tolerance, individual initiative, self-confidence and self-respect, dynamism, risk-taking, efficiency, punctuality, organization, communication and cooperation, open-mindedness and respect for new ideas, innovation and creativity. At the same time development has weakened values that support respect for tradition and hierarchy, seniority and authority, self-effacement and humility, patience and perseverance, generosity and self-sacrifice. The nineteenth century tolerated values based on the exploitation by people over people through slavery, colonialism and war, and the domination of nature by man. The guiding values for the coming century are freedom and respect for the individual, social equity, tolerance of human diversity and harmony with the environment.

Development is widely regarded as the cause of moral decline and increasing corruption, crime and violence. These negative consequences are primarily due to the fact that freedom has been extended to vast sections of the population which were confined in the past by rigid social barriers and minimum expectations, so they never had need or occasion to embrace the values they now eschew. The earlier self-restraint has been replaced by a self-assertion that has not yet acquired the productive values needed for achievement. Rising expectations enhance this tendency. While it is true that corruption is more prevalent today than ever before, it is also true that the entire global economy functions on the basis of a faith, honesty, openness and tolerance that would have been inconceivable in the past. We mourn the loss of cloistered values, which were very often accompanied by narrow rigidity and provincialism, while failing to recognize the enormous growth in positive human values that has made possible the incredible progress of the past few decades.

In past centuries cultural values were handed down to future generations through the family. Education, which now focuses on the transfer of information, ideas and mental skills, can also impart development-oriented values such as open-mindedness, initiative and innovation. Integration and tolerance of diversity are crucial values for the further development of the human community. Yet the increasing speed of globalization has accentuated a contrary tendency toward increasing fragmentation. The pull of fragmentation cannot be countered solely at the political level. Education – both formal and public – is the best means for rapidly communicating and imparting the benefits of integration to the largest numbers of people.

In order fully to harness cultural potentials for development, we need to understand better the natural process of value formation in society, to discover the circumstances and conditions under which new values are accepted, and the factors that retard or facilitate this process. In other words, we need to evolve a theory of value formation which will ultimately enable us to consciously identify and instil values that are most conducive and supportive of a peaceful, prosperous life for all humanity. The collective progress of humankind will achieve its maximum velocity when we have discovered how to consciously accelerate the process of values acquisition. The role of the UNESCO Commission on Culture and Development can make a valuable contribution to our understanding of this most important issue.

Strategies for Developing Human Resourcefulness

The following strategies can be carried out by both governmental and non-governmental agencies at the national and international level to achieve the goals set forth in this report:

International level

Shift resources from defence to human resource development: Worldwide, massive investment is needed to improve the quantity and quality of education and training. A substantial portion of these resources will have to come from reduced military spending. But as recent experience illustrates, savings in defence spending will not automatically go to this sector. The UN Social Summit should adopt specific goals for reducing military expenditure worldwide and channelling a specific percentage of the savings into education, vocational training, public information and other programmes for development of human resources. Each country should set similar goals. The Commission recommends that a minimum of 10 per cent of the reductions in defence expenditure be invested in education.

2 *Comprehensive, human-centred theory of development:* An important shift in thinking has taken place from regarding development primarily in terms of economic growth to greater emphasis on the human welfare and development of people. But development is not only a set of goals or material achievements – it is a social process by which human beings progressively develop their capacities and release their energies for higher levels of material achievement, social and cultural advancement, and psychological fulfilment. New theory is needed that focuses on the dynamic role of information, attitudes, social institutions and cultural values in the development process. An international effort should be initiated at the forthcoming UN Social Summit to evolve a comprehensive, human-centred theory of individual and social development that will lead to the formulation of more effective strategies to accelerate the development process. UNDP's approach to human security and sustainable development is an important contribution to this effort.

3 *Social organization index:* It is now widely recognized that a country's social organization or 'social capital' is a key determinant of its development. Measures and indices such as UNDP's Human Development Index that provide a comparative national assessment of progress on key dimensions of development generate greater awareness and stimulate greater political will and social initiative to improve performance. In a similar manner, UNDP should commission a programme to construct a Social Organization or Social Capital Index consisting of one or more scales to measure the organizational development of countries covering major sectors such as commerce, industry,

agriculture, education, health care, and technical training. The index should evaluate the level of social organization in terms of its overall support to activities in each of these fields as well as the number and quality of institutions providing this support. Where objective measures are not possible, a rank or relative scale will suffice. These scales can then be utilized by countries to assess their own level of organizational development and to identify key areas where improvement is most needed.

Scale of Productive Skills: UNESCO should commission studies to construct a series of scales to measure the level of key skills in societies at different stages of development. The scales should assess the quantitative and qualitative development of key physical, technical, vocational and organizational skills, so that countries can more accurately identify high priority areas for training.

4

Developing countries

Eradicate illiteracy: All developing countries should commit themselves to achieving UNESCO's goal of eradicating illiteracy by the year 2000, engaging the participation of educational institutions, non-governmental agencies, military and national service corps personnel.

5

Educate the girl child: Central and state governments should give the highest possible priority to raising the educational achievements of female children. The benefits of educating girls on health, nutrition, population control, and family welfare should be widely publicized. A comprehensive strategy for achieving this goal should be drawn up and presented at the Fourth World Conference on Women in Beijing in 1995.

6

Emphasize techniracy: While we have argued strongly for the importance of general education, rising numbers of educated unemployed justify a shift in government spending toward greater investment in vocational training. Basic technical and vocational skills are in short supply in most developing countries and this shortage acts as a significant constraint to more rapid growth in incomes and jobs. Efforts must be intensified to deliver these skills in an accessible

7

manner to all sections, especially the rural workforce, by establishing an extensive system training institutes at the local level throughout the country, offering a wide range of basic technical and vocational training. Each country should prepare an inventory of key physical, commercial, educational, organizational and technical skills needed to raise the country to the level of nations at the next higher level of development. Place maximum emphasis on investments to raise the quality and quantity of skills to that level.

8 *Development-oriented education:* The growing problem of educated unemployment in developing countries reflects the wide disparity between the knowledge taught in the classroom and that required for self-employment and individual achievement in society. Development education should be introduced at all levels of the curricula of schools, colleges and universities in every country to impart a greater knowledge of the process of development the society is passing through and the opportunities which it presents for individual accomplishment, with emphasis on entrepreneurship and self-employment.

9 *Disseminate information:* Governments, in cooperation with public foundations, research institutes, universities and voluntary agencies should identify gaps in public awareness regarding opportunities and achievements in agriculture, industry, trade, management, science, technology, nutrition, health, education, employment, law and social welfare. National, state and local programmes should be initiated to promote wider dissemination through governmental and non-governmental channels and the media.

10 *Enhancing social capital:* Introduce measures to increase the velocity (speed of transmission and utilization) of productive social forces – including money, information, decision making, the application and dissemination of technology, transportation and communication – to increase productivity and stimulate development. Identify missing organizational links needed to raise the country's performance to that of more developed nations in agriculture, commerce, industry, exports, invention, marketing, distri-

bution, consumer and commercial credit, housing, health, education, training and other key activities. Combined teams of researchers and business professionals in each country should identify innovative systems successfully employed by other nations to improve performance in key sectors of the economy and propose steps to introduce as many as possible.

Industrial nations

Raise minimum standards of education: Unemployment is highest among those with the least education. Extending the minimum compulsory level of education by two years will improve the educational qualifications of the workforce, slow the entrance of youth into the labour market, generate new jobs in education, and better equip the next generation for coping with the increasing complexity and sophistication of life in the coming century. Intensify efforts to reduce high school drop-outs and encourage greater enrolment in higher education.

11

Management training: The ability to manage people, time, technology, money and other resources has become a critically important skill for achievement in modern society. The emergence of free market forces and globalization of business require new and improved management skills in every country. Introduce management training as an essential part of the high school and college level curriculum in order to impart essential planning, organizational and financial skills to all students.

12

Education for the future: Accelerate efforts to evolve new educational systems adapted to the needs and conditions of life in the next century. Emphasis should be placed on developing the capacity for original thinking, acquisition of higher values, and psychological attitudes that lead to achievement and personal fulfilment.

13

8

A CALL FOR LEADERSHIP IN THOUGHT THAT LEADS TO ACTION

The vision of opportunity presented in this report is based neither on blind hope nor on scientific projection. Mere wishing has no power to accomplish and science has not evolved far enough for projections with regard to the complex processes that govern global political, economic and social development. And although it is true that very often our hopes have been disappointed, it is equally true that frequently our fears have proved misplaced. Our attempt has been to present what is imminently possible, not what is immediately inevitable – though we believe that much of what we have written will inevitably come to pass in one form or another, because it represents a natural fulfilment of social movements that have been preparing for a long time and continue to gain momentum.

The next two years are a propitious time for creating the leadership in thought that leads to purposeful collective action. Three major events will bring together world leaders from both governmental and non-governmental agencies to develop strategies for meeting the major challenges confronting humankind. At the International Conference on Population and Development and the World Conference on Women, concrete steps must be taken to generate greater educational, training and employment opportunities for the poor, and most especially for females – the best-known methods for eradicating poverty and bringing down the rate of population growth. In the absence of effective measures, expanding population will pose increasing threats to human security worldwide. Therefore, substantial resources must be transferred now from defensive military preparedness for some possible future conflict to an all-out war on poverty today. That is the best investment in the future security for all people.

Fifty years after the founding of the United Nations, world leaders will come together in Copenhagen in March 1995 to examine the impact of the UN on global politics, economics and human security, and to develop strategies for converting the unfulfilled social aspirations of the UN into reality. Issues of international governance are now pressing and ripe for action. Although they may be too complex and important to be dealt with comprehensively at the Social Summit, the occasion should be utilized for placing the restructuring of the United Nations and the international security system at the top of the international agenda.

Strong measures are needed at the national level to generate sufficient employment opportunities in both industrial and developing countries. But international cooperation and coordination are essential to ensure we are actually creating more jobs and not just intensifying competition for those that already exist. The Social Summit is also the right platform for launching a World Employment Programme to generate one billion new jobs worldwide during the next decade.

Ironically, the passing of the Cold War has heightened the incidence of violence in human affairs, partly because of greater freedom and removal of the external constraints that had earlier prevented people from expressing pent-up frustrations over their unfulfilled expectations. Tolerance of diversity and pluralism is an essential foundation for the exercise of democratic freedoms and achievement of economic prosperity. The greatest achievement of the twentieth century has been the growing recognition of the pre-eminent value of the human being. In recognition of the need for promoting greater tolerance in societies around the world, the UN has declared 1995 the Year for Tolerance. This can only be achieved by recognizing that the forces which oppose us are not other people, but our common enemies – ignorance, egoism, poverty and greed. As world leaders at the Earth Summit in 1992 supported a Convention on Biological Diversity designed to protect and preserve genetic diversity in the living world, at the upcoming Social Summit a similar Convention on Human Diversity should be adopted to protect and preserve the rich variety of human cultures, which are the finest fruit of civilization and the moving force for our future progress.

Governments alone cannot accomplish these goals. It is the collective responsibility of all humankind. The advance guard of those who have already achieved high levels of prosperity in both the industrial and developing countries have a special responsibility to assist the rest of humanity to do so as well. Nor is it any longer feasible for a portion of society to benefit to the exclusion of the majority. A world in which 20 per cent of the population enjoy 84 per cent of the income, while another 20 per cent struggle for survival on a mere 1.4 per cent, can never provide a secure and sustainable way of life for humankind. Poverty is the greatest source of instability and strife and it will not honour any boundaries. We have all the resources necessary – intellectual, financial, technological, and organizational – to arrive at a system that guarantees the right of each individual to human security in its widest meaning – peace, food, employment and education for all. Those who now possess and enjoy affluence hold it temporarily in trust with a responsibility to use it to build a better world for all. An investment by the one billion people already living in affluence in all countries of $1000 *per capita* could form a trillion dollar Trust Fund to create a world without poverty.

Looking back over the past decades, centuries and millennia, we certainly cannot say that our progress has been as rapid as it possibly could have been. What we have achieved by the last decade of the twentieth century could have been accomplished decades or perhaps even centuries earlier. There was no compelling necessity that we fight two world wars before recognizing the need for global governance. It was not inevitable that we fabricate more than 50,000 nuclear weapons before realizing that they have robbed us of the very security we sought to achieve by them. We cannot say that the collapse of the Eastern European economies was an essential and unavoidable step in their transition to greater freedom and prosperity.

On the other hand, wherever humanity has set itself with determination to achieve something great, sooner or later it has accomplished its goal. In fact, that inner determination and commitment seem to create external resources and opportunities where earlier there were none. The intense effort of countless dedicated individuals and institutions to grow more food at a time when explosive population growth threatened the world with unprecedented famine leading to the creation of the high-yielding varieties of wheat and rice is a consummate illustration of this truth. So too, in looking forward, what justification do we have for saying that it need take decades to eliminate war or hunger or poverty from the face of the earth, just because it has not gone more quickly in the past?

It is this latter truth that we would wish to become the guiding principle of the next millennium. Instead of waiting for calamity to compel our progress, we can consciously and collectively develop the inner determination not only to overcome the problems that presently confront us but also to seek out every opportunity to better our present accomplishments and discover more of our as yet unborn human capacities.

The choice is ours and, if we choose, what would otherwise take decades or centuries can be accomplished much sooner. Standing on the verge of the third millennium, we have the capacity to bring the future towards us by seeking with greater eagerness and determination to discover more of the infinite resources within ourselves.

9

Executive Summary

The report examines the global issues of international security, employment, food and transition in Eastern Europe and identifies a range of 'uncommon opportunities' that have arisen since the end of the Cold War to evolve lasting solutions to these problems. It brings out the linkage between peace, democratization, development and the environment; calls for a restructuring of the UN on democratic lines; proposes a shift from a state-centred, competitive approach to national security to a global cooperative security system supported by a standing world army; calls for acceptance of employment as a fundamental human right; traces the positive contribution of technological development and trade to job creation; sets forth the basic elements of a world employment programme to generate one billion new jobs in industrial and developing countries; views the Third World as a driving force for expansion of the world economy; argues that agriculture can be a powerful engine for employment generation and economic growth in the developing world; presents an alternative approach to transition in Eastern Europe; and stresses the fundamental role of education, information and organization in development. The report challenges the view that external factors are the main determinants of social progress. It approaches development as a human process by which individuals and societies acquire and express greater awareness, knowledge, skills, values and institutional capabilities to promote their material, social and psychological progress and views diversity and pluralism in human societies as a potential force for integration. The Fiftieth Anniversary of the UN is the time to act on all these opportunities, and to establish a global convention on human diversity and a global trust fund for a world without poverty.

The astonishing events of the past few years, beginning with the fall of the Berlin Wall and the lifting of the Iron Curtain, make this a time of uncommon opportunities for accelerated progress on issues of concern to all humankind. These events removed the physical barriers to freedom for hundreds of millions of people and the physical threat of nuclear war that loomed over the whole world. But they have also shattered decades-old ideas, beliefs, attitudes and conceptions, leaving us without a clear vision either of our past or our future. Without an understanding of the forces and processes that have brought us to the present, and without an intellectual map to the opportunities and challenges of the future, there is a real danger that the remaining fragments of out-moded ideas, attitudes and structures will lead us backwards rather than forwards or, at the very least, prevent us from seeing, seizing and fully benefiting from this unprecedented occasion.

International commissions set up by governments, or international agencies, such as the UN, which study pressing issues of global concern are bound by the views and policies of the governments that constitute them. Thus, Robert McNamara proposed the establishment of the Brandt Commission as an independent initiative nearly 20 years ago to look beyond the horizons fixed by government policy and priorities, which resulted in a new vision and perception of an interdependent world. The International Commission on Peace and Food is such an independent initiative to seek a fresh perspective that extends beyond the present purview of governments. Like the world in general, the Commission has been overtaken by events. Originally conceived to utilize the growing international consensus on the need to abolish hunger as a lever to promote disarmament, recent progress on disarmament has outpaced our highest expectations. Eradication of poverty has emerged as the most essential condition for building a stable peace.

Several factors make this an auspicious time for breaking new ground and seeking higher accomplishments. The peaceful termination of the confrontation between East and West has lowered the mental barriers that divided the world into opposing ideological camps and prevented either side from critically evaluating their own and opposing viewpoints. This provides us with an opportunity to experiment boldly with new ways to reconcile and synthesize the forces of individual freedom and social responsibility. This is evidenced already by the movement of economic liberalism spreading throughout the developing world and the revolution of democratization that began in Latin America during the early 1980s, then exploded into prominence to sweep away authoritarianism in Eastern Europe, and is now washing away three decades of post-colonial authoritarian rule in Africa, where it has already raised 15 new democratic states in four years. South Africa is the most recent and inspiring example of this new freedom movement.

The aftermath of the Cold War has also given greater impetus to another powerful current that is stirring the world from below – a revolution of rising expectations that gained prominence among the

Western middle-class after the Second World War, but has now acquired global proportions among the masses on every continent – reaching peak intensity in the great cities of Asia, Latin America and to a lesser extent Eastern Europe and Africa – unleashing an unprecedented burst of human initiative, a clamour and striving for more comforts and better lives, and a growing impatience and assertiveness, as reflected in the growing incidence of urban and ethnic violence and mini-wars. No longer are the poor satisfied or resigned to their condition, or willing to wait indefinitely for improvement.

These powerful currents, triggered and supported by the onset of the Information Age, are quietly sweeping through the world at the present time, awakening aspirations and stirring energies to action. They bear with them great potentials and grave challenges. A global community of democratic nations is the greatest safeguard against war, for history confirms that liberal democracies do not wage war against one another. So too, is it the greatest safeguard against famine, for no democratic nation with a free press has suffered from famine in the past five decades. The climate of freedom which democracy generates is highly conducive to the market economy and rapid economic development. Rising expectations are a product of growing political and social freedom, and more education translating into higher economic aspirations. They move people to cast off the shackles of inertia, complacency and resignation, which are the handmaidens of poverty, and rise up to fulfil their own economic destiny. The energy and aspirations released by these two movements, if properly harnessed and directed, are enough to rebuild the world in a brighter image; if left blocked from constructive expression and frustrated in their seeking, they are enough to destroy the fragile peace and limited prosperity we now enjoy. Both the potentials and the challenges unleashed by these two great forces urge us, indeed compel us, to a more far-sighted vision and to bolder enterprises.

The new international political climate has also created the possibility of a massive redirection of resources from defence to development. Already military spending has declined by one-third from a peak of $1200 billion in 1987. The hoped-for windfall peace dividend has not met expectations, primarily because a large portion of the cuts were absorbed by the decline in economic activity in the USSR and Eastern Europe, and by efforts to control the US budget deficit. However, an additional $400 billion a year in savings is practicable and could generate substantial cash resources for deployment to address pressing problems. Combined with a conscious and creative effort to utilize for development purposes other resources possessed by the military –

personnel, R & D capacities, training facilities and teaching staff, organization and management, logistics, transport and communication, engineering and technical facilities – we have the material capacity to generate prosperity and a safe environment for all in the coming decade.

The perspective the world seeks must be based on a greater understanding of the inextricable linkages between peace, democratization, development, equity and the environment. None of these great goals can be achieved without corresponding progress towards the others. Today, the greatest security threats are social in origin and cannot be mitigated or controlled by greater defence preparedness. Partial solutions will lead, at best, to temporary achievements fraught with unwanted side-effects that perpetuate the problems we seek to solve or generate new problems in their wake, such as the environmental pollution generated by application of industrial technologies, the population explosion resulting from improved public health, and the economic collapse generated by a uni-dimensional approach to a complex political, social and economic transition in Eastern Europe. Viewing famine in narrow terms as shortage of food ignores the important role of democratic institutions, a free press and employment opportunities in eliminating famine. Comprehensive, integrated solutions alone can unravel the knots that make it impossible to establish peace when more than a billion people remain hungry and impoverished, while at the same time making peace an essential precondition for the eradication of hunger and poverty. ICPF has approached major problems by viewing them as parts of an integrated whole that can only be addressed by concerted action on multiple fronts. The report emphasizes that human attitudes, values, awareness, energy and skill are prime movers of the development process.

What are the foundations of this new intellectual perspective and what sort of strategies, actions and results will it lead to? It requires a change in the way we look at and think of familiar things like war, weaponry, security, the role of the military, developing countries, democracy, agriculture, industrialization. First, we have to awaken from the millennia-old nightmare that war is a natural and inevitable part of human existence, which can perhaps be mitigated or kept far from our shores, but never really mastered or eliminated. In a world now free from major opposing military blocs fighting proxy wars in the developing world to maintain their perceived security interests, *there is no insurmountable material or technical or political obstacle to the complete abolition of war as an instrument of national policy and of the incidence of war in international affairs. It requires a determined will and the fashioning of effective institutional arrangements for enforcement. The complete abolition of the production, possession or use of nuclear weapons is a first essential step toward this most desirable goal.*

Second, in the interests of human rights, global peace and prosperity, the movement of democratization must be carried to its logical conclusion. The sovereignty of nations, derived as it is from the sovereignty of their people, has to be based on a form of government that grants self-determination to those people. Whatever its inadequacies, representative democracy is the only proven system for extending these rights to all citizens. *A representative, democratic form of government should become the norm and standard in international relations and the minimum requirement for participation in the institutions of the UN system.* Furthermore, this principle that is so essential to achieving peace and prosperity at the national level is also vitally important to the creation of truly viable and effective institutions for global governance. The rule of law, democracy and universal human rights are incompatible with an international system that is still governed by the principle of rule by might. The world fast approaching is a multi-polar world with many centres of economic growth and political influence. An expansion of the Security Council and abolition of the veto power are necessary but not sufficient steps in this direction. If our aspiration is for the establishment of a settled and secure peace and prosperity for all people, and not merely a precariously unstable and temporary absence of war, then *nothing short of a complete restructuring of the UN system along democratic lines will suffice.*

Third, there must be a shift from the egocentric, state-centred competitive security system that has governed relations between nations over the past century. This system is founded on the premise that each nation should strive to arm itself militarily against possible sources of aggression, which in turn creates a greater sense of insecurity in other countries, thus leading them similarly to arm themselves. This inherently destabilizing approach to international security was a natural outgrowth of the security arrangements put in place after the two world wars, resulting in the arms race and the confrontation between East and West. It must give way to a new cooperative security paradigm based on the principle that the security of each nation can be enhanced by measures that provide greater security for all nations through lower, rather than higher, levels of defence expenditure and armaments, and by the establishment of a permanent standing military force, a world army, that guarantees the security of all member nations against external aggression.

A fourth new perspective is a change in the way the industrial and developing nations perceive their mutual interests. The old view of a Third World of politically and economically weak, aid-dependent countries is a vestige of the past that blinds us to immense opportunity. While growth is slow or stagnating in much of the West, it is gaining momentum in one developing country after another. The phenomenal progress of the East Asian 'Tigers' is now being outdone in speed and sheer magnitude by China. India and other nations are destined to follow these examples within the decade. *In the coming years, the so-called Third World will be the major engine driving the growth of the world economy and, as a result, the greatest potential source of economic growth and job creation for the industrial nations.* The measures presented in this report to accelerate development and employment generation in developing countries can be a highly effective strategy for ensuring growth and prosperity for all in the next century.

Fifth, nowhere are we in greater need of fresh thinking than when it comes to the issue of employment. So much have we come to accept the inviolability of the economic rules and systems fashioned haphazardly, and often unthinkingly, for our convenience that we now feel helpless to improve or alter the structures we have created. The very notion of an economic system that provides security and wealth for some while denying it to others – regardless of whether that denial is on the basis of heredity, first discovery or superior capacity – is an idea unworthy of a world that speaks of reason and justice, in the same way that slavery and colonialism are now considered unacceptable. Furthermore, it is unsustainable in an increasingly democratic world, where political leaders cannot resort to force to suppress the outrage of a rapidly growing minority of the economically disenfranchised unemployed. In a world where people are responsible for their own livelihoods and economic well-being, employment is not a privilege, it is an absolute necessity. The system that fails to offer job opportunities to all is a failed system. Nor can we cast blame on some inevitable flaw in the market system. Like all others, it has been fashioned from our ideas and values. If we change the priorities, we can make it work differently. *The change that is needed is first of all a recognition that employment is a fundamental human right that must be guaranteed to all.*

Full employment would seem more appealing if it were not so widely believed to be impossible. The Western world has come to accept the myth that technology is inevitably eliminating jobs. Again, it is intellectual limitations that stand in the way of progress more than material constraints. Although it is certainly true that technology eliminates jobs, at the same time it creates them, and on balance it creates many more than it destroys. Otherwise, how can we account for the 400 per cent increase in employment in the technology-intensive United States during this century, or the projected 21 per cent increase expected over the next 15 years? While the total percentage of the workforce employed is near to historical peak levels, unemployment has risen in the West due to historically high labour force participation rates coupled with a number of temporary factors that will subside during the decade. The notion that the amount of work available in society is fixed has to give way to the realization that society can create real demand for more employment. *This report presents a series of practical strategies to stimulate greater demand for labour in industrial and developing nations and provide a viable basis for full employment economies.*

Out-dated thinking about food and agriculture conceals a vast hidden potential. For too long, food has been considered primarily as a means to abolish hunger and meet people's minimum needs, leading the governments and people of many developing countries to overlook its greater role in the process of economic development. Historically, it was rising agricultural productivity and surpluses that gave birth to the Industrial Revolution in Europe. In this century a strategy based on increasing productivity in agriculture has been a driving force for industrialization, job creation, and rising incomes in the fastest-growing nations of East Asia. *Accelerating agricultural development, with the emphasis on value-added commercial crops, is a highly effective strategy for employment generation and industrial growth in developing countries today. Coupled with the elimination of subsidies and protectionist policies for agriculture by industrial countries, ICPF's country-level research indicates that this strategy may be sufficient to stimulate the creation of the billion jobs needed to abolish poverty and unemployment throughout the developing world.* Whatever loss this may entail to the four per cent of the work-force engaged in agriculture in industrial nations will be compensated for many times over by the surging demand for imports of industrial goods and services in developing countries. A structural adjustment is needed in industrial as well as developing countries to abandon anachronistic policies that benefit a few, but curtail the progress of the entire world community, including the nations that employ them.

The need for fresh perspectives and comprehensive strategies is graphically illustrated by the economic decline and social upheaval that has rocked the transition states of Eastern and Central Europe. The courageous initiative of these people to abandon dead rhetoric, reverse narrow attitudes, cast off decrepit structures to embrace new ideas, accept new attitudes and adopt new systems marks the greatest peaceful revolution in history. Yet our common inability to look beyond the mental dichotomy of two out-moded systems – a statist communism that stifled the vitality of its people and a rampant free market capitalism that lives on in Western thought long after it has been abandoned in practice in favour of a more humane system – has led to untold human suffering and a wasteful squandering of the economic potentials of these countries. The temporary supremacy of economic doctrine in human affairs has blinded us to the need for solutions that are at once politically, economically and socially viable. Efforts to guide a multi-dimensional social, political and economic transition through reliance on uni-dimensional strategies, particularly those focused on manipulation of macro-economic policy, are bound to fail. *An alternative approach is needed for the transition in Eastern Europe that builds political and social consensus for rapid change, introduces all the essential elements of a market economy in a balanced manner, gives priority to developing the essential micro-level institutions and skills, recognizes the essential role of government regulation and the special status of agriculture, and reduces reliance on external assistance.*

The most difficult mental shift of all involves our conception and attitudes about ourselves. Humanity has become so creative and prolific in its external accomplishments that we have lost sight of the greatest of all resources – the human being. It is from within ourselves that have sprung all the ideas, technologies, innovations, organizations and activities we regard with such admiration and anxiety. *Most of all, the new perspective the world seeks should be based on a recognition that humankind is the master of its own destiny, that the external limits are not binding on us if we tap the unlimited creative potential of our own inner human resourcefulness.* Educating every human being to see the opportunities beyond the present limits and to discover the potentials within themselves is our most important task, *for true education is leadership in thought.* This education should help us shift from our present preoccupation with problems to a grasping of opportunities and an insistence on actions to exploit them; from an emphasis on meeting minimum needs to a commitment to achieve the maximum which our inner resources and outer potentials make possible.

This leadership in thought necessitates that we first come to understand fully the process by which humankind has evolved to the present level of development, the forces that have propelled or compelled that growth, and the stages and levels of that ascension. Our achievements have been the result of the initiatives and contributions of countless individuals and communities, an unconscious, or at best semi-conscious, process of haphazard trial and error experimentation. In order to proceed more surely and rapidly than in the past, this unconscious process of growth has to be converted into a conscious process of human self-development. We must become conscious of our past achievements so as to hasten and multiply our future accomplishments. *The cumulative experience of many countries over the past five decades needs to be freshly examined to evolve a comprehensive theory and model of development which will clarify the process of human self-discovery and development and serve as an instrument for evolving more effective development strategies to meet the challenges that still confront us.*

These perspectives have been applied in the report to generate specific strategies for accelerating progress on peace, food security, poverty eradication, full employment, social transition and human development. Although the number and range of recommendations is too great to be briefly summarized, the following fifteen strategies represent the central thrust of the Commission's proposals.

Summary of Key Recommendations

Restructuring the UN: The opportunity provided by the Fiftieth Anniversary of the UN should be utilized to examine the restructuring of the UN to make it a more representative and democratically functioning system of international governance, by increasing the number of permanent members of the Security Council, abolition of the veto power, a redefinition of the respective roles and powers of the Security Council and the General Assembly, enhancing the status and powers of the UN Secretary General, and the establishment of democratic guidelines for membership and participation of states in the UN system.

1

Global cooperative security system: The present state-centred competitive security framework must be replaced by a cooperative security system that unconditionally guarantees the security of member nations against acts of external aggression by means of a standing world army, similar in constitution to NATO but open to all countries that practise democratic principles of national governance, contribute financial and defence resources to a common armed force, accept ceilings on national defence expenditure and eschew possession of nuclear weapons.

2

3 *Peace dividend:* A detailed plan should be drawn up by the Security Council for a further 50 per cent reduction in global defence spending before the end of the decade, to a maximum of $400 billion. In addition, all states should conduct studies of the opportunities to re-deploy resources – manpower, educational, scientific and technological, productive and organizational – controlled by the military to combat rural and urban poverty as well as national and global environmental degradation.

4 *Nuclear weapons:* The use of nuclear weapons should be declared by the UN a crime against humanity. Based on the precedent of the Chemical Weapons Treaty, the proposal for a universal ban on the possession of nuclear weapons by any nation should be placed before the Security Council. The five permanent members should agree to the suspension of their veto power on this issue so crucial to the future of humanity.

5 *Full employment:* Partial or incremental measures will not solve the growing problem of unemployment in industrial nations. A radical change in values, priorities and policies – a structural adjustment – is required, based on the recognition that *employment is a fundamental right* of every human being.

Comprehensive strategies coordinated among OECD countries should be implemented to increase public investment to spur economic growth, remove tax disincentives for job creation and the bias towards development of capital-intensive technologies, promote small firms, raise minimum educational and training standards, reorient social security programmes, increase labour market flexibility, and make income distribution more equitable.

6 *One billion jobs in developing countries:* A comprehensive strategy based on the promotion of commercial agriculture, agro-industries and agro-exports, improved marketing, expansion of rural enterprises and the service sector, dissemination of commercial information, extending basic education and upgrading skills can form the basis for creation of one billion jobs in developing countries over the next decade. Achievement of this goal requires that the industrial countries adopt agricultural trade policies designed to enhance the export opportunities of developing nations.

Global employment programme: Neither the industrial nor the developing countries can resolve the problem of unemployment in isolation. The industrial nations require a significant increase in demand, which only the faster-growing developing countries can provide. The latter require greater investment and access to markets, especially for agricultural products and textiles. A global employment programme should be adopted at the 1995 UN Summit, setting forth a plan to expand job creation dramatically worldwide during the rest of the decade. The plan should focus on elimination of protectionist trade policies, debt rescheduling for the poorest debtor nations, accelerated transfer and dissemination of technology, and international cooperation to encourage labour-friendly tax policies.

7

International sustainable development force for food deficit regions: An international development force should be constituted under the UN, consisting of demobilized military personnel and young professionals, trained and equipped to promote people-centred, sustainable development initiatives. The technical and organizational capabilities of this force should be employed to design and implement integrated programmes to upgrade food production and distribution in famine-prone nations by the introduction of effective systems and institutions for planning, administration, education, demonstration and marketing.

8

Model districts: At the forthcoming UN Social Summit, a plan should be adopted for establishing model district programmes in many countries. The central approach is to improve the usage of available natural, technological, human, managerial, institutional and financial resources in a sustainable manner to optimize production, productivity, farm incomes and employment, non-farm occupations, self-employment opportunities, agro-industrial development, exports and expansion of the service sector. The programmes should also cover depressed urban and rural areas in the industrial nations.

9

10 *Eliminate crop losses in the CIS:* In Russia and the other republics of the former USSR, highest priority in agriculture must be given to implementing a comprehensive programme to reduce crop losses, which average between 25 to 50 per cent of total field production for major crops. A viable plan is now available to reduce losses for foodgrains, vegetables and potatoes, eliminating food imports and food shortages within three to five years. The plan requires acquisition of foreign production and storage technology, but depends only marginally on the import of equipment, most of which can be manufactured in domestic defence facilities. In order to be effective, it needs to be supported by a massive public education campaign on the use of new technology to eradicate crop losses combined with demonstration plots on both large-scale and small private farms throughout the country.

11 *Institutional development for economic transitions:* Macroeconomic policy reforms must be complemented by parallel efforts at the micro-level to build up new social institutions to support education and training in entrepreneurial and management skills, a free flow of commercial and technical information, access to credit and marketing assistance for small enterprises, business incubators, industrial estates, quality standards, leasing, franchising, and a wide range of other basic commercial systems.

12 *Global education programme:* A worldwide programme should be launched to improve the quantity and quality of education in both developing and industrial nations. The programme should focus on the achievement of six objectives: eradication of illiteracy by 2000; raising the educational standards of female children to that of males; expanding techniracy by improving basic technical information and productive skills through a network of basic technical institutions using methods of instruction appropriate to the recipients; changes in the school curricula at all levels to reorient education to promote self-employment; raising the minimum levels of education in industrial nations by two years; and evolving education systems now to prepare youth for life in the twenty-first century.

Master plan for debt alleviation: An international agreement should be negotiated to provide debt alleviation for the 60 poorest, most indebted countries. Debt reductions can be based on the current market value of country debt, directly linked to investment by these countries in programmes to expand education, upgrade vocational skills and other investments that attack the root causes of poverty. **13**

Comprehensive, human-centred theory of development: An important shift in thinking has taken place from regarding development primarily in terms of economic growth to greater emphasis on the human welfare and development of people. But development is not only a set of goals or material achievements – it is a social process by which human beings progressively develop their capacities and release their energies for higher levels of material achievement, social and cultural advancement, and psychological fulfilment. A new theory is needed that focuses on the dynamic role of information, attitudes, social institutions and cultural values in the development process. An international effort should be initiated at the forthcoming UN Social Summit to evolve a comprehensive, human-centred theory of individual and social development that will lead to the formulation of more effective strategies to accelerate the development process. **14**

Tolerance, diversity and small arms proliferation: The dramatic increase in the availability and use of small arms has become a highly destabilizing factor, both in industrial and developing countries. Often these weapons are utilized against other ethnic, religious and linguistic groups. Highest priority must be given to controlling and reversing the proliferation of small arms on a parallel with the determined international measures employed to curb hijacking. These weapons should be classified and a UN register created to monitor their manufacture and sale; agreements should be negotiated between major arms suppliers to severely restrict production and sales; and strong sanctions must be instituted to discourage states from abetting small arms proliferation. The year 1995, declared as the International Year for Tolerance, will be an appropriate time to establish a global convention on human diversity and a global trust fund for a world without poverty. **15**

THE COMMISSIONERS

Chairman
M. S. SWAMINATHAN, India – Chairman, M. S. Swaminathan Research Foundation; first World Food Prize Laureate; formerly Chairman, UN Committee on Science and Technology for Development; President, International Union for the Conservation of Nature and Natural Resources; Independent Chairman, FAO Council; Director General, International Rice Research Institute; Secretary of Agriculture, Government of India.

Member Secretary
GARRY JACOBS, USA – Partner, MIRA International Management Consultants, California; Assistant Secretary, The Mother's Service Society, India.

Members
A. T. ARIYARATNE, Sri Lanka – Founder-President, The Sarvodaya Shramadana Movement.

DRAGOSLAV AVRAMOVIC, Yugoslavia – Governor, Central Bank of Yugoslavia; formerly Director of Economic Studies, European Centre for Peace and Development, Belgrade; Director, Development Economics Department, World Bank; Director of the Secretariat, Brandt Commission; Adviser to Secretary General of UNCTAD.

ROSALYNN CARTER, USA – Former First Lady of the USA; co-founder of The Carter Center, Atlanta, Georgia.

UMBERTO COLOMBO, Italy – Chairman, Aurelio Peccei Foundation; formerly Minister of Universities and Scientific Technical Research, Government of Italy; President, European Science Foundation; Chairman, Italian National Agency for New Technology, Energy and Environment; Chairman, Italian Atomic Energy Commission.

ERLING DESSAU, Denmark – Resident Representative, UNDP, Somalia and formerly in Bangladesh, India and Myanmar; Deputy Resident Representative, UNDP, Turkey; Deputy Director, MIS, Bureau of Administration, UNDP Headquarters; Board of Directors, Data for Development, France.

ROBERT VAN HARTEN, Netherlands – President, MIRA International, Netherlands.

JAMES INGRAM, Australia – Visiting Fellow, National Institute of Development Studies, Australian National University; formerly Executive Director, UN World Food Programme; Director General, Australian International Development Assistance Bureau; Australian Ambassador to Canada and Philippines.

LAL JAYAWARDENA, Sri Lanka – Former Director, World Institute of Development Economic Research; Honorary Fellow, King's College, Cambridge; Secretary, Ministry of Finance and Planning, Sri Lanka; Ambassador of Sri Lanka to Belgium, Netherlands, Luxembourg and the European Community.

MARY KING, USA – President, Global Action, Inc.; formerly senior US government official in the Carter Administration responsible for the Peace Corps and domestic national service corps; Winner of 1988 Robert F. Kennedy Memorial Book Award for *Freedom Song*.

MANFRED KULESSA, Germany – Director, Association of the Churches Development Services, Bonn; formerly Managing Director, German Development Service; Director, UNDP, Nepal and China; former Lecturer, University of St. Gallen.

R. MARTIN LEES, UK – Director General, International Committee for Economic Reform and Cooperation; Member, China Council for Cooperation on Environment and Development; formerly UN Assistant Secretary-General for Science and Technology.

UMA LELE, India – Graduate Research Professor, Food Resource and Economics Department, University of Florida; Director, Global Development Initiative of the Carnegie Corporation led by President Carter; Member of the Technical Advisory Committee of the Consultative Group on International Agricultural Research; formerly Manager, African Technical Department, The World Bank.

ROBERT J. MACFARLANE, USA – Partner, MIRA International Management Consultants; Treasurer, The Mother's Service Society, India.

JOHN W. MELLOR, USA – President, JMA, Inc.; formerly Director, International Food Policy Research Institute; Chief Economist, United States Agency for International Development.

VICTOR I. NAZARENKO, Russia – Director, Research Institute of Information and Technical-Economic Studies of Agro-Industrial Complex, Russia. Member of Russian Academy of Agriculture, Economics and Informational Sciences.

ALEXANDER NICONOV, Russia – Director, Agrarian Institute of Russia; formerly President, All-Union Academy of Agricultural Sciences; Director of Stavropol Agricultural Institute; Minister of Agriculture, Latvia.

HER MAJESTY QUEEN NOOR AL-HUSSEIN, Jordan – President, Noor al-Hussein Foundation.

GENERAL OLUSEGUN OBASANJO, Nigeria – Former President of Nigeria; Chairman, Africa Leadership Forum; Member of Eminent Persons Team for Ending Apartheid in South Africa; Africa Prize Laureate for the Sustainable End of Hunger.

ABDUS SALAM, Pakistan – Nobel Laureate in Physics; President, Third World Academy of Sciences; President, Third World Network of Scientific Organizations; formerly Director, International Centre for Theoretical Physics.

JASJIT SINGH, India – Director, Indian Institute for Defence Studies and Analysis; Air Commodore (retired), Indian Air Force; Member, National Security Advisory Board of India; Member, International Commission for a New Asia.

BRIAN W. WALKER, UK – Executive Director, Earthwatch Europe; formerly Director General of OXFAM; President, International Institute for Environment and Development.

EUGENE F. WHELAN, Canada – President, Agricultural International Development Associates Inc. of Canada; formerly Member of Parliament and Minister of Agriculture, Canada; President, World Food Council.

EDWARD L.WILLIAMS, USA – Executive Director, Kilby Awards Foundation; formerly Senior Associate, Winrock International; Administrator, The World Food Prize.

ACKNOWLEDGEMENTS

The work of a Commission such as ICPF could not have been carried out without the active support and assistance of many individuals and organizations. We wish to express our appreciation to the institutions that hosted meetings of the Commission: Third World Academy (Italy), All-Union Academy of Agricultural Sciences (USSR), Agricultural Research Council (Norway), Carter Presidential Center (USA), Gorbachev Foundation and Agrarian Institute (Russia).

In addition to those individuals named in the Chairman's Preface, we are especially grateful to the following persons for participating in the meetings, contributing to the preparation and review of working group papers, and meeting personally to discuss ICPF's agenda of issues: Ajit Bhalla, Director of the World Employment Programme, ILO; Marco Vianello-Chiodo, former UN Assistant Secretary General; Harlan Cleveland, President of the World Academy of Art and Science; Nitin Desai, UN Under Secretary General for Policy Coordination and Sustainable Development; Luis Gomez Echverri, Director, Environment, and Gus Edgren, Assistant Administrator, Bureau for Programme and Policy Evaluation, UNDP; Ettore Gelpi, UNESCO; President Mikhail Gorbachev, President of the Gorbachev Foundation; James Grant, Executive Director, UNICEF; Solomon Hailu, Director of Executive Office, UNESCO; Nural Islam, International Food Policy Research Institute; Stanley Johnson, Director of CARD, Iowa State University, USA; Richard Jolly, Deputy Executive Director, UNICEF; V. Kurien, Chairman of the National Dairy Development Board, India; K. N. N. S. Nair, M. S. Swaminathan Research Institute, India; B. S. Raghavan, former senior Indian administrator; G. Rangaswami, former Adviser to the Planning Commission of India; Richard Reid, Director of Public Affairs, UNICEF; Timothy Rothermal, Director, Division for Global and Inter-Regional Programmes, UNDP; Linda Starke, Consultant, USA; Lars Sjoflot, Agricultural University of Norway; C. Subramaniam, former Finance Minister of India; R. Sudarshan, Assistant Resident Representative, UNDP, India; Lance Taylor, Professor of Economics at Massachusetts Institute of Technology, USA.

The Commission would also like to acknowledge the researchers, advisers and consultants who have contributed to the preparation of the working group papers: Man Mohan Agarwal, Jawahalal Nehru University, India; Sidney Bailey, international law expert, UK; Sam Daws, Head of Research, UN and Conflict Programme to UN Association of UK; Major General Eustace D'Souza (Retd), India; Brigadier Michael Harbottle (Retd), UK; Major General Leonard V. Johnson, Chairman of the Canadian Pugwash Group and Project Ploughshares, Canada; Terry Kelly, University of Florida, USA; Kenneth Kirkwood, Emeritus Rhodes Professor of Race Relations, Oxford University, UK; Severie Lodgard, Director, UN Disarmament Research Institute; Sir Anthony Parsons, former UK Ambassador to the UN; Anatol Rapoport, Professor of Peace and Conflict Studies at the University of Toronto, Canada; Demeiza Stubbings, Oxford University and the Oxford Project for Peace Studies, UK; Sir

204

Crispin Tickell, former UK Ambassador to the UN and Warden, Green College, Oxford University, UK; General Sir Timothy Toyne-Sewell, Commandant, The Military Academy, Sandhurst, UK; Peter J. C. Walker, Head of Research, League of Red Cross and Red Crescent Societies, Switzerland.

The meetings, working groups, and research projects were funded by generous support from UNDP and UNESCO and from the following institutions and individuals: Agricultural Research Council (Norway), All-Union Academy of Agricultural Sciences (USSR), Arca Foundation (USA), Nirwano Foundation (Japan), Carter Presidential Center (USA), Earthwatch Europe (UK), Ford Foundation (USA), German Foundation for International Development (Germany), Gorbachev Foundation (Russia), International Development Research Centre (Canada), Mere Cie. Inc. (USA), Mira International (Netherlands and USA), The Mother's Service Society (India), Third World Academy of Sciences (Italy); and John Banks (Canada), Frederick Harmon (USA), M. Nandagopal (India), and Donald Wheeler (USA).

The Commission would also like to acknowledge the support to our work provided by Mohammed Hassan, Secretary, Third World Academy of Sciences in Trieste, Italy; Arnie Hole, Programme Coordinator, Agricultural Research Council, Norway; Suresh Kennit, The Mother's Service Society, India; Oxford Project for Peace Studies, Oxford, UK; Svein Sundsbo, President, Norwegian Research Council; Lynne Twist, Hunger Project, USA; Steve Catlin, Save the Children (USA); and Joan Key, ICPF Secretariat.

Our publisher, Zed Books Ltd (London and New Jersey), has offered great cooperation in expediting the publication of this volume. We are grateful to Robert Molteno, Editor, and his colleagues at Zed Books for their assistance.

INDEX

208 • INDEX